CONTENTS

FOREWORD

JONATHAN KAY

EDITOR-IN-CHIEF, *THE WALRUS* MAGAZINE

Blue-chip law firms present themselves to the world as calm, collegial white-collar workplaces. But under the surface, the reality can be very different—especially at the highest levels of law-firm governance.

The most powerful lawyers in a firm often tend to be the most successful and well paid. They are used to being the smartest and most influential person in every room. Put a dozen of these high-ego specimens into the same space (say, for a Compensation Committee meeting), and professional courtesies can quickly give way to bickering, recriminations, and ultimatums. Unlike in most other high-value businesses, which tend to be run by a specialized managerial class, lawyers manage themselves. And it's not something most of them are good at.

Even so, the dissolution of Heenan Blaikie in 2014 was, by the standards of Canadian business, an extraordinary event. Large, full-service law firms are not in the habit of just going away. Sometimes, they merge with one another, or change the names at the top of the letterhead, or subsume themselves to foreign behemoths. There is no modern Canadian precedent for a firm of Heenan Blaikie's size simply falling apart.

What makes this story more unusual still is that it does not involve the elements that typically spark the sudden and spectacular collapse of name-brand business entities: there was no large-scale scandal, no allegation of criminal conduct by Heenan Blaikie partners, no scheme to cook the books. Journalists who came looking for a quick and simple self-destruction narrative to the story came away disappointed. Yes, there was an unsuccessful African gambit, a general sagging of revenues, one or two lapses among senior partners—but nothing that the firm couldn't have easily survived if its management team had retained the trust of the firm's rank-and-file lawyers. It was their exit— at first, lawyer by lawyer and then, team by team—that truly caused Heenan Blaikie to go under.

The story that Norman Bacal tells in this book is essentially the human equivalent of a classic bank run: just as account holders at a financial institution become more likely to demand their funds when they see neighbours lined up outside the local branch, so too did Heenan Blaikie's lawyers scuttle to the exits when they saw their officemates make the first move.

In some cases, these moves were quite profitable. Many second-tier law firms seek to vault themselves to the status of 'full service' by filling out their missing practice areas. But developing these departments from scratch can take years, or even decades. With the demise of Heenan Blaikie, firms suddenly had a chance to go lawyer shopping at the wholesale level, taking on whole departments at one stroke. Better yet, these lawyers already knew one another—coming on board with established internal hierarchy, esprit de corps, and, most importantly, client lists.

The question is: Why did *any* significant number of lawyers begin to leave Heenan Blaikie in the first place? Moreover, once the exodus began, why wasn't the firm's management able to reassure those still on board? When the lawyer-exodus 'bank run' was at an early stage, the Heenan Blaikie client base was still largely intact. A decisive intervention by a competent leadership team could have saved this law firm.

And here we get to the real business lessons of Bacal's book—all of which extend far beyond the legal realm.

First, the experience of Heenan Blaikie shows that while an informal, egalitarian command structure may be appropriate for a small start-up entity, it can cause serious problems once the organization grows large. In the early days of Heenan Blaikie, Bacal and his colleagues were able to make important decisions on the basis of trust, consensus, and goodwill. But eventually, that became impossible, because larger firms must be organized into subunits, each of which inevitably will lobby management to advance its own interests.

In the case of Heenan Blaikie, the transition from small to large firm became especially problematic because power within the firm was divided between the Toronto and Montreal offices. So the firm became tribalized on the basis of not only practice area but also geography. At one telling point in Bacal's narrative, things become so nasty that the Montreal-based managing partner isn't permitted to even physically set foot within the Toronto office. Perhaps that extraordinary fact alone foreshadowed Heenan Blaikie's fate.

This second lesson from Bacal's book—that healthy firms must manage territorial divisions before they become toxic and unmanageable—is especially pertinent in the context of Quebec and the rest of Canada. Heenan Blaikie is far from the only Canadian company whose internal relations have foundered on the differences in business culture between French and English. This is not something that is spoken about much in polite Canadian corporate circles. But from several examples I have observed as a journalist, I can attest that the phenomenon is very real.

A third lesson—and perhaps the most obvious one to emerge from Bacal's book—is that at moments of crisis, firms must be able to rely on vigorous leaders as their last line of defence. In this regard, Heenan Blaikie didn't have the men it needed. One key figure was well meaning but indecisive. Another was decisive but polarizing. And the chairman who sat at the very top of the firm, at least symbolically, was simply too far along in years to rouse the troops.

— ● —

As a journalist, I have been waiting for someone to produce a truly authoritative account of Heenan Blaikie's failure. Now that Norm Bacal has done so, I would urge Canadian business leaders to heed the lessons of this unique cautionary tale.

THE END

FRIDAY, FEBRUARY 14, 2014

Dusk is setting in on the Toronto skyline as I stare blankly out the tinted windows of my office on the twenty-eighth floor of the Bay Adelaide Centre. Around me, an entire floor of office suites lies empty, stripped of any sign of life. This is not a standard Friday evening in the life of a law firm, where office etiquette varies according to the personal habits and schedules of its attorneys: some with desks neatly organized in anticipation of the coming week, others with papers and files strewn on surfaces, client matters abandoned mid-thought, to get started on their weekends. This is a day unlike any I have ever experienced. Packing boxes litter the hallways in a royal-blue and grey mosaic. Desks lie bare, shelves stand empty. Photos, desk toys, reference books, files, notepads, knickknacks—evidence of life in the law firm—all gone. Secretarial stations clear of all personal effects. Partly filled bottles of single malt Scotch, orphaned on a boardroom table, missing the social drinkers. It is moving day at Heenan Blaikie, and unlike previous moves, everyone has left permanently. Forever.

"The greatest failure in Canadian law firm history." That is what the country's national and local papers are reporting concerning the closing of Heenan Blaikie, a firm that recently celebrated its fortieth anniversary. It has been home to two retired prime ministers, one provincial premier, various Cabinet ministers, a retired Supreme Court of Canada justice, and the former CEO of one of Canada's largest construction companies, as well as a breeding ground for judges across the land, including one of the most recent appointments by former prime minister Harper to the Supreme Court.

I was one of the poster boys of the firm's success. It encompassed my entire adult life, as a student, associate, partner, founder of the Toronto office at the tender age of thirty-three, and later as national co-managing partner for almost sixteen years. Over the course of time I celebrated successes, rallied the troops, fought valiant fights, and spun the mythologies that gave the firm its special niche in the market. I retired from management at the end of 2012 and handed over the keys to others, returning only as we ushered in 2014 to take on one last great challenge: salvation of the business and the legacy.

Had I succeeded, I might have basked in the glory of the victors.

Instead I have spent the last few hours reflecting on the past. Over a period of thirty-nine years we built an empire from the ground up. As one of its leaders for a quarter of a century, I was personally involved in its development and growth. After I stepped away, we watched the incoming tide absorb it, like a castle of sand, in almost no time at all. My fears over the past six months have become reality. What has taken me so many years to build is being dismantled swiftly and mercilessly.

—— • ——

This is a tale of a young lawyer's growth: how I evolved from law student to successful lawyer and then leader. In some ways it is the potential story of every student graduating from university, a real-life case study of the skills required to survive in the business world. This is also a journey through the building of a remarkable enterprise. It represents my perspective on the birth, adolescence, and maturity of a business from its infancy as a small, regional firm through to its glory days as a recognized international brand and ultimately to its shockingly swift demise.

Who are its heroes and where are the villains? What compulsions were at work throughout? Was it a case of greed, as portrayed by some of the newspaper coverage surrounding the demise, or was there something more complicated at work? Perhaps the end was driven by pedestrian matters, suggesting that this could happen to any professional services firm at any time? What factor did bad timing and bad luck play in all of this? What was my role in the legacy I handed over to new management that it could all erode so hastily and with such harshness? Most important, could it all have been avoided?

In writing this book I have embarked on a personal journey to trace the roots of the firm, its values and business approach, and the winding road we followed to its success, as well as the events of that final year that led to its collapse. We grew up together, Heenan Blaikie and I. Many of the valuable lessons learned in the firm formed the basis of my management philosophies as a firm leader. Above all, this is a story of leadership and how it develops, of the importance of people to an organization, of the stories we tell about ourselves and what those stories reveal of our value systems. These stories will be told through my eyes, with my voice, and with my own biases. Others may have experienced the events I describe differently. As I cast my gaze over my thirty-four years at Heenan Blaikie, I do so with a high degree of nostalgia and with the benefit of considerable hindsight.

If you are reading this book, you are probably wondering how this could happen. How could a firm with a solid reputation and a storied past just disappear? As I lead you through this journey I remind you this is a cautionary tale. I leave it to you, the reader, to come to your own conclusions as to the reasons for our demise.

PINNACLE OR **PRECIPICE?**

PARIS, 2011

"*Bienvenue à Paris*, Norm. How was the voyage from Toronto? We are so pleased you were able to make it for the opening." These are the warm words of greeting from my newest partner, Jean-François Mercadier, as I arrive early for a cocktail reception at Palais de Chaillot on the Trocadéro facing the Eiffel Tower. Jean-François is well known locally as one of the finest commercial lawyers in Paris, with a strong reputation in the mining industry. His multinational clients buy and sell projects across French-speaking Africa. This past January we opened Heenan Blaikie's tenth office, located just off 'Le Triangle d'Or' with a great view from its terrace of the Eiffel Tower on the other side of the Seine River. Tonight, business clients from Europe and Africa, French politicians, and international and Canadian diplomats stationed in Paris have come to celebrate the opening and to chat for a few minutes with our counsel, former prime minister Jean Chrétien.

This is our first venture outside North America, but we have become the experts at opening small offices and growing with them. When our Montreal firm opened its second office, a four-lawyer operation in Toronto back in 1989, we could never have imagined becoming the fifth largest firm in the country. We did it in our inimitable Heenan Blaikie fashion, stressing local autonomy and the importance of people in our growing family. We started a labour boutique in Vancouver and satellites around Quebec through the 1990s. We experimented for ten years in Beverly Hills, and most recently we achieved great success in the oil and gas market in Calgary.

I sidle up alongside my co-managing partner, Guy Tremblay, who has also flown in for the evening. My wife, Sharon, refers to Guy as my 'second wife,' based on the amount of time—days, nights, and weekends—we've spent on the phone together.

We proudly talk to one another of our achievements over thirteen years of working together. Paris is the next step in our expansion. And it has all been done our way, starting small offices, following opportunities, and growing them patiently. This time we are adding fifteen new lawyers and taking our first step at becoming truly global.

Guy has been continually reminding me that Paris is a different animal than Hollywood or Calgary, where we experienced success in markets far from our original bases in Montreal and later Toronto. This time we crossed the ocean, and we have our work cut out to show our partners back home that this is a smart decision. We agree that if our assessment is correct, a movement into Europe and the lucrative French-African mining market will open a door to opportunities we cannot yet imagine. This has been true of every previous expansion that we sponsored together.

Yet it was laughable how little we knew about running a firm when we started working together in 1997. Guy was a veteran labour lawyer who knew nothing about operating a business. I was a tax expert in film finance who didn't even want the job of managing partner. Jean Potvin, my mentor, was doing a great job running the operation, and if not for his illness, he might have been running the firm forever. When

Guy and I took over, we were a $60 million business with about 165 lawyers and Guy didn't know how to read a balance sheet. Now we were a firm of over 575 lawyers on two continents.

We had both come a long way together, as had the enterprise, but we were now both reaching the end of our respective terms running the firm. The partners had decided a number of years before that by the end of 2012 we would be rotating two new managing partners in to replace Guy and me. Guy's term was set to expire at the end of 2011, and I would be retiring from management a year later. Roy Heenan, the long-serving firm chairman, was also set to resign at the end of 2012. I had high hopes of succeeding him as chair of the firm.

Guy and I had established a few shared secrets for success. We agreed from inception that we would always support one another, we would never disagree in public, and we would talk every day. Guy was fond of saying, "Norm, you are my brother." I never forgot the words Guy used about our role: "We are the fiduciaries of our partners. Our job is to make every decision putting their collective interests above all." That served us well over the years.

Roy Heenan comes over to join us as we are chatting. "Gentlemen, I believe this is going to be a great success. We've really chosen well with Jean-François and his team. I feel very buoyant about where we're headed. At this point, we're all nearing the end of our terms in leadership, and I really want to leave something of value behind for all the young people."

Guy and I nod in agreement.

"This is the future," Roy continues. "You know, we've never been afraid of going after opportunities. That's been the hallmark of the firm from the beginning when I started with Peter and Don. I've always felt, though, that it's more important to bring in the right talent who are focused on collegial practice, rather than the greed you see in so many firms these days. I hope our partners continue to retain that as a guide."

"We've always tried to be a different kind of law firm, and to try novel approaches," I add. "We pioneered billing for value, rather than associate or much later when I had taken up the managing partner role. It was a tone he would equally use with his largest client.

Here was a man who had graduated from Oxford and returned to his native Shawinigan to teach high school English, before finally going off to law school and then beginning his career as a junior to Donald Johnston at Stikeman Elliott. He called things the way he saw them: blunt, to the point, brilliant, and well spoken. Peter also felt strongly that a lawyer only had a value if he maintained some balance in life, whether through the arts, politics, sports, family, or, in his case, all of the above.

Roy Heenan, the second founding father, contrasted with Peter in almost every way. Roy operated on emotion; he was a storyteller and a dreamer. While he could be a brilliant litigator, he abhorred confrontation in his personal life. When challenged he would become petulant. It was as if Latin blood coursed through Roy's veins. Raised in Mexico, son of a wealthy industrialist, Roy was fuelled by his passions, whether for the law, Canadian artists, great food and wine, or social conversation. He possessed a powerful legal mind and took a keen interest in the entire world. He wrote voluminously; studied Canadian, American, and international labour law; and spoke publicly at every possible opportunity, becoming prominent not only in Canada but also around the world. As a result of Roy's efforts, the firm became one of Canada's dominant labour law firms.

Roy believed in the firm with an undying passion. He had a vision for building it, but had no natural ability to develop its talent. I don't think it ever occurred to him that this was a role he could or should play. He was the undisputed head of the labour group, and its beacon. He cast a giant shadow and was not an easy man to work for, particularly if you disagreed with him on a point of law. Yet Roy possessed a heart of gold when it came to protecting his people and would often take less than his share of money if it meant rewarding a more junior partner who he felt was deserving.

Donald Johnston had been the gold medalist in his law class at McGill University; he was an up-and-coming star income-tax lawyer training under Heward Stikeman and Fraser Elliott when he decided to leave that firm, which at the time comprised only sixteen lawyers. He had a vision of starting his own firm and had already established some wonderful connections with serious Canadian and American businesses. He and Peter departed from Stikemans along with Gerald McCarthy and Jean Monet to form the new firm in early 1968 under the name of McCarthy Monet Johnston. A year later Roy, who was at another firm, joined them, along with Guy Dufort and a couple of other lawyers.

The firm split five years later. Don, Roy, and Peter left to found Johnston Heenan & Blaikie (JHB). Roy liked to joke that during the first two years with McCarthy and Monet they went through sixty drafts of a partnership agreement that never got executed. After the separation, the notion of a written partnership agreement was anathema to the original three and would not be seriously reconsidered for another twenty years. It became part of the firm lore that we were unique in not having one. Roy drew from this two corollaries that, for him, became the basic tenets of the firm: first, that we would spend our time and energy fighting our competitors and not one another; second, that we would have no rules. The second was Roy's own take on the situation. Peter preferred to say that while we actually did have rules, "goddamned Heenan would never follow them." Over the years the regular repetition of these and other stories became woven into the fabric of the firm.

Besides deciding against a written partnership agreement, Peter, Don, and Roy laid out a few basic principles at the outset intended to govern the firm: as soon as feasible with new clients, both the work and the client relationship should be delegated to younger partners and lawyers; there should be no great differences in compensation between the partners and non-partners whose strengths were in different categories; among the partners themselves the differences in compensation between the highest remunerated and the most junior should be modest; and the firm should be as diverse as possible in its composition, as well as impeccably bilingual. These principles were also very much part of the culture I encountered when I arrived at the firm.

Don's legal career as a partner of the firm ended between the time I committed to join the firm and before I started work when the Trudeau Liberals were swept back into power after Joe Clark's crushing defeat in the spring of 1980. Don was appointed president of the Treasury Board, and his name had to be removed from the name of the firm in accordance with Quebec bar requirements. He left behind an impressive array of client relationships from which many lawyers in the firm would benefit in the years to come (myself included).

Don was as scrupulous as a Montreal summer day was long so there were no favours forthcoming to Heenan Blaikie clients while Don was in Ottawa. The closest thing to a scandal that Don had to endure resulted from a fundraiser for his re-election campaign as a member of Parliament. He held a cocktail party at one of Montreal's leading hotels where he entertained his guests with a piano recital of contemporary hits. The Revenue Quebec authorities attempted to impose their 10 percent amusement tax on the admission cover. Peter remarked that "there was nothing amusing about Don's performance that night," although I'm not certain whether that had any impact on the assessor's decision to ultimately drop the claim. Don was ever charming and brilliant, and a wonderful after-dinner speaker. As a student and junior lawyer of the firm, I rarely had a moment when I did not feel intimidated by the sheer intellect of the firm's three founders.

Don and Peter were both fond of saying that one thing that set Heenan Blaikie apart from other firms and that made them proud was that at our firm, "if there were any knives, they went in the chest." That quip evokes all kinds of bloody images, but it spoke boatloads about a firm where backbiting and secret jealousies were to be shunned. While the line very much described Peter's method of operating (if he had a problem he would deal with it honestly and face to face), it really didn't seem to apply to either Roy or Don, both of whom avoided confrontation wherever possible. I doubt either of them had ever sparred with more than a butter knife. Nevertheless, this was an attribute of the firm that I actively publicized. The firm folklore would benefit from the telling and retelling over the years, and the reference to the "knife going in the chest at HB" was particularly useful in explaining what we were about when I was recruiting senior lawyers from other firms.

— • —

I learned early on that every organization needs a conscience. Not every business has one. When I joined the firm, I discovered its conscience was a senior associate named Danny Levinson. The one common characteristic of the people playing that role is that they are a thorn in the side of management. They have a tendency to challenge decisions made out of expediency without regard to the values of the organization. They act as the check and balance that ensures the organization actually has meaningful values and measures its decision-making against the backdrop of those values. In so doing they can become very unpopular but are generally unfazed by that fact.

Danny was a brilliant lawyer. He had a strong grasp of tax law, and while in law school had written a detailed paper on surplus stripping, an area of the law that was barely intelligible, even to sophisticated tax practitioners. While a McGill undergraduate, Danny studied quantum physics (not a prerequisite for law school) and failed. He would laugh about the experience, but I knew how smart you had to be to even enrol for the course. He was also an excellent draftsman and a thoughtful commercial lawyer. Danny originally followed in the footsteps of his father, a journalist, writing copy for the *Montreal Gazette* before turning to law.

My first memo as a student was written for Danny. It was a three-page memorandum on yellow paper, the colour of memos at Heenan Blaikie, constructed carefully with all the talent I had honed in four years of McGill law school. When he called me in to review the work and its conclusions, he handed back a document awash in red ink.

"I've made a few suggestions you may want to look at," was all he said. I've hung on to that yellow memo as a keepsake. I could barely make out any original text left untouched. What few lines had emerged unscathed were left with various questions and suggestions attached to the end of long, snake-like red curves. It was only on the third read-through that I noted a message in the top right-hand corner of the cover page: "Good work."

A rigorous approach to the practice of law is what Danny taught and what I learned very early on in my fledgling career. It was not enough to be smart and talented. As lawyers we also had to be meticulous. Every word has a meaning and every meaning must be applied with precision. Ideas are meant to be expressed in a particular way. As lawyers we craft with words, and our task is to master them. I began my training under his friendly but demanding tutelage.

Danny's sheer talent, wry sense of humour, and charm made him a favourite among clients. He could also swear like a sailor. Unfortunately, Danny convinced himself early on that he hated clients. Danny loved the law, loved analyzing and solving problems, but found many of his clients to have unreasonable expectations; some he believed to be downright stupid. They insisted on negotiating points that Danny considered frivolous and occasionally required him to advance positions he knew to be untenable.

In fairness, some of the clients Danny inherited from Don when the latter entered politics were unremitting jerks. Don had a talent for managing all of them while Danny did not. This created a conflict that ate Danny up inside. Danny's most interesting client relationship was with Wayne Drury, the Royal Bank vice-president responsible for film and television finance in Canada. Wayne was famous for his hot temper, his support for his banking clients, and his passion for undressing idiots and frauds, of which there were many to rail against in the industry. He and Danny shared an unusual mutual respect that saw them alternately agreeing on strategy or screaming at one another when they disagreed. I marvelled at the ability of lawyer and client to aggressively go at one another and the next day get on the phone as if nothing had happened. This was one of many lessons I would learn in my formative years about the different ways to manage clients based on their unique personalities.

Although he was my first career mentor and became a very good friend, Danny was often his own worst enemy. He was haunted by occasional fits of darkness that would envelop him for days and sometimes weeks on end. Once, at the end of a particular tirade, a phone came flying out his office door. While there were no casualties, from that point on we all exercised caution walking by Danny's office. Danny was also fond of arguing arcane points of tax law with Richard Lewin, a chartered accountant as well as a lawyer. He was my other mentor and a man who never made an error on a technical point of tax law. I found it laughable and intimidating that Danny would call me in to arbitrate their disputes. Fresh out of law school, I could barely follow the argument, yet Danny seemed to think I might actually have an informed opinion without six hours of research on the matter. You can bet I would spend the night figuring out the answer for myself. Perhaps that was the point of the exercise!

While he occasionally displayed contempt for those he did not respect, Danny taught me something valuable about dealing with others at the firm. He treated everyone equally, whether partners, students, support staff, or administrative personnel. He didn't just treat them with courtesy. Those that he liked became friends for life regardless of status.

Reflecting upon Danny's influence has led me to reconsider the lessons that I absorbed over the years without really thinking about them. I discovered early on that in dealing with people, words, actions, and even facial expressions matter. Things we say and do, and the way we say and do them, are being observed, evaluated, and judged on a daily basis by superiors and subordinates. The higher we rise in the organization to positions of mentorship, leadership, or other forms of authority, the more the attitudes of the entire organization will key off the subtle cues we give out about who we are. We are continually on display as role models, and every word, every gesture, every omission can carry weight. Danny also taught me that everyone matters regardless of standing or station. While he may not have intended it, he planted the seeds that were to grow within me and shape some of my own philosophies of management.

THE **TRUDEAU** EFFECT

I am a classic introvert. Growing up, I was never the raconteur type, and my public speaking skills were average at best, though I took my first lessons from my uncle Irving, who taught the Dale Carnegie Course to my class when I was in sixth and seventh grade. I was not particularly effective or comfortable in new social settings and rarely blew anyone away with a first impression. In short, I was an acquired taste. Quiet, friendly, but somewhat awkward in social situations, I would not have been voted on by high school contemporaries as the person most likely to run an organization.

A 2012 book by Susan Cain, *Quiet: The Power of Introverts in a World That Can't Stop Talking*, takes an in-depth look at the differences between introverts and extroverts and concludes that there are many reasons why people who consider themselves introverts make excellent leaders. This is somewhat counterintuitive in that our paradigm of leadership is linked to obvious charisma and shows of public charm or outspoken reaction. In reality some of the best leaders are quiet and thoughtful, promote the achievements of their followers, and possess high levels of self-awareness and low levels of narcissism.

In hindsight, my career path to leadership at Heenan Blaikie could not possibly have been predicted. While a second-year law student at McGill University, I and others with solid grades who were looking for summer jobs applied to Montreal's seven or eight major law firms. In 1978 these included Clarkson Tétrault, which is now McCarthy Tétrault; Martineau Walker, destined to join Faskens[1]; Ogilvy Renault, which would join the international giant Norton Rose Fulbright after the millennium; and Stikeman Elliott, which had grown in the seven years since Don and Peter left into a major firm of about sixty lawyers. In my wisdom I had decided that the only firm that interested me was Johnston Heenan & Blaikie, a firm of sixteen lawyers, which seemed large enough for me. Roy, Don, and Stuart "Kip" Cobbett, who led their commercial group, had been lecturing in the law faculty at McGill and creating a great buzz about Montreal's next up-and-coming firm. I didn't have a second choice, which perhaps was not very forward thinking, since I was about to marry my college sweetheart and needed a job.

I was, however, expecting to follow the trend set by many anglophones who grew up in Montreal to witness the FLQ terrorist crisis; the rise of René Lévesque, the Parti Québécois, and Quebec nationalism; and the slow deterioration of Montreal as the business centre of Canada. I assumed that after graduation I would be heading west on Highway 401 to Toronto, so the notion of establishing roots in the Montreal legal community was a low priority in my life. After having given what I thought was a dynamic first interview at JHB, I was called back for a second one. The lawyers interviewing me were lovely people, all very friendly, down to earth, and charming. I was impressed, and satisfied with the rapport I believed we were creating. As it turns out, they were less impressed with me, which I intuited

---

[1] On occasion, I refer to the major firms by their current nicknames, taking the first name on the letterhead and adding an *s*; hence, for example, Faskens for Fasken Martineau, Blakes for Blake Cassels, and McCarthys for McCarthy Tétrault.

from the fact that I never heard from them again. There was to be no final interview. Though passed over in favour of others considered more suitable, I recovered quickly from the rejection. Unbeknownst to me, fate would eventually reunite us.

At the end of second-year law school I got married, at twenty-two, to Sharon, my sweetheart of three years. She had just started her career as a chartered accountant with Coopers & Lybrand. If I was the introvert who couldn't get hired at JHB, Sharon was at the other end of the spectrum: she'd applied to ten accounting firms and been solicited with ten offers. In addition to being smart and charming, she had a natural gift for handling interviews. I would try to learn her secrets a year later when it was my turn to attend articling interviews in Toronto.

— • —

At the end of third-year law school, I desperately needed a job. Sharon was working as a junior accountant earning $600 a month, and rent for our basement apartment was eating up about a quarter of that sum. By the time we got through with the monthly bills, we barely had enough money to shop for groceries. Some weeks it was heavy on the peanut butter and Kraft Dinner, which we could still procure on sale at Steinberg's for twenty-five cents a box. I learned to love chicken livers, which were rich in iron and only about a dollar a package for dinner for two.

There were no summer job opportunities in the legal community, so I reached for the *Montreal Star* classifieds at the end of April. One particular ad caught my eye: "Demonstrate our unique product to customers and get paid. Car required." So I set out in our brand-new Honda Civic, a car that then retailed for only $4,500 and struck fear in the heart of my mother, who was convinced the tiny 1979 "made-in-Japan" model would provide no more protection than a transistor radio when we were crushed in the inevitable highway fatality. I crossed the city from the safe anglophone confines of Hampstead to the east end of Montreal, heading for the vicinity around the Olympic Stadium, built for the 1976 Olympics, where the only language spoken for miles was French. I had no idea of the breadth of the east end, having rarely crossed the legendary 'Main' (Boulevard St-Laurent), much less Parc La Fontaine, rue Christophe Colombe, Pie-IX, and the many landmarks of the 'other side' of Montreal. In the hour-long drive to the interview, I saw neighbourhoods I had never explored.

My journey ended at a storefront on Hochelaga Street, where I met a man who would unknowingly have a profound impact on my professional development. Alfred was a big African-American man with crooked front teeth and a disarming smile. He looked like he might have played US college football at some point in the past. With a soft upstate New York accent, sounding a little like you might imagine Morgan Freeman would when speaking the language of Molière, he not only greeted me in French but also insisted on conducting the entire interview in what was obviously his second language. His French grammar was atrocious, which didn't seem to bother him one bit. Alfred owned the Filter Queen vacuum cleaner distributorship for half of the east end. I had never heard of Filter Queens. I knew Hoovers from television ads, and Sharon and I were using a fifteen-year-old no-name brand on the few hand-me-down area carpets we had in the apartment. Alfred, who'd been successfully selling for years, had been promoted to his own distributorship, with about a dozen salesmen who reported to him.

The pitch to newcomers like me was simple: attend a morning training session to learn about the product, then start giving door-to-door demonstrations and earn a modest $25 fee for each successful demonstration. "You don't have to sell if you don't want to" were the magic words that led me to accept his offer.

Sales might have been in my father's blood, because he was an incredible insurance and mutual fund salesman, but there was no inner voice whispering that my future was in sales. I wanted to be a tax lawyer. I was certain of that from the first day of second-year law school, when I took my first course in tax law. I had always been mathematically inclined, and the course material, while deadly boring and complicated for most of the law students, intrigued me as much as solving a problem in advanced calculus did. The math gene came from my father, although he did everything in his power to dissuade me from becoming a CA, his chosen profession. Tax law was an acceptable career compromise and one that excited me. But selling? I was convinced I would never possess even an ounce of my father's talent for salesmanship.

Little did I know that day that everything in life is about sales, and that Alfred's pitch had been made over and over for years to timid people like me who either dropped out after a week or became salesmen in order to earn a living.

The next morning I arrived, filled with a combination of eagerness to accept the challenge and trepidation at making a presentation in a second language. Fortunately, according to Alfred, I didn't need to close a sale to survive in this job. The training session focused on learning how to make the presentation, including outlining the machine's features, and various first-level tricks of the trade. I had to master the names of every part in French (not that I knew what they were called in English). The second part of the training involved a group session that took place every morning before the salesmen went out on their calls. They would discuss sales challenges and would always end with a fiery exhortation by Alfred. Just like the Notre Dame football team soaking up every last word of a Knute Rockne speech before heading out of the locker room to beat opponents on the gridiron, our salesmen would head out the door shouting "Pump, pump, pump!" on their way to their appointments.

Off I drove to my first house. I clumsily felt my way through the presentation by trial and error, then with a little more confidence later in the day and over the next four days until Friday, payday, when the other shoe was about to drop. Alfred called me in to ask how the demonstrations had gone. I told him I thought I was doing very well, leaving out the details of the few where the presentations had been abbreviated. In one case the woman was depressed and lonely and

learned some of my most valuable life lessons. Failure and rejection were good things. Selling one machine a day meant that I was failing six or seven times a day. Most people have great difficulty dealing with rejection. Psychological profilers have conducted studies showing that lawyers are four times more sensitive to criticism than the general population. Personalities driven towards the practice of law are mostly hypercritical and cannot accept the risk of failure. That is why they are drawn to the law: as lawyers we are trained to ferret out and analyze risk. Our clients make the decisions that most of us are not capable of making. Law school experience intensifies that bias, focusing on disputes that might otherwise have been avoided. It is rare to find a lawyer with sales expertise, as the vast majority of them prefer to analyze risk rather than take it.

Judy was very kind to have offered me the job. She remembered that I had nothing lined up in May and she was now drowning in research. The resulting two-month legal experience might have been a footnote in my life, but for a series of coincidences that would lead me to Heenan Blaikie. Judy's husband, Danny Kaufer, was two years senior to us at law school and was an articling student at the young law firm under the wing of Roy Heenan in the labour group. Danny would go on to have a stellar career with the firm, becoming a leading rainmaker there. Bullish, personable, outgoing, and always the showman, he and Judy were polar opposites: she was quiet, thoughtful, kind, caring, and nurturing, while he could be loud and intimidating and could pour on the aggression when it was needed—and often when it was not. While we knew each other socially, Danny was otherwise someone I avoided.

Towards the end of that summer it was time to follow the career plan and head to Toronto for interviews for an articling position. Applying for student positions at law firms in Toronto is, was, and will always be about making a strong first impression. Today the major law firms receive as many as a thousand applications annually. In my day there were still three hundred or four hundred applications for a mere four or five positions. I might have been in the top 10 percent of my graduating class, but I was competing with countless strong academic records from across the country. How was one to stand out? The question puzzled me. I was the classic quiet but steady, solid but not flashy candidate. It didn't matter that I was smart. I didn't shine, sparkle, take command of interviews, or otherwise project myself as indispensable.

I will never forget my experience at Davies Ward & Beck, my first choice of firms. The interviewer was so busy selling the firm that I couldn't get a word in edgewise. I still remember sitting there, half-listening, wondering when it was going to be my turn. Couldn't he read the pleading in my eyes? Was he ever going to shut up and let me speak? This was a familiar theme in other interviews with eight of Toronto's prestigious law firms. It seemed the Filter Queen experience had not yet translated to impressing lawyers enough to hire me.

My salvation was McDonald Hayden, a boutique commercial and tax litigation firm that called with my first and only offer, and only because the gold medalist in my class had turned them down to accept another offer. The experience left a giant chip on my shoulder that would eventually make me a worthy adversary for all those other firms later in my career. Quiet, pensive, oblivious to pressure, and smart, I was an ideal candidate, but it remained the best-kept secret on Bay Street for many years.

— • —

Throughout my fourth year of law school, Sharon and I were experiencing buyer's remorse about the decision to move to Toronto. She had not yet begun to work out her transfer within Coopers & Lybrand, and she was beginning to make her own mark in the organization as a dedicated, smart, and hard-working woman. She had partner material written all over her. I was committed to McDonald Hayden; after all, they were the only firm to offer me a job. But we had made a decision together to get out of Quebec with its separatist tendencies, so each week during the fall when one of us faltered, we reminded each other of our commitment to leave.

One Sunday in January 1980 we were once again revisiting this decision. Despite my failure to get hired as a second-year summer student, JHB was still the Montreal firm of my dreams. If I could get a job in the tax group working with Don Johnston, my life would be set.

Sharon asked me why I didn't call. "What do you have to lose? Besides, you know Danny Kaufer. Why don't you call him and ask?"

She remembered well my serial failures at interviewing, and when juxtaposed with her own success, she felt very confident telling me to follow her script in approaching Danny and the firm. I was now the experienced salesman, but she was the one giving the sales advice. I shut up and listened.

"Tell Danny you're planning to move to Toronto, but that the only place you'd risk staying for is JHB's tax department." So far we were on the same wavelength. "Then tell him you need an answer by Friday. If they can't make up their minds quickly, then you'll pass because you need to give the other firm notice. Be firm and show some backbone here. They need to need you, not the opposite." Here I was on shakier ground. The Filter Queen experience had not sunk that deeply into my bones as yet, but Sharon had enough nerve for the two of us.

I made the call that day, and Danny called back Monday night to let me know I had an interview on Friday. That was a shock. I showed up at JHB Friday afternoon after classes in my only suit, with my long-flowing brown hair and an untrimmed socialist beard. In those days I was living the student-bohemian lifestyle, and I felt more comfortable in jeans and a lumberjack shirt, faded forest-green knapsack on my back, spouting legal theory and voting for the NDP.

Still, I thought I had a good discussion, moderated by Danny Levinson, with Richard Lewin—the lawyer who was also a CA— and Jean Potvin. Jean had been convinced by Don Johnston to leave a successful career at the Department of Justice to join, and soon after to become the head of the JHB tax department. By then Don was sitting in Parliament in the Liberal opposition to the Joe Clark minority government. Times were not great for him or for his buddy Jean Chrétien, who had lost his Cabinet post and the salary that went with it. Roy and

Don persuaded Mr. Chrétien to take a counsel job in the firm, which would provide a nice economic supplement to support his young family. This was a favour that the young Chrétien would never forget.

At the end of the hour, Potvin turned to me and asked, "When can you start?" I knew the Filter Queen sales had helped, but I didn't expect this kind of miraculous turnaround. I raced home to share the good news, and Sharon and I shelved our Toronto plans. This was the dream job. Unbeknownst to me, Kaufer, who was now a first-year lawyer, had approached Levinson, Potvin, and Lewin and explained that Judy had worked with me and he was certain they were looking at the next Wayne Gretzky. They divided the hyperbole by two and still felt there was likely enough talent there to justify hiring a student for the department. As Potvin later put it simply, "We needed another tax guy." It was a $3,000 risk. Levinson later confided that my interview skills had not significantly improved since our first meeting.

— • —

The firm occupied the top floor of the Richardson Greenshields building, a stubby, five-storey building next door to the landmark tower at number 1 Place Ville Marie—a.k.a. PVM to Montrealers. The latter had become the icon of what was left in Montreal of corporate Canada after the banks had all but abandoned their Montreal head offices on St. James Street (now Saint Jacques Street). The top floor of the PVM building looks out over all the other major Montreal landmarks, including the gigantic cross at the top of Mount Royal, and Saint Joseph's Oratory, reminders of Quebec's Roman Catholic origins. The proud Scottish blood in Peter Blaikie would likely not have permitted him to be caught dead in the much more expensive space of the main PVM tower.

Don Johnston was a fan of La Popina, the classy restaurant-bar on the plaza floor of what was then the IBM Building, also part of the vast PVM complex. He could often be found there with clients or, on late afternoons, buying drinks for the firm's lawyers. At the

Friday afternoon get-togethers, the lawyers would linger there into the evening, telling and retelling stories about the foibles of the name partners and the exploits of clients, which would become the legends that were fed to newcomers. JHB also encouraged practical joking, for which certain partners were famous. They were not averse to childish pranks, like sending roses in Don's name to Barbara Miller, a student who went on to make her career in Toronto as a partner at Faskens. Barbara, the young student, was touched by Don's chivalry. Don, of course, was speechless when Barbara showed up at his door to thank him for the gesture.

By the time I arrived in May 1980, Don had returned to Ottawa to join the Trudeau Cabinet as president of the Treasury Board, along with Jean Chrétien, who returned to the Cabinet. Eight months into Joe Clark's Conservative minority, Clark had lost control of the budget process, and I lost contact with the man I had assumed would be one of my career mentors. While I was fed a constant diet of Don legends, I didn't actually meet him during my first year in the firm.

Kip Cobbett, another star McGill law graduate, was known through the office grapevine to have been made a partner the day after he joined the bar. His prematurely silver hair—when I joined the firm, he was only in his early thirties—added to the WASP mystique that surrounded him. Always unreadable, with cold blue eyes and a charming smile, he scared me. It was years before I would do any work for him and I considered it a blessing.

After Kip, Claudette Bellemare was the most serious commercial lawyer in the firm. A model of decorum, perfectly bilingual, and sharp as a razor, she would size up the students and junior lawyers very quickly. If you failed Claudette's first test, you were toast, marking time until you finally figured out you had no long-term future at the firm. The time lag could be a number of years before a few of the more thick-headed associates realized this and moved on.

Among other things, Claudette considered herself responsible for the dress code at the firm, dictating that only suits and ties were acceptable for men. It was anathema, the height of impropriety, to show up in a sports jacket and slacks, and Lord protect any young lawyer—and even some of the partners—from a Claudette tongue-lashing for breaking the code. This was a challenging standard for my first few years at the firm when I could afford no more than three suits, including the winter corduroy that was particularly damp and uncomfortable in the humid Montreal summers.

In my book Claudette was one to avoid. I stuck to my cloister in the tax group, but that was possible for only so long. Claudette's son Alexander was a couple of years older than my son Brian, so after a barbecue at her home in Westmount, we struck up a relationship outside of the practice of law that eventually developed into a long-lasting friendship.

Claudette was so serious that she was an easy butt for numerous practical jokes and endless teasing, especially from Blaikie and Cobbett. Danny Levinson would tell the story of the day he walked the halls in a sports jacket and open-necked shirt, deliberately striding by Bellemare's office three or four times and watching her grow progressively purple with undisguised exasperation. That was Claudette's signature reaction, one that made her such a tempting target. Five minutes later she dragged Blaikie into Levinson's office so he could dole out a lecture and punishment. Danny, now wearing both a suit jacket and a tie, looked up innocently from behind his desk with only the slightest hint of an impish smirk. Claudette was speechless. She had to be wondering when Levinson had changed into proper attire. Blaikie took a look at Claudette and bellowed, "What's gotten into you, Bellemare?" Of course he was in on the gag.

— • —

Jean Potvin, a stunningly handsome man in his mid-thirties, ran the tax department, which fed me all my summer work. Before joining us, Jean had litigated many big tax cases while at the federal Department of Justice. Given his political-career plans, Don was looking for a talented successor for his lucrative client base, which included companies like United Technologies Corporation, Lockheed Martin, and various construction industry clients who had made their fortunes building the Olympic Stadium. Don's construction-industry clients used us regularly to help negotiate their contracts, but tended to handle disputes on their own. "Don't worry, Don—don't call your litigators. I'll handle it myself," one of Don's most important clients, born in southern Italy, would tell him. We used to joke about what that meant.

Jean was the golden boy, servicing clients in English and French, including many Americans inherited from Don. He spoke English with a Parisian-French inflection that belied his origins in Roberval, a salmon fishing village on Lac Saint-Jean in northern Quebec. Jean's father was the local judge for the town, which attracted hundreds of US fishermen each year to the local motel on the lake. During the time of the FLQ crisis in 1970 when nationalists were agitating all over the province, Judge Potvin would sit on his front porch in the evenings with his loaded shotgun on his lap, reminding the fractious youngsters marching up his street that it would be best they get along home. They got the message.

Potvin was a model of French elegance, with a good sense of humour, though you did not want to be around him when he was tense, facing an unreachable deadline, or awaiting an overdue answer from Richard Lewin on a point of law. When Jean became uptight, his field of vision narrowed and his peripheral vision would disappear. If you unwittingly stepped into his path in the halls, he would walk right into you. In those moments, we sought shelter in our offices and shut the doors.

Jean had an incredible touch with clients. When faced with client problems in the boardroom, he could skate as gracefully as my childhood hero Jean Béliveau. Whether or not he knew the answer, Jean radiated confidence and projected a depth of knowledge and understanding far in excess of what he actually understood at the time. Occasionally he left these meetings where he'd been particularly convincing and would ask, "Do you know what those guys were talking about in there?" I learned quickly that the most important task for the guy at the bottom of the pecking order was to make Jean look good and insure that he was never wrong. There were more senior people around, like Danny Levinson and Richard Lewin, to handle the sophisticated tax issues.

I spent that first summer researching every outstanding issue that any of the three of them could not agree upon. Occasionally they had me act as insurance, researching points they already knew the answers to. Jean, like other great litigators, could quickly synthesize new information and make it his own, convincing a client or a court-room judge that he had spent many hours doing the research and writing the research papers that I was penning and feeding to him the night before he presented them.

Life with Danny and Richard was considerably more challenging. While Jean taught me about managing clients and thinking on your feet, allowing me to follow him to court and to his meetings, Richard and Danny instilled in me the kind of rigour required of an excellent tax lawyer. Good was never good enough. Writing without precision was unacceptable. You had to edit and re-edit until you achieved perfection. Danny believed in the power of the written word. While a lawyer can get away with murder in an oral argument or debate, the true test of an idea is to express it in writing and subject it to criticism. Only then can you determine its underlying value. Richard would never allow me to re-enter his office without the answer to any question he had posed. If I had some doubt, he insisted I stake out a position and support it. There was no sense ever having a discussion with Richard if you were unprepared.

While Richard was technically excellent as a tax specialist, his claim to fame was his culinary expertise. He had been trained in the kitchens of some Parisian grand chefs, including Alain Ducasse. Richard, then in his mid-thirties, was complicated and brilliant. His clients over the years would follow him as much for his tax planning expertise as for his palate and sophisticated wine cellar. Dinner at Richard's was a treat reserved for his best clients and, on the rare occasion, for the tax department.

Given that we were a small vibrant firm, lunchtime was a central theme in our lives. Young lawyers from various practice groups would get together, occasionally with partners, to frequent the various downtown haunts. Most famous among them were Bens Delicatessen and the lunchroom in the Sun Life Building, where ancient waitresses served us toasted club sandwiches and their famous mincemeat pie at prices affordable to young professionals earning very small salaries. I often went with my former McGill classmates who had also joined the firm: Ken Atlas, who finished third in our law school class and invited me to be the best man at his wedding; Neil Wiener, who joined as a first-year lawyer and would become the leader of our securities group; and Bruce McNiven, whose lineage traced back to the Drummond family, for generations a leading name in the Montreal business community. When Danny Kaufer was at the lunch table, he would regale us with stories about Roy's exploits in the labour group while we munched on inexpensive club sandwiches. Occasionally Levinson would join us and allow us to catch up on gossip from the more senior members of the firm.

While I sat at the bottom of the tax totem pole, the position had its advantages from time to time. Jean was very generous with client allocation. While a first-year lawyer, I was handed Donald Sutherland to look after his occasional Canadian and Quebec tax issues. Though he was a California resident he always maintained a Quebec domicile. We communicated by phone at the start. He was one of the few actor clients who spoke to me directly rather than through agents, accountants, or lawyers. He always struck me as well grounded, the salt of the earth. Not what you would expect from a Hollywood star. I recall meeting him for a strategy session at his New York hotel when I was still a young lawyer, impressed by the fact that he travelled under an assumed name. Years later he asked me to do some work for his son Rossif, and finally in 2011 the three of us met for lunch at the Four Seasons. The arcs of our respective careers had taken us both in interesting directions and now the next generation of acting Sutherlands was making its mark. I expressed my gratitude for the patience he showed a very young and wet-behind-the-ears lawyer so many years before when he was already a screen star. If I learned one lesson from *that* Donald and a number of other senior people in my early years, it was how appreciative I was of the respect that was shown to me when I still knew very little and that far exceeded anything I was entitled to expect. This was a lesson I determined to pay forward for the rest of my career.

Don Johnston may not have known it at the time, but he indirectly launched my career in film and television finance. Don had a partnership with Canadian film star Geneviève Bujold, most famous for her Golden Globe award and Academy Award nomination for *Anne of the Thousand Days*. In addition to being a tax lawyer and politician, Don was an aspiring film producer in the late 1960s and early 1970s, though he and Bujold produced only one film of consequence together, *Mon oncle Antoine*. These were the days of the 'wild west': a fledgling Canadian industry trying to copy successful American concepts. Don was among the pioneers of Canadian film-financing techniques, cleverly created to take advantage of the Canadian tax system, which led to the production of numerous television shows and motion picture films that no one can recall, such as *Professor Moffat's Science Workshop*. Revenue Canada[2] did not like any of these tax schemes and challenged them all. My job as a student in 1980 and then as a young lawyer was to follow these cases, which ran all the way to the Supreme Court of Canada.

The original concepts could be understood by anyone, and it so happened you could make money on a money-losing Canadian film, thanks to the Canadian tax system. This was a sure-fire way to get a solid, 100 percent return. You ran only two risks, that the Canadian government would close the tax loophole, and that the movie would actually make money. Virtually all of the Canadian movies in those days lost money, so it was a good bet.

---

[2] This is the term I use throughout (except in direct quotes) when referring to the entity established in 1927 as the Department of National Revenue and subsequently known as Revenue Canada in the 1970s, Canada Customs and Revenue Agency (CCRA) in the 1990s, and Canada Revenue Agency (CRA) in 2003.

It worked like this: Say you invested $100 in a Canadian film. In those days marginal tax rates were as high as 60 percent and you could write off the entire investment, so you saved $60 in tax by investing. But here was the beautiful twist: You didn't actually pay the full $100 in cash up front. You only had to put up $30 in cash, and you'd sign a promissory note for the balance of $70—payable *only if the movie made money*. If it didn't make money—and you could be pretty sure something like *Professor Moffat's Science Workshop* wouldn't—you didn't have to repay the $70. The rest of the deal was right out of *The Producers*, except you were not buying "Springtime for Hitler." If the film generated zero dollars, your $30 cash investment made you $60, a 100 percent return. It wasn't nearly as good a deal if the movie made money, though. Say the film generated $70 of revenue. Now you'd have to pay the moviemaker the $70 you'd promised, plus $42 in taxes on the film revenues. So instead of making $30 on your investment, you'd lose $12. You can see why investors needed these pictures to fail. And fail they did! You can also understand why the government hated them.

The first generation of these deals was thrown out by the courts. As a result, the investors ended up losing their money and their tax benefits. These were not just any investors. Many of them now have their names on buildings on university campuses across the country. I was still a nobody, but I was representing some of Canada's corporate elite on these tax litigation files.

The bottom of the totem pole also gave me my first direct exposure to the film business. Up until the end of 1984, American actors who shot movies in Canada did not have to pay Canadian tax even though they were providing services in Canada. This was one of the quirks of the old tax treaty between Canada and the United States. Very often, however, Canadian producers withheld tax at source on these payments, so the actors' agents would hire us to recover the tax withheld. The files ended up on my desk with a note from Danny Levinson that read something like "Please figure this out." It was scut work, of no importance to a senior lawyer, but great fun for an aspiring tax lawyer like me who was just learning the ropes. Within a year I became a Canadian expert on the subject of US and other foreign actors working in Canada, mostly because almost no one else in the country had enough file work to bother.

— • —

My first serious error occurred in my second year as a lawyer—when I felt the impact of the sophomore jinx I had read about in sports magazines. My years as a student and then a first-year lawyer had been outstanding, but suddenly my brain hit a wall. I was having difficulty focusing on problems, and slowly my confidence began to erode. I was responsible for drafting the arguments in a case that Danny Levinson argued before the Income Tax Appeal Board for a significant real estate client. We lost the case at trial in the spring and the client wanted us to file an appeal. While on summer vacation I had the sickening feeling there was a deadline to file the appeal that I had never diarized. I didn't know when it was, but I became convinced I had missed the date. This was in the days before our insurers insisted we institute formal systems to diarize all the key dates on our litigation files, but there was no question it was my responsibility to remember. Sick with worry, I returned from vacation and immediately went to see Danny. I suppressed my misery and admitted the mistake.

Danny's immediate reaction surprised me. He blamed himself for not exercising the proper oversight and hauled us over to Jean's office. I was prepared to make my confession when Danny beat me to the punch and admitted the error. Jean was not a stupid man. Fully expecting to be fired, I was shocked when Jean picked up the phone and advised the client of the mistake he had made in missing the deadline. My name never came up in the conversation because the two partners shouldered the blame. Due to Jean's excellent connections and relationships with the Department of Justice, his adversaries waived the default. Danny forced me to handle the appeal on my own, and while I'm still quite critical of my performance, I won the case on a legal technicality having nothing to do with the merits. I learned two of the most valuable lessons of my career from that experience, which I used as teaching material once I was in a position of authority in the firm.

First: admit to your mistakes as soon as you become aware of them. It is a sign of strong character. Yes, we all make mistakes, but it requires backbone to step up and own them. In any event, that is now a requirement of law firm insurance coverage. The tangled web of lies required to hide an error slowly eats away at the fabric of your personality.

Second, and even more important in terms of philosophy and approach to building young lawyers: the partner takes responsibility. Never hang a junior lawyer out to dry, especially in front of a client. No salary increase, however large, or performance review, however favourable, could have engendered in me the kind of loyalty I felt to Jean and the firm as a result of his act. From that day forward, he owned me. This story, repeated over a period of years, would add to the mythology of the organization. We were a firm that took care of its own. The United States Armed Forces have a motto, "No man left behind." From that day on, I believed Heenan Blaikie stood for a similar principle.

— ◉ —

The firm attracted little public attention until the day in 1984 when Peter announced that former prime minister Pierre Trudeau, who had recently retired from politics, was joining the firm as counsel. This was a real coup for the young firm. We were just past our tenth anniversary when we shared the auspicious news with the world. Roy and Jean Potvin, who in 1978 had inherited from Don the role of personal tax advisor to the prime minister, had spent many months explaining the firm ethos to Mr. Trudeau. They were able to convince him that their firm, given its nature and its camaraderie, was the right place for him when he returned to private life. He would play a statesmanlike and outward-facing role for the firm vis-à-vis the public. No unpleasant or onerous demands would be placed on him, and in particular, he would not be focused on client work, which would be considered mundane for a former head of state.

Mr. Trudeau gave the firm instant credibility internationally. He was well known in every corner of the world, and based on his presence in the firm most people made the assumption that we were a high-powered, New York–style firm, rather than a more family-like group of thirty professionals who just wanted to have some fun working on sophisticated files. Until the day it was announced that Mr. Trudeau was joining Heenan Blaikie, we were relatively unknown in the business community outside Montreal. As an added benefit after he joined, I no longer had to spell the name of the firm to Americans.

After a half-dozen years, Mr. Trudeau went to Peter and asked that we stop paying him a salary. The office and secretarial assistance were sufficient. "I have never been beholden to anyone, and I do not want to be beholden as an employee of Heenan Blaikie." From that point on, he served the firm entirely on his own terms, making himself available for client lunches and other receptions, doling out sage advice in situations where we needed a completely different perspective on a problem, and meeting his political friends from all over the world.

While we were not close, I did have the chance to spend some time with Mr. Trudeau and found his assessment of situations—whether world crises, domestic politics, or legal issues—to be filled with insights that no one else could have. He could conduct a geopolitical assessment of a problem in light of his own experience as a world leader. A student of the law and of history, he could analyze problems in unique ways. I also found him to be a shy man in crowds, though not at all unfriendly. He was not an attention seeker and would never be the life of the party, because he felt no need to impress others publicly or privately. His door was always open to those who wanted to talk with him, and when approached, he showed a genuine interest and was impressive on virtually any subject.

Mr. Trudeau dispensed with his security team one year after leaving government. Unlike his American counterparts, who had security officers for life, he had no interest in being followed around or chaperoned. His house on Pine Avenue, classified as a historical monument, was high on the downtown-facing slope of Mount Royal, a healthy walk from the office. But walk it he did, downhill to work and steeply uphill on the way home in the evening. He had no fear of being approached by strangers on his journeys and would always stop to speak to any passerby when recognized.

I had my 'life moment' as a young associate one evening when Roy had a reception at his home in Westmount in September 1984. I was heading out the door to get home to my wife and young son at the same time as Mr. Trudeau was also making his early departure, so I politely offered him a lift home. Somewhat to my surprise, he accepted. Knowing that I was not a particularly good small-talker, I had a low-level panic attack. We had never spoken before, other than perfunctory friendly greetings in the corridors. I struggled on the way to the car to find a subject of common interest.

"How are your children?" I finally asked as we settled into our seats. The one subject we had in common. Justin was probably around twelve at the time, while Sacha and Michel were younger than my son Brian.

"It's very interesting," Mr. Trudeau replied. "When I was a boy growing up, I was reading Dostoyevsky and various philosophers. There was no such thing as television, and while I would listen to the odd radio broadcast, I spent most of my spare time reading. My children are far more interested in *Star Wars*. I have no idea what will become of them." I could not have imagined that the *Star Wars* fan would eventually succeed his father, ushering in the 2015 instalment of the sci-fi franchise.

We spent the rest of our short time together chatting about family and the value of being close with our children. I told him about our house rule, imposed by Sharon, that we had to have dinner together as a family every night. As he left the car and said good night, I felt very proud that I had survived the conversation unscathed.

Mr. Trudeau's legacy to the firm was in putting us on the global map of law firms. I learned an important lesson in business through his association with us. While most lawyers are expected to make their contribution through a combination of legal skill and an ability to generate work, there is a rare breed of individual that can help establish and build the firm's brand. Mr. Trudeau gave us instant worldwide credibility. An organization that is able to attract a prime minister must be doing something right; it projects an image of quality. While the linkage of his name with ours did not create immediate financial gain, he helped us build a reputation greater than the sum of our collective legal skills. This became an important precedent for me years later when I was considering whether to hire Jean Chrétien.

— • —

While the idiosyncrasies of Jean, Richard, and Danny Levinson and our interactions could fill an entire book, one anecdote involving Jean deserves repeating because of its impact on my career. An important file had come in from a major accounting firm. They wanted us to review a particularly complicated tax-related matter. The head of the tax department in Montreal had invited Jean over to make a presentation, and I had been asked to complete the research on the technical tax points. I worked around the clock with Neil Wiener, who was responsible for the commercial law issues. After a week of solid work, I produced a lengthy memo for Jean outlining the main points and conclusions. There were four key issues. He reviewed the memo the night before the meeting, and the three of us sat down to discuss it the morning of the meeting.

I had a process for dealing with Jean in these briefings, so I had to explain to Neil the way our meeting with Jean would progress. Jean was an extremely quick study, but unless I got him to repeat the arguments back to me so that they became his answers, there was a risk he would get things wrong in front of the client. We followed the protocol and Jean was kind enough to bring me along with him to the meeting to sit in "and keep my mouth shut." I was there to observe.

The accounting firm offices were located in one of the towers on Dorchester Boulevard (now known as René Lévesque Boulevard), beside the landmark Queen Elizabeth Hotel. I knew it was critically important for Jean to shine in this key meeting. The head of tax was trying him out for the first time, and if the meeting was successful, there would be other opportunities and more work. Jean performed well going through the first three issues, exactly as rehearsed. The fourth issue was a very technical argument, and I understood it was probably the most critical issue. Jean wound his way through the argument and concluded confidently that the answer was "X." The argument was not simple, however, and my own conclusion was the opposite of "X."

The head of tax raised his eyebrows. "You're prepared to opine that the answer is 'X'?"

He looked pleased, and I began to feel sick to my stomach. What was I to do? Jean kept on speaking while I quickly reviewed my options. I could follow his orders and say nothing, and wait until we got back to the office to explain to Jean how he had gotten it completely wrong. That would involve a very embarrassing retraction call to the head of tax. Or I could attempt to correct Jean's conclusion there in the meeting, or at least make it clear that Jean might have glossed over some of the risks associated with "X," thereby adding a degree of qualification to that conclusion. That would make the follow-up less embarrassing.

This was truly a moment of truth and I was no longer listening to the conversation. Instead I was weighing my career options, standing on the precipice and deciding whether to jump. I waited until there was a lull in the conversation. I understood how I could fix this problem and plunged ahead. To this day I have no idea what I said, except that whatever it was made it clear that I did not agree with my boss: not very politic for a third-year lawyer, even if I was right.

The head of tax saved us both from immediate embarrassment by saying, "So you really mean that Jean's point does not represent a likely court conclusion, just an aggressive tax argument?"

"Yes," I nodded, believing I had successfully threaded the eye of the needle. The meeting ended shortly afterward and I congratulated myself for showing such fortitude.

We stepped out of the building into the frosty mist of René Lévesque Boulevard. It was bitterly cold and I could see my breath. Instead of heading for the crosswalk on the west side of the Queen Elizabeth Hotel, Jean forged directly ahead across the six lanes of René Lévesque, stepping over the two-foot-high concrete median designed to discourage jaywalking. As I stumbled over the median, thanking my lucky stars there was no oncoming traffic to crush me, Jean looked at me with those steely blue eyes, now penetrating my soul like icicles.

"Norman, if I had a gun right now, I would shoot you through the head." Those were the last words I would hear from him during the endlessly long and chilling walk back to the office. Jean eventually sent a letter with the correct opinion, and we never heard from the head of tax again, other than at social functions.

I came home that night firmly believing three things: that I was right; that I had done the right thing regardless of the outcome; and that I would be fired the next day. Sharon agreed with me on none of the points and reminded me that, at the very least, I had learned a valuable lesson about contradicting the boss in public. I grudgingly gave in, thinking to myself that had it been Levinson instead of Potvin, the scrum in front of the client would have been perfectly acceptable.

The matter was never raised again in the office, and Jean began speaking to me again after about a week. I don't think I ever apologized.

Jean waited until after I became a partner three years later to begin telling and retelling the story to anyone who would listen. It always ended the same way: "Can you believe that guy contradicted me in a meeting with such an important client? I still don't know why he changed his mind on the point from our briefing. He clearly told me 'X' and then he waits for the meeting to change his mind and contradict me. If I'd had a gun, I would have shot him in the head right then and there on René Lévesque, and I would not have lost a moment's sleep over it."

All I could do was keep my mouth shut and smile.

— • —

As young lawyers, Ken Atlas and I would go to lunch together regularly and exchange stories about the progress of our careers. He had moved out of the litigation group and into the commercial department, where he often worked for the intimidating Kip Cobbett and Claudette Bellemare, focusing on bank finance and insolvency, areas where he slowly developed a strong reputation. Our favourite lunch joint was Mister Steer on Saint Catherine Street, where they served their famous Steer burgers and curly french fries. Many times I would tell Ken, "I can't believe they pay me to do all this tax research." He'd looked at me quizzically, and years later admitted he thought my career was in a stall, that I was lost in the theoretical world, and that reality would eventually come crashing down on my head. As it turns out, it was about to. Jean Potvin's marriage fell apart and his personal life went into a tailspin. For almost two difficult years the strain impacted his work life and severely diminished the amount of new work coming into the department and landing on my desk.

Jean's career eventually got back on track, so much so that one day he would succeed Peter as the managing partner of the firm. We used to joke that Jean had been 'out to lunch' for an extended period, but the firm's management taught me yet another valuable lesson. While we associates would joke, belying our concerns about what was going on, management showed patience. No one voiced complaints while Jean went through his life crisis and came out the other side. No partners gossiped about him in the hallways, no one took steps to chastise or get rid of him, and no one complained about him behind his back. In fact Danny let us know about the trouble in Jean's life, and Peter and Roy advised the partners that they would have to pull together to help Jean. There was no issue, no question, no doubt. We were a family, with all the quiet support that went hand in hand with the dysfunction.

Over the years I've heard many people say, "It's just business," to support their harsh decisions. Peter's treatment of Jean always reminded me that business could be conducted another way. We all might make a little less money, but we were always proud of where we worked and who we were. This would factor into my long-term management philosophy. Many years later Sharon would remind Roy that this particular story was a reason why she always encouraged me to stay at the firm.

3

SHERIFF OF **DODGE CITY**

My cohort had been practising four years when the reviews and salary adjustments came out. For years we had all moved in lockstep, and the partners thought it was time to start drawing distinctions based on performance. My new salary was set at $61,000, which I thought was fair. In my review, Jean mentioned that he felt I wasn't reaching my potential. "Norman, something is missing, but I can't put my finger on it" was all I could remember of the entire review. Not particularly helpful advice either.

I was slightly bewildered and a little frustrated. Danny Levinson had always told me that the firm made partners once associates were behaving as if they were already partners and owners of the business. Partnership was no more than the recognition of a new status quo, rather than a brass ring or reward for hard work. I was still two years away from consideration, and I had not yet made the connection between Danny's assertion and Jean's observations.

That might have been the end of the story for me but for a discussion I had with Ken Atlas a couple of days later at Mister Steer.

He asked how my review went and whether I was satisfied with the increase in salary.

"I was a little disappointed to get only $63,000," he added. "I thought I had a great year and worked really hard."

I could feel my stomach muscles clench and my teeth grind as the number 63 hit the most sensitive corner of my psyche. The size of the discrepancy, the $2,000, was irrelevant. This was not about envy; it was about rejection. The partners had made the conscious decision that Ken was now more valuable than I was. What else might that mean? Was I no longer on a partnership track? I hid my feelings through lunch then brooded in my office, door shut, for the rest of the afternoon.

That evening I waited until the kids were tucked in and Sharon and I were in bed before raising the subject with her. After I blurted out the whole story, she reflected for a moment and then took charge.

She started off sympathetically, and then slowly began analyzing the situation. For four years I had been a good employee, did what was asked, stepped forward when called on. She pointed out, though, that I had not really taken control of my career, that I was a bystander watching it from the sidelines. I had to take more initiative, step up and focus on my strengths. I had a creative mind and a soft-spoken skill with people. My brain could analyze complex problems and break them into simple, solvable issues. I never gave up. This she had observed, and this other people needed to see. For two hours she spoke, she challenged, she encouraged, and she pushed to force me to really see myself. I could feel the depression lifting and slowly being replaced by a new enthusiasm, a new spark.

In my entire life I could never hope for a better friend than Sharon. That night she didn't change who I was, but she completely altered the perspective from which I saw myself. I was going to march into Jean's office the next day and demand a more thorough review. From this point forward, every meeting, every phone call, and every client experience would be a new opportunity for me to show Heenan Blaikie, and myself, exactly what Norm Bacal was all about. Sharon had the utmost confidence in my abilities. It was time for me to shine.

For some people, their life-altering moments are brought about by deep religious or spiritual experiences, visions, or dreams. For me, my wife's wise advice, which I spent that night absorbing, set my future on a whole new course.

I visited Jean the next morning and told him the review was unacceptable—it left me hanging without direction. He sat back and reflected—or, in his own words, "cogitated"—over the problem, then told me that it basically came down to initiative. I was doing everything asked of me. I had even published my first article in the Canadian Tax Foundation's prestigious *Canadian Tax Journal*, on the Canadian film industry, which established Richard Lewin and me as the experts on foreign actors, entertainers, and athletes coming to Canada. The partners knew, however, that I was capable of much more, and they just hadn't seen it.

I left his office and I was no longer depressed. If they wanted initiative, I was going to demonstrate it in spades. The second half of 1985 and 1986 represented my transition from young lawyer with unrealized potential to aspiring rainmaker.

A chance to prove myself soon arose. One of Jean's contacts was a player agent who was trying to get retained by Montreal Expos all-star outfielder Andre Dawson. Andre was a key ingredient, along with Ellis Valentine and Tim Raines, in a Montreal Expos outfield that had transformed the expansion franchise into one of the finest teams in major league baseball. In 1981 Richard Lewin and I watched in dismay from behind the plate as Rick Monday of the Los Angeles Dodgers took a Steve Rogers pitch over the wall to end the Expos' dream of going to a World Series.

Andre was about to become a free agent, and Jean was asked by the player agent to come up with an efficient tax plan that would make it worth Andre's while to stay in Canada in a higher tax bracket. The idea would then be sold to the Expos, who would use it to keep Andre from moving to the United States. My task was to design something original that would work for both Canadian and US tax purposes. I spent over a month on the plan, and for me the experience was a game changer.

I was forced to transform myself from a strong technical lawyer into a tax planner, and that required imagination. In the tax world, this is what separates the planners from the lifetime technicians, the men from the boys.

I came back with a plan that threaded the eyes of the Canadian and US tax needles and would allow the Expos to sign the "Hawk," as he was known, for the balance of his playing career, and past that into retirement. The plan satisfied everyone's objectives, but it was novel by Major League standards in that it provided for a unique structure of payments deferred until after the end of the contract and into retirement. So it would take some salesmanship. That was Jean's department. My reward on the file was lunch with the Hawk, who towered over me. I had no idea from watching him at a distance just how big his hands were. His shoulders were broad and he was built like a football player. He spoke softly and thoughtfully. He did not fit the image I had of a ballplayer. If there was ever an athlete who represented the ideals of my childhood hero Jean Béliveau, it was Andre Dawson. Soft-spoken and classy, both men let their actions, on and off the playing field, speak for their great skills, integrity, and humility. These were qualities I wanted to emulate in my own career.

The lunch was positive, but the ultimate outcome was not. Andre had decided that maintaining the health of his arthritic knees was more important than money. The artificial turf in Montreal was going to prematurely end his playing days. He opted for free agency, but Major League owners colluded against free agents that year, so there was no auction for his services. In the end he selected the grass at Wrigley Field in Chicago, where he spent the next few years.

More important, I had made the breakthrough. Perhaps the neural connections in my brain were firing differently, but I began to see the tax world as a series of puzzles I could now solve. It was very much like being a research scientist. Most scientists spend their careers trying to prove or disprove the work of others. The true trailblazers are those who deliver breakthroughs, typically spending years looking for new insights. Their brains function differently. Einstein relied on his imagination, performing thought experiments that others then proved or disproved. Tax planning is all about thought experiments. Today's analogy would be the worlds created in video games. You are walking down a lonely road, blocked with brick walls. You spend weeks running at the walls relentlessly, obstinately, until one of two things happens: either you get a very bad headache, turn back, and embark on a different road or you finally see the crack in the wall that you missed in all your previous efforts. You pick at the crack until you've made a hole, which in our profession we call the loophole. Once the hole is established, you create an entire scenario to take you from one side to the other.

Success at tax planning is like being in love. There's no way to explain the feeling to someone who has never experienced it. Once it happens, you learn to recognize the signs the next time. It cannot be taught, but once you've successfully designed your first plan, you have a methodology to work with and are energized by the success in whole new ways. You need to hold onto the memory of that breakthrough moment to carry you through the hours, days, weeks, and months that it will take to realize your next breakthrough. Some of my ideas would sit on the shelf for as many as ten to fifteen years, waiting for timing and opportunity to coincide in the elaboration of a new structure. Other ideas I abandoned along the way. Tax planning, like lab research, requires the learning experience of repeated failure to generate an ultimate groundbreaking concept that may take years. For those with a "fertile imagination," as Jean called it, there was nothing more fulfilling.

— • —

While Danny, Jean, and Richard mentored me in my early years, it was Michael Prupas who was the catalyst for the rapid upswing in my career. He sponsored my continuing development, taking me under his wing and contributing greatly to my success.

In 1982 Michael joined us from his own entertainment boutique with a coterie of film and television producer clients who would become Canadian legends. Denis Héroux, John Kemeny, and occasionally Robert Lantos, Roger Frappier, John Dunning, and André Link were among the most prominent members of Michael's clientele. André was the producer of Canada's first serious commercial film success, *Meatballs*, an early Bill Murray summer camp film.

Michael Prupas was a hard-nosed lawyer/businessman with a charming smile whose greatest talent was in holding a deal together during negotiations. Film producers are for the most part artistes, with hot tempers and creative insight, but not particularly good business skills. Michael filled that business gap for many of his clients, sitting through long negotiations, keeping bankers comfortable, making regular visits to the Hollywood studios and talent agencies, and generally holding his clients' hands from the time deal discussions commenced until the money funding the production was in the bank. No crisis was too great, no stumbling block too large. Michael's deals closed.

In the mid-1980s, in addition to government-agency funding, private investment was necessary to finance Canadian movies. Investors relied heavily on tax incentives, which they insisted be backed by the assurance of a formal tax opinion from a reputable law firm. In 1984 Michael needed such opinions for the deals his clients were involved in, and Danny Levinson decided that I would be the lawyer to provide them.

For many years one of our largest Canadian clients was a company called Astral Bellevue Pathé Limited, run by the Greenberg family. They were a Montreal success story. The company began in the photofinishing business and grew from a lab that processed the film negatives for some of the worst Canadian movies ever made to become one of the most powerful film distribution and pay television companies in Canada. Harold Greenberg, the family patriarch, was a good friend and client of Don Johnston. Don passed the client along to his protégé Kip Cobbett, and the file was run for years by Kip with the assistance of Danny Levinson. Shortly after Michael and I began working together, Kip left the firm to join Astral as president of its entertainment group, perhaps with the hopes of one day becoming Astral's CEO. At first this appeared to be a blow to our firm because we were losing our leading commercial lawyer. Danny Levinson reminded me that every departure created new possibilities for the younger lawyers in the firm. Sure enough, in this case Danny moved up to be the lead lawyer on the account and I moved to second position.

Any concerns I had were quelled when I recalled the wise advice my uncle Harry Bacal, one of Montreal's leading doctors, had given me on his deathbed: "Follow the current of your career, don't fight it." Uncle Harry had wanted to be an obstetrician, but opportunities arose for him in pediatrics and as an allergist. For his radical idea to inoculate Canadian troops heading overseas, a procedure that became standard in the Commonwealth, he was awarded the Order of the British Empire. Now here I was, an aspiring tax lawyer, with a chance to expand my horizons into the entertainment industry. Who would have guessed that would put me on the trail to becoming one of the leading entertainment lawyers in the country? Certainly not me.

One event was crucial in establishing my credentials in the film industry. Because I handled the files for foreign actors shooting movies in Canada, over the years I represented a number of Hollywood stars. I never got past their agents or accountants, though, so other than the name-dropping value within the firm, there was no glamour. At the beginning of 1985, Canada's new tax treaty with the United States came into force. One of the major changes meant that Canada became entitled to tax American actors filming in Canada.

I might still be an obscure Canadian lawyer if it weren't for Raymond Burr, the Hollywood actor who made famous the role of the defence attorney in *Perry Mason*, and later that of the wheelchair-bound private detective in the hit series *Ironside*. One day in 1985 in the middle of filming in Vancouver, he stormed out, refusing to return until the producer agreed to cover him for any taxes Canada now wanted to impose on his fee as an actor. No one had advised his agent that the rules had changed on January 1. Suddenly there was a crisis. Many producers feared news of this scandal would spread and that all producers would be asked to swallow the Canadian tax as a cost of getting the top US actors to come to Canada.

An industry lobby was assembled, and within a year the advisors to the lobby were two very young professionals: Mark Prior, who ran a growing payroll service out of Toronto, and me. We were thrown together to help lead the charge in educating Hollywood and achieving some compromise with Ottawa. I began publishing articles on the subject, and by 1986 I was recognized as *the* Canadian expert. In May 1986 I made my first trip to Los Angeles at the urging of Michael Prupas and gave a speech along with Neil Harris of Goodmans, who was far more senior, to a room full of film and television producers. It launched my reputation there. I could not yet appreciate the importance of that speaking engagement, since Sharon and I made a vacation out of it. We drove through Big Sur, along the spectacular Pacific Coast Highway, and then along the Ventura highway in the sunshine. While in the process of becoming the Canadian expert on the thinnest wedge of tax law, I was about to embark on a journey that would take me down a career-defining path in the film and television industry.

Between 1979 and 1984 film investment had fallen into disfavour. The structures of the previous decade had been abandoned. A number of public movie syndications without any gimmicks were floated. In those deals the investors paid $100 cash and were entitled to write off the cost of the investments, but by and large the films performed poorly. The most famous of the lot was *Running* with Michael Douglas; most of the others are still completely unheard of other than by the angry investors who lost the balance of their investment.

Before he left to join Astral, Kip Cobbett asked me to do a piece of research that would become the cornerstone of my career. He noted that for years mining companies had been raising money in the public markets by issuing flow-through shares. This gave investors tax deductions along with shares they could sell. The appetite of Canadian investors for the product was insatiable.

Kip asked whether we could design something analogous for a film or television investment. Film was still a four-letter word to most investors. It had never been done before, "but if the resource guys could figure it out, why couldn't we?" I spent six months researching the question. Astral was paying for the research, and if we came up with a product, they would be the prime beneficiary. Fresh off my Andre Dawson success, I felt confident as I refined the idea with input from Richard and Danny. For the first time, a Canadian film production would be syndicated to investors through a Canadian limited partnership. The liquidity in the deal would be provided by a subsidiary of Astral. The structure was simple and elegant, but it was also revolutionary. Would it sell? Would the other law firms reviewing our tax opinion accept or reject it?

I was responsible for every aspect of the deal; I was a veritable one-man band. For the first time in my career, I was in charge: responsible for the tax opinion, the offering document, all the contracts, and the closing. The experience had me working around the clock with Claudette Bellemare, whom I had feared as a junior lawyer. Her role was to review all my work that was not tax related. In my career I never worked with a lawyer with greater endurance for all-nighters or with a greater ability to catch typos at four in the morning.

The plan itself was not all that complicated, but it was revolutionary enough to change the face of film finance in Canada. The original premise had not changed. The tax plan I had learned from Don Johnston worked brilliantly for Canadian movies that failed financially. But now we lived in a world where investors would likely recover most of their investment, so we came up with a new plan that would work whether or not the film made money.

The core of the new scheme was a buyback option. If you invested $100 in a film through a limited partnership, the producer would promise to buy back your investment within two years for $85. If the film was a success you could keep the partnership unit. If not, you could exercise the buyback option and limit your loss to $15.

That does not sound very good—until you factor in the magic of the Canadian tax system. Capital gains tax was one-half the ordinary tax rate, so this was an arbitrage. You saved tax on the purchase at a

60 percent tax rate, but you paid tax on the sale at a 30 percent rate. If you were a high-income earner, after counting the tax savings and capital gains tax, you ended up with a profit of $13, or over 20 percent of your after-tax cost, *regardless of whether the film made any money*. Who would not want an investment like that? The tax system made the whole investment risk-free.

This was a primitive version of a structure that by 1986 would become known in the Canadian film industry and in Hollywood as "the buyback." The tax plan involved many hurdles and challenges, the last of which was worked out at the eleventh hour. We had broken new ground in Canadian film finance. While those at Astral were convinced that Astral owned the plan's design, Michael Prupas had other ideas. This would become a bone of contention between Harold Greenberg, Astral's CEO, and the firm, and it would later entail a personal cost to me and to the firm.

In the meantime, Michael Prupas began to see the value I could be creating for his clientele, and I felt as though I was being given a new life. My new outlook, the product of my conversation with Sharon, was about to be engaged. A few days after my performance discussion with Jean, Michael spoke to me about a problem his clients Frank Jacobs and André Link were having with the financing of André's newest movie, *National Park*. Frank was the financier and André the producer. They wanted to do the buyback deal that Michael had bragged about, and Michael had sold me as the expert on the subject, which happened to be true, since the mechanics of the structure were still locked in my head. I was now the master of my own career, and I vowed I would never attend another meeting as second fiddle. From now on, if I was attending a meeting, I was not the tax geek. I was going to own the meeting and run it.

I moderated a meeting of about ten people sitting around a boardroom table, including André and his production team and Frank, as well as the brokers and accountants. I was all of twenty-nine and my baby face made me look even younger. The barrage of questions began. Instead of waiting to be called on by someone more senior, today I was running the entire show. I 'owned' the structure, but questions were popping up about issues that I had never considered. Jean's skating ability, which I had observed for years and apparently absorbed, kicked in, and I found myself able to comfortably answer questions on the spot or to simply take note of them, typically in the case of non-tax related issues, and undertake to get back to people with answers later. I began to realize that being a good lawyer was as much about being a good leader as having a brain.

The key was to show confidence without arrogance, to not be afraid to admit that I didn't have all the answers at my fingertips, and to take responsibility for follow-up and delegation of tasks. These were skills that I could see our clients valuing. The meeting ended well and I was on my way to completing my second deal. Frank Jacobs is still a steady client, almost thirty years later.

In short order Danny announced that he too was leaving the firm to join Kip at Astral. While my mentor and security blanket was departing, he was going to become my client, since suddenly I had taken over one of the largest and most historic accounts in the firm. I wasn't certain I was prepared to handle this challenge, but there was no looking back. Kip and Danny were both very encouraging, and I had begun to see that perhaps I had misjudged Kip. My fear of him had turned into a genuine respect, which I sensed was mutual.

— • —

Meanwhile Michael had made the acquaintance of Joseph (Joe) Cohen, a New York financier with some interesting connections to Hollywood. Joe had a finance background and spent a number of years working on US production financing for a number of studios. He was a student of US film financings, which had been prevalent since the late 1970s. Joe also idolized the man he considered the dean of US tax structuring, Peter Hoffman, the name partner of Gipson Hoffman & Pancione in Los Angeles. Joe and Peter wanted to explore the possibility of relying on my new structure to raise funds in Canada to produce films for the US market.

Peter was the embodiment of a classic New York–style lawyer. Brilliant, tough, impatient, aggressive, and filled with ideas, he seemed the type that ate Canadian lawyers for lunch. He had been the brains behind a series of US syndications in the early 1980s that raised hundreds of millions of dollars for the US studios. He knew everyone and everything about the US tax aspects of film finance. A fast talker, Peter had pushed every limit and experimented with every scheme. His aggressive style had an impact on his structures and his human relations. After our first deal, Peter left the practice of law to become CEO of Carolco Pictures, Inc., an independent studio, which went on to make some blockbuster movies, including the *Terminator* series. Things would not end well for Carolco. The company overspent and underperformed, and its recordkeeping was suspect for a public company. This led to Peter's first indictment by the United States Department of Justice a number of years later.

But back to 1986: life was still sunshine and roses for Peter and Carolco, although Peter was to hold my relatively inexperienced feet to the fire.

Joe Cohen's idea was to create the first serious Canadian film fund. Joe was bringing his US relationships with Peter and Carolco, and he expected Michael Prupas to supply the Canadian producers and the tax formula to make this work. The natural place for Michael to begin, since he had no working relationship with Astral, was Alliance Communications, based in Toronto.

Alliance had recently been formed as a true alliance of some of Canada's biggest names in film and television production. Robert Lantos and Victor Loewy had first made their mark together as university students, filming excerpts of the New York Erotic Film Festival and selling the package for great publicity and profit. Robert's claim to fame had been the film *In Praise of Older Women*, along with a few film productions based on the novels of Mordecai Richler and a slew of television productions, including the series *Night Heat*, which notably had played on the CBS television network. Denis Heroux and John Kemeny, two of the other partners, were among Quebec's acclaimed film producers.

With my help, Joe Cohen spent months figuring out the Canadian tax system and was fascinated by the buyback I had designed. He retained us to work on putting a deal together involving up to four productions to be made by Alliance and financed in part by Carolco. A major Canadian investment house, Richardson Greenshields, would be retained to market the deal to investors. We had numerous phone conversations with Peter Hoffman. He grilled me on the limits of the Canadian tax rules and wanted to know whether we could import into our structures certain concepts he had built into his US deals. As I had learned through my own diligence, most of what Peter had designed in the United States had been outlawed there. But there was a fertile field of old ideas to borrow from, since Canada's rules were nowhere near as advanced or sophisticated.

Our cast of characters now included a burgeoning Canadian production company (Alliance), America's most aggressive new film studio as distributor (Carolco), a major European bank, a letter of credit, a Canadian bank that agreed to lend money to the investors, and an 'Omnibus Agreement' linking all the parties together—as well as a multitude of law firms, whose input added depth and sophistication to the documentation. The plot for the buyback investment could be summarized as follows: Carolco was permitted by Canadian tax law to guarantee future revenues to the investors. The future payment obligation as well as the buyback were secured by a letter of credit issued by a major European bank. That additional security allowed investors to borrow a large portion of their investment from the Canadian bank, safe in the knowledge that, regardless of Carolco's future ability to pay the guarantee, the proceeds of the letter of credit, when drawn, would pay back the bank loan. In a matter of eighteen months I had progressed from creating a basic étude for my first deal, an Astral made-for-television movie called *Half a Lifetime* (starring Gary Busey), to composing and conducting a full symphony called Canadian Entertainment Investors (CEI), the first prospectus film offering in Canada in five years. Michael handled the film-related agreements between Alliance and Carolco, while I was in charge of all the tax aspects for Alliance and the investors, coordinating between Canada and the United States. In May 1987 we finally filed the prospectus, attempting to finance four pictures simultaneously with a goal of raising $45 million. The brokers only managed to raise about $20 million to fund two pictures. Nonetheless, they considered it a success, opening the doors to seven years of successful film finance in Canada.

During numerous phone calls spent working on the CEI structure, Peter Hoffman tried to push every limit imaginable. He cross-examined me on the Canadian rules, challenged my assertions, and asked hundreds of questions about various features permitted at one time in the United States and which he hoped to add in order to gain every possible advantage. I was the gatekeeper and we were breaking new ground on virtually every issue. While the rules relating to the production of the films were black and white, most other issues fell into a grey zone where there were no firm answers. A successful tax planner understands the difference between setting up structures to lawfully reduce taxes payable by investors through legitimate structures, and abusive tax plans that involve avoidance or evasion of tax. The demarcation line is often blurred. Clever tax planners need to develop instincts and judgment to keep their clients on the right side of the line.

This called on parts of my personality that had never been tested. I had to know where to draw the line. It was going to be an arbitrary line, based on my limited experience and judgment, but I was not going to be bullied into crossing that line. There was no one else in the country to ask, since we were making this up as we went along. I knew for certain that one day the deal would be scrutinized and would have to be defended as reasonable, and that on that day there would be no Joe Cohen, no Peter Hoffman, nobody except Norm Bacal and Heenan Blaikie. So I drew a series of perpendicular lines. These lines became my box, and I was not going to permit anything outside that box. In my conversations with Peter I had to draw on an inner strength to push back, to defend the box, to set the limits, and to end up with a transaction that would stand up to the closest scrutiny.

In hindsight, if I had not established these standards, my career would have been over before it began. I understood that I was the sheriff of Dodge City. To preserve the town, I would have to create and then defend the law. Peter was the gunslinger, and I instinctively understood the nature of the threat and the damage it was capable of wreaking if not restrained. The structure would ultimately stand up to the diligence of countless major law firms. Eventually Revenue Canada approved the concept, issuing many advance tax rulings for variants of the basic structure, which helped spur Canadian television production.

— • —

After the first CEI transaction closed, I began spending nights and weekends working on my second article for the Canadian Tax Foundation. It would be a history of film and television tax-based finance in Canada. This was really a compendium of all the research I had done at the firm since 1980, following Don Johnston's old cases going back to the late 1960s and right through to CEI. I had hoped that this work would push me to the forefront of film finance, not only in Canada but in the United States as well. Early in my career I had read the works of Richard Wise, a CA who wrote about the early days of film finance in Canada and had been involved with Don and a number of others on the earliest tax structures. As I read them, I remember thinking that one day I hoped to become the film industry's new Richard Wise, someone who, along with Don, was a recognized authority on the subject. My article and the spinoffs generated for US legal and film-finance periodicals added to a very busy year. CEI was launched and was the first of nine deals over the next few years as my independent client base continued to grow. I spent hundreds of hours (many between 9 p.m. and 4 a.m.) on the development and refinement of my expertise.

The use of bank leverage in these investments and the security to back the repayment unlocked Pandora's box. For the next sixteen years the Department of Finance would change the rules to try to restrict our abilities to limit the investor risk on these deals. The tax rates changed, the capital gains tax rates changed, rules restricting how to limit risk were added, and debt restrictions were imposed. They could slow us down, but nothing could stop us. All these changes simply resulted in an ongoing evolution of our technology.

From my perspective, while the changes were frustrating, they also presented a huge opportunity. Each time the law changed, a new level of ingenuity was required to survive. In light of any proposed changes, I had to go back to the drawing board and rethink the theory of each deal, making adjustments in order to complete the financings. The first change was made in the middle of the *National Park* financing. The tax rule changes were announced late in the day mid-week, and the brokers and producers went into a panic. I told them to give me the evening to analyze the changes, and by the next morning I had engineered a workaround. Ironically, the first change prevented buybacks from taking place at a pre-agreed fixed price. The new "at-risk" rules would, however, permit purchases at fair market value determined at a future date. I was on the phone the next morning with Richard Wise with a novel idea. By lunchtime, we had developed a change that required Richard's firm to perform an independent valuation, a modification to the buyback that would be acceptable to all the parties and would form the basis of all our future deals.

That was the story of my career. Each change pushed my back up against the wall, requiring imagination and guile to survive and flourish. Our structures financed billions of dollars of production and helped to build a Canadian industry. Yet there was always a tension between the two arms of the government: one that wanted to support a successful domestic film and television industry and understood that financing had to be encouraged from the private sector; and the other that preached fairness in the tax system and worried about rich

Canadians not paying their fair share of taxes due to the elaborate schemes that were evolving.

While the beginning of 1985 posed all kinds of questions about my career, within eighteen months I had begun to convince myself that come January 1987 I might become a partner of the firm. The size of my practice had grown to the point where I was generating enough revenue to put me on a par with one-third of the partners. There was only one problem: Ken Atlas, Neil Wiener, Bruce McNiven, and I had come through the system together, and there were many good reasons not to rush all of us into the partnership at the same time. At this point, would the partners really advance one of us ahead of the others? Over time, as my confidence in my abilities increased, I slowly convinced myself this was a possibility.

Danny Levinson, who had left the firm for Astral in the middle of 1986, had drummed into us the HB philosophy of partnership: one became a partner of the firm only when one was already behaving like a partner. The act of admission to the partnership was no more than an acknowledgment of the new, already established reality. Partnership was not a new timeline, not a starting line, but merely another point on the continuum of a successful career arc. Most partnerships spend countless hours debating the merits of new admissions. Danny's view had been that a candidate's name should not be on the table for more than thirty seconds. If a debate ensued, then the candidate should have to wait. The 'thirty-second test,' as it came to be known, always got us our best partner material. In principle, the decision was instinctive and based on the unanimously shared view of the partners that the candidate was outstanding. After all, isn't that what you want from a partner?

Alas, the firm rarely applied the test uniformly; to be fair, I am not certain how many other firms espouse this philosophy, but I expect most would find it difficult to apply, particularly as they become large and have to cater to the views of many partners in multiple offices. There had been, and in the future there would continue to be, debates over some excellent candidates. A reasonably safe conclusion, however, was that the longer a particular debate lasted, the more likely it was that the candidate should not be admitted. Often, battle fatigue set in and mistakes would be made.

Between October and December 1986, I had convinced myself that the firm had no choice but to admit me. I received the greatest vote of confidence from Sharon, who stood beside me at my lowest moment, focused me on my strengths, and helped to point me in the direction she was certain I should be headed. Ken Atlas and I had a number of discussions about the partnership issue over Steer burgers, and he was considerably more pessimistic. He also expected to be a shoo-in on an individual basis but was certain the partners would make the four of us wait what had now become the standard six years. The rational corner of my brain knew he was right, but the emotional side, which I usually kept under tight check, was taking over. An inner voice whispered that if I continued my ascent, there would be no choice but to admit me to the partnership now. Knowing that a seat at the partnership table was mine, I kept pushing, doing outstanding work on a litigation-related file for Max Bernard, one of our best commercial litigation partners, a true contrarian and someone I believed would be an ally.

When Jean and Richard sat down with me in mid-January to explain they were thrilled with my progress but I was going to have to wait one more year, I was devastated. The disappointment ignited a tinderbox of anger. I wasn't prepared to accept this defeat. As I walked out of Jean's office all I could blurt out was "You've just made a very big mistake." The statement was minimalist yet rash. Was it an open-ended threat or simply an echo of frustration? I only cared at that moment that they would not be able to know which it was.

Did I mean that they'd made a mistake not distinguishing me from the other three candidates? Or perhaps that they were underestimating the depth of my disappointment? Were they taking it for granted that as a consummate team player I would accept this decision and wait the year, at which point partnership was more or less guaranteed? I eventually calmed down, and judging from the results in 1987, the partners had taken an excellent calculated risk. The rejection I experienced might have demotivated me and dragged on my performance. Instead I spent every moment of the year proving them wrong. My practice continued to blossom, and by the time they made the four of us partners together a year later, my billings were among those of the top ten lawyers in the firm. By the end of my first year as a partner in January 1989, my practice was second in size only to Roy's.

By spring 1987 I had gotten over my tantrum and slipped back into a work rhythm that would underlie my operating philosophy for the next twenty-five years. I stopped trying to grasp for what was out of reach, instead allowing success to come to me. My new mantra: work smart, take every opportunity that presents itself, stay a step ahead of every client, then allow things to work out for the best. This strategy was a modification of my earlier laissez-faire approach and required not only quiet confidence in my own abilities but also great faith that my clients, colleagues, and friends would recognize my abilities and respond accordingly. Over the years I had observed various negative role models who were in it for themselves, insisted on hogging the glory, and surrounded themselves with weak personalities. They might have become very rich or powerful, but in my eyes they were not worthy of respect. So I learned to steer my ego out of the way and push credit onto others. I had to trust that the rewards would find me. This would be a core tenet of my development as a leader. And while there might have been moments when I did not feel particularly humble about the achievements I helped to bring about, I understood it was important to remain understated.

— • —

The CEI experience had given Michael Prupas a relationship with Alliance that he deeply wanted to maintain. Their chief financial officer, Jay Firestone, just six months my junior, continually peppered Michael with tax questions, and Michael would continually hedge before coming back to him with answers in a day or two. Jay is the type of client who doesn't just ask questions. He is ready with a hundred follow-up questions, and rarely accepts an answer without reasoning it through. In these cases Michael was playing a shuttle role and keeping me in the background, while Jay was getting frustrated because it was becoming apparent to him that Michael was being prepped by someone else. Eventually Jay wanted to speak directly to this "Norm Bacal the Heenan tax expert," assuming I was a sedentary tax nerd in his late sixties.

No one would ever accuse Jay of being laid-back. He was a bundle of energy, exploding in bursts, always studying new schemes and challenging the status quo. He sported a Groucho Marx moustache and spoke quickly and occasionally without a pause. Alliance Communications had grown dramatically from humble beginnings when Robert Lantos, the passionate Hungarian, joined forces with Victor Loewy, his Romanian university buddy, to produce and distribute films and television shows. Robert ran the company and Victor ran distribution. In Jay's opinion, Robert and Victor knew how to spend money while Jay was the only one worrying about how to conserve it. Industry insiders speculated that during the ten years after Jay became established as the CFO of the company, often when they disagreed, Jay would simply ignore Robert's wishes. Jay felt that Victor, who ran the distribution division, was spending too much money that the company didn't have. Victor felt Jay was no more than a bean-counter, without any creative vision. Robert was the passionate Hungarian and Victor the short-tempered Romanian with a seldom-used verbal filter. Whatever Victor's thought at a particular moment, he expressed it out loud, for better or worse. As a result he and Jay would go at one another regularly, neither one holding anything back. The two played cat and mouse around Robert, each showing complete disdain for the other. Somehow the dysfunction worked for many successful years.

Eventually Jay started calling me directly. Having mastered Peter Hoffman, I knew I could handle anyone. Many hours of my professional career would be spent in the Alliance offices on Yonge Street just north of Davenport Road. While the premises were modest, the support staff looked as if they had been recruited from a modelling agency. Perhaps they had. I would not put it past Robert to figure that film-industry types waiting for meetings would appreciate the view.

My first few years were spent assisting with their film-finance business. Eventually, with Jay's support, I worked with Jay, Robert, and board member Ellis Jacob, now CEO of Cineplex Inc., handling the Alliance initial public offering (IPO) in the early 1990s. But I'm getting a little ahead of the story.

— • —

The Canadian income tax system is guarded by a two-headed dragon. The Department of Finance sets tax policy and is responsible for any changes to the tax system, reflected in amendments to the *Income Tax Act* or its regulations. Revenue Canada is responsible for interpretation and compliance with the law and regulations crafted by Finance. Support of a structure by Revenue Canada may be of great value, but occasionally it is the harbinger of bad tidings. When Finance institutes new rules, Revenue Canada may subsequently interpret them in a manner that Finance believes is not intended. In those cases, Finance will go back to the drawing board to correct the perceived problem. As a result of this process, the taxpayer or tax planner can be burned either by a sudden change in the law or regulations, or by a reversal in interpretation by either head of the dragon.

By 1987 the buyback had become a mainstream form of film and television finance in Canada. In fact it had become so popular that the Department of Finance decided to take steps to curb the flow of too much investor funding into the Canadian industry. The 100 percent fast write-off was designed to encourage risk-taking. It was never intended to be part of a strategy to eliminate investment risk, which is what the buyback had achieved.

Production may have been at an all-time high, and job creation in the industry had also risen to its highest levels, but Finance wanted the risk put back into investment. The department issued a press release announcing a major change in 1988. They eliminated the 100 percent write-off and replaced it with a 30 percent deduction. Most experts believed that the change would kill private financing of the Canadian film and television production business.

The Canadian film and television communities went into a panic. From this experience, which threatened to have a severe impact on my livelihood, I learned some new, indispensable lessons. The first was that anyone who lived by government policy was sure to die on that cross. The second was that every roadblock presented new opportunities.

Leaders in the industry quickly banded together to fight the perceived injustice and to lobby the politicians not to change the rules. Since all of this was tax related, the industry needed input and leadership from the tax community. I quickly offered to lend my services to the cause. Though not yet a partner, I was involved in meetings with production company leaders from across the country, and mine was the only voice that could speak the language of tax. Producers, distributors, and provincial and federal funding agencies all would come to know me and listen to my views and strategies, which gave me the chance to lead a coalition urging Ottawa to fix the rules. The CEO of Telefilm Canada, Peter Pearson, blamed me for the change in the first place and referred to me as the *bête noire* of the industry. I wasn't sure whether this was a compliment or an insult, but at the very least the buyback had lent me, a thirty-one-year-old tax lawyer from Montreal, a certain notoriety. The contacts I made with Toronto producers gave me an industry prominence I could never have planned.

The lobby effort failed, and I returned to my drawing board to see what I could do with the newly announced rules. It took a few months of research, but I eventually came up with a novel financing structure that I intended to roll out in the second half of 1988 (once the grandfathering period for the old rules expired). The new structure would not be as generous to the producers, but a growing audience of investors had come to believe that Canadian film and television was a good investment. So if we came out with a product that provided tax advantages similar to the buyback model, private-sector finance of the industry could continue. This may not have been what Finance was anticipating, but I was following the new rules. By accepting the new structure, producers could immediately earn their producer fees and reinvest them in their next productions. The gears that turned the wheels of the industry could continue to move. All I needed was a blessing once more from Revenue Canada. If I could quietly get it, I would have a six-month head start on all the competitors. Since we did not want any copycat structures, we kept the new formula under close guard, like any industrial secret. I understood the value of an idea when it was a monopoly.

— • —

After Kip Cobbett left, Roy's sense of disappointment in the senior commercial lawyers in the firm was palpable. He loved them all but respected none. The frustration over the commercial group's perceived inability to grow might have driven a serious wedge between the partners at most firms. Ironically, patience—perhaps procrastination would be the better word—was the remedy in our case. The firm's recruiting of young, homegrown talent over the years had been impeccable. Ken Atlas, Neil Wiener, Bruce McNiven, and I would form a solid core going forward, as would Danny Kaufer, Robert Dupont, and Robert Bonhomme in the labour group and Clément Gascon (a future Supreme Court judge) and Marie-Josée Hogue (a future justice of the Court of Appeal of Québec) in litigation. They would in turn be followed by a superb group of future firm leaders, including Manon Thivierge and Andrew Cohen, to name just a couple. Like a great sports franchise, the firm would only hit its true maturity when its draft choices matured and came of age. Reliance on free agents alone was no solution.

Tensions between the departments rose and fell with the seasons, but the gravitational forces holding us together always superseded the tensions pushing us apart. We were bound by our common values, which we saw as creating a unique environment where individual creativity was nurtured and where we were all encouraged to develop as individuals, not just as lawyers. More important, the experience of coming through the system together from our infancy as lawyers meant we had an abiding respect for one another that survived the minor spats between departments or the sparring between Peter and Roy.

One of our budding young stars in those days was a student whom Danny Levinson had recruited from a class he taught at the McGill Faculty of Law. Arthur Evrensel trained in the commercial group until adopted first by Neil Wiener as a workhorse for his securities practice and later by Michael Prupas for his entertainment practice. Arthur had a keen mind and an incredible ability to crank out the work. Neil trained him well, and over time they became close friends and drinking buddies given that they were both single and free on Friday nights after work.

Neil was as straitlaced as they came, with a wry sense of humour and a fierce temper that reared up every once in awhile. Back at McGill, we had played on the law school touch football team, and Neil occasionally had to be separated from opposing arts or engineering students after a rough play that threatened to lead to fisticuffs. When he and Arthur were out carousing on Friday nights, the odd parking-lot brawl would ensue. Arthur was built for a good fight. He was a tough, heavy-set Armenian, still brooding about the holocaust wrought by the Turks on his people in the early part of the century. He made a formidable wingman and sparring buddy. There had to have been a few broken noses, but neither of our two heroes ever felt the pain until Saturday morning. Who said the securities bar wasn't tough? Arthur was chosen to implement the newest tax structure I had dreamed up, which came to be known as the 60:40 structure; it later became the dominant Canadian film-finance structure.

— • —

Situated on The Main, Moishes Steakhouse has been a Montreal landmark for over sixty years. Opened by Moishe Lighter in 1938 on Saint

Laurent Boulevard a few blocks north of Pine Avenue, it was for many years one of the prime steakhouses in the city. This was where the Jewish elite gathered for important business lunches and to celebrate family occasions. The decor in the second-floor walk-up was simple. After climbing the steep staircase from the bustle of the street, heading to the elongated, noisy dining room, you passed the fully stocked bar—and the candy bowls that you couldn't help reaching into on your way out after your meal. Eventually you were greeted by the maître d'. As you walked through the narrow entrance into the dining room, the waiters in their gold waistcoats hovered like bees.

Aside from their uniquely flavoured charcoal-broiled steaks, Moishes was famous for various Jewish specialties, like chopped liver smothered in fried onions, dill pickles, coleslaw, verenikas, and knishes, along with the classic Monte Carlo stuffed baked potato and some of the best french fries in the city. The eatery was a hit with the Jewish and French-Canadian communities and had gained a following among the American convention planners, who regularly sent tourists to the restaurant.

When Neil Wiener, Ken Atlas, Bruce McNiven, and I were made partners, a group of senior partners led by Max Bernard took us to Moishes to celebrate. This was where we learned about the first HB partners' tradition. It seemed that the new partners' first contribution to the firm was to pick up the bill for lunch. A fine welcome indeed!

A few months later I was back having lunch with Jay Firestone, the CFO of Alliance Communications, who was introducing me to Jeff Rayman. Jeff had been one of the top fundraisers in the film industry in Toronto for years. Alliance was in the process of developing a slew of new television series, building on the successful relationship with Sonny Grosso and Larry Jacobson, the executive producers of the *Night Heat* series. They were bringing out many new shows to Canadian prime-time television with dramatic and comedy series. The Alliance feature film division also required financing. Jay had seen the profits that the syndicators had been making on their productions, while the producers were taking all the business risks. He concluded that the volume of Alliance production was more than enough to feed a pipeline that he could vertically integrate into Alliance. If successful, Alliance could also compete in the syndication business for the projects of independent producers, including those that had other relationships with Alliance's distribution business.

We were young and eager and anything seemed possible, so the purpose of the lunch was to evaluate just how good a salesman Jeff really was and whether he might be the right person to build a sales division at Alliance. Could he make the transition from sales to management?

Most important, could we trust him?

The chemistry between us was immediate. Jeff was charming and well spoken. His father had died when he was a toddler and he had grown up with a stepfather, Bram Morrison, only ten years his senior. Bram was the lead singer of Sharon, Lois & Bram of *The Elephant Show* fame. Jeff was an English major who set off at age twenty to make his fortune. His handsome looks got him into marriage at a young age, and the breakup had left him with a couple of children whom he was now raising.

He started telling me about his sales background. "You know, Norm, after I moved out to Calgary I was recruited to start selling Filter Queens. Have you ever heard of them?"

I bolted to attention. "Heard of them?" I chuckled. "One summer I sold them in the east end of the city. Most fun I ever had!" and added proudly, "I used to sell one a day."

"I was their top salesman in Canada." He said it matter-of-factly, with no trace of boasting, but I was intrigued.

"How did you manage that?"

He shrugged and smiled. "I was selling four or five a day on average. The key for me is to befriend first-time acquaintances and make them feel as though we've known each other for years. Once inside a house to make a sales pitch, I'd gather up husband and wife, let the husband's aggression play itself out, and quickly convert him into an advocate. The harder they fought, the faster they fell."

I nodded as I took in his strategy. "But Jeff," I said, "none of that explains how you were able to sell so many. Even in my most successful moments I could only sell two a day."

Jeff leaned in as if sharing a confidence with me. "That was just the beginning. Once I made the sale to the family, I'd ask them to do me a favour and call over their friends. In the tight suburban neighbourhoods around Calgary, everyone knew one another. My goal was to turn one sales call into a block party. The guy who just bought the machine was my biggest advocate with his neighbours. I could sell six or seven machines at a time. After all, once you'd decided you couldn't live without the machine, how could you let your friends miss this incredible opportunity?"

I felt as though I understood him and I couldn't help liking him. I was certain he'd become a good friend. Jay and I later discussed whether Jeff was the right person to build the financing division and concluded that hiring Jeff was a risk worth taking. Jay set about persuading Robert Lantos that bringing Jeff on board was a good idea, and within a few months Equicap was born, as a subsidiary of Alliance, combining Jay's business skills, my creativity, and Jeff's sales and strategic abilities.

— • —

The year 1988 proved golden for me. I was a newly minted partner at Heenan Blaikie and had come up with the next new tax structure for film financing. My ring of acquaintances in Toronto had blossomed through the lobby process and now included a sizable group of Eastern Canada's English-language film and television producers.

We were all young, developing an industry together. Many of the names I worked with to build their companies would go on to be industry leaders: Michael MacMillan, Michael Hirsh, Michael Donovan, and Robert Lantos. Atlantis Communications, Nelvana, and Alliance Communications would all go public over the next few years, having built film libraries on the backs of the structures that we were devising and selling. In Montreal, though we lost Danny Levinson to Astral, their in-house legal counsel, Sam Berliner, decided to go into private practice and joined Michael and me in the entertainment group. He brought with him an assortment of Quebec client relationships and expertise in international co-productions, which made him very useful to Alliance, Robert Lantos's production company in Toronto. Between Sam and Michael Prupas, we represented clients such as Telescene, Cinar, Coscient, Claude Héroux, Tom Berry, Roger Frappier, and many others in Montreal, both French and English. It had reached the point where half the office was working on our deals. We were a small core group, but our influence within the firm was beginning to grow. By the end of 1988, billings from our practice had grown to levels never seen outside the scope of our labour practice— and we were only three partners generating all the work. Between film-industry committees and regular visits to various production houses, I was commuting back and forth to Toronto, where I was beginning to establish a solid reputation.

Throughout all this, I had taken a six-week leave of absence in winter 1988 to study for my Ontario bar exams. Given the political situation in Quebec, and in the event of another Quebec vote on sovereignty, I felt it was a wise insurance policy in case I needed to leave on short notice. There were to be six exams over four days in the spring, to be written in Ottawa. The leave of absence was actually more like the establishment of an office for me at the library, since I was spending a few hours each day on files that required structuring advice. Sharon and I had just moved into a newly built house on the West Island of Montreal, and our baby daughter, Vanessa, had raised our contingent of children to three.

My business in Toronto had now become quite extensive and diverse, and clients began to ask whether I planned to stay in Montreal. I recall a dinner with Peter Sussman and youthful CEO Mike MacMillan of Atlantis at Il Posto in Yorkville, during which they were extolling the value to me of being in Toronto on a permanent basis. Jeff and Jay at Alliance were now in daily contact with me by phone, and a host of other clients were committed to send work if I relocated. I had no plans to leave Montreal, though I had now passed the Ontario bar. The little voice inside of me was beginning a whisper campaign, questioning whether Montreal made sense on a long-term basis. My richest relationship, however, was still with Astral in Montreal, where Danny and Kip were sending work. A regular commute to Toronto seemed to be covering the bases.

— • —

Many have claimed that success is not all that it's cracked up to be. I would put it that success has its dark sides, which can manifest themselves in strange ways. In early 1986, though I had recently published my first film-industry article, I was still a relative unknown, just another obscure tax lawyer with potential. In the space of two years, the introvert had been catapulted to a leadership position in an industry with a significant public profile, at least in the professional world of which I was a member. It was partly a question of being in the right place at the right time, armed with a unique skill set and some quickly developing marketing instincts. I hadn't gotten any smarter, handsomer, or more charming, and I was no genius. But this was the entertainment industry, and like the sports business, it revolves around a star system. The media revere sports and entertainment icons and the fans pour on the accolades, not recognizing the difference between the person and the talent. Unlike lawyers in any other practice area, elite entertainment and sports lawyers are almost as well known as their famous clients.

I was not prepared, though, for the counterintuitive way my brain handled the sudden notoriety. I was becoming an icon, and while I could have been basking in the glory, the fame was having the reverse effect on me. I knew the accolades were overblown. I was not nearly as smart as some people gave me credit for, and I depended on a huge team of great lawyers to get the job done. While part of the success was the result of a creative mind, the rest was circumstance.

I had very supportive partners, a great work environment, and client opportunities that I could never have achieved on my own. I knew that my reputation had quickly grown out of proportion to reality. I was no superstar, just a smart lawyer and an opportunist. But this was a Hollywood-like phenomenon and fame had come knocking, so I opened the door and marched through, knowing that my time in the sun might be fleeting. All of this left me with the deep sense that I was a fraud. No one could be as good or as smart as others were giving me credit for being. I was no industry saviour, no genius, and ultimately I was no better than my next mistake or failure or the next Finance rule change that I would not be able to work through. I could not shake the feeling that I was deceiving people.

The stories parents read to their children over and over sometimes have as much impact on the parents as on the children. Our home library featured a number of Dr. Seuss titles, including my favourite, *Yertle the Turtle*. Yertle lived in a community of turtles and one day decided that he would become the leader of all the turtles. To be their true leader he needed to build a pyramid of all the turtles in the community and perch himself at the top as it rose into the sky. As Yertle continued to climb, the view improved until he had risen to the very top, having achieved everything possible. Yertle surveys his dominion, pleased with himself, still not grasping the reality of what lies underneath. Blinded by ambition, caught up in the quest for success, he does not foresee the tragedy about to befall him. The total weight of all the turtles at the top is too much for the base to bear and the entire pyramid collapses, leaving Yertle to wallow in the mud. Wanting to be king of the turtles, he finds himself king of a collapsed domain, of nothing.

The story of Yertle had an unexpected impact on me for years. As my career continued its upward trajectory, I would always feel Yertle's forlorn glance just around the corner. It would take no more than a simple change to the *Income Tax Act* to bring about the collapse of the Canadian film-finance industry, destroying all my fancy designs and returning me to the obscurity from which I had recently risen.

4

OUR **FIRST** BIG STEP

October 1988 was an auspicious month for Sharon. Coopers & Lybrand were announcing their new equity partners and Sharon had been nominated. Prior to that announcement there had never been a woman admitted to the partnership in the Montreal office. Our careers were set … or so we thought. We were happily ensconced in our brand-new house, and Sharon was pregnant with Meredith, our fourth child, when Quebec politics finally intruded into our lives. We had lived through the rise of Quebec nationalism in the sixties, the separatist movement that followed, and the shocking election victory of René Lévesque's Parti Québécois in 1976. I later worked for the "No" side on the first referendum held in 1980. We were constantly irritated by a steady stream of language issues affecting the English-speaking community, including actions by the so-called French-language police (l'Office québécois de la langue française), restrictive rules relating to the language of education, and the push for prominence of French on signs. Seeing lead stories in the English news media every day on these and other like subjects was a constant annoyance.

This was the life of an anglophone in Quebec. Some of my partners, like Michael Prupas and Peter Blaikie, actively engaged in the battle against linguistic intolerance through Alliance Quebec, whose raison d'être was to protect minority English-language rights in Quebec. I still remember the tongue-in-cheek, but biting, exhortation of one of my nationalist partners: "It's not that we don't like you anglophones, we just want you to leave."

My ancestors had heard that one before, all the way back to the Spanish Inquisition. Columbus was discovering America while the Jews of Spain were, if they were able to do so, uprooting and fleeing to Eastern Europe. Some eventually emigrated from there to America in the nineteenth and twentieth centuries to escape the oppression that culminated in the Holocaust annihilating a staggering number of those who remained behind. The Jewish community was particularly sensitive to the dangers of nationalism, and this sensitivity led to a drastic exodus from Quebec beginning in the 1960s, picking up around the time of the FLQ crisis in 1970, and gathering steam between 1972 and 1976. The business community also reacted strongly to the perceived nationalist turmoil, with the result that a number of prominent head offices, particularly in the financial services sector, departed from Montreal for Toronto.

Despite what was happening around us, Sharon and I had determined to stay and make our lives in Montreal. We had adjusted to a series of governments that brought us Bill 22 and Bill 101 to protect the French language. By 1988, Robert Bourassa's Quebec Liberal Party was ruling the roost in Quebec City when the *Ford* case made its way to the Supreme Court. The case concerned Quebec's rules requiring French only on exterior business signs. Valerie Ford, along with a number of other business owners, had posted English signs, thus setting up a challenge under the Canadian Charter of Rights and Freedoms to the constitutionality of the language law as it applied to signs.

In late 1981, as part of a last-minute concession to provincial premiers to forge agreement on the repatriation of the Canadian Constitution, Prime Minister Trudeau had agreed to allow a "notwithstanding clause" to be inserted into the Charter to the effect that any law could validly infringe Charter rights for a five-year period, which was renewable, so long as that law contained an express declaration that it would be effective notwithstanding the Charter rights violation. Premier Bourassa had publicly stated that if Quebec lost the court challenge on signs, he would not invoke the notwithstanding clause to override the court's decision. Nevertheless, once the judgment over-turning the sign-law requirement was released on December 15, 1988, the premier gave in to political pressure and reneged on his promise.

His decision to do so upset me. For the first time in years I seriously questioned the future of anglophones in the province. Was this a place where my children would want to live as adults? Were we witnessing just one more in what would be a never-ending series of concessions to Quebec nationalism, concessions that would just get worse? The daily grind of media scrutiny on minority language rights had never really had an effect on my life, but now it was front and centre. What an impact Mrs. Ford's court challenge was having on my psyche and my future!

The voice in my head, the same one that had urged me to follow the stream from general tax into film finance, was now beginning to whisper that it might be time to leave. I was feeling out of place in the Montreal fishbowl. As a member of a minority that seemed to provoke suspicion at best and hostility at worst in a significant seg-ment of Quebec society, I was now sensing that I would never truly be accepted, never truly feel at home. Even though my French was quite functional, I would never have the cultural grounding to be considered as any more than one of *les autres*, an outsider.

On my previous business trips to Toronto, my clients had been subtly—and not so subtly—tugging me in their direction. They were unanimous. Peter Sussman put it succinctly: "Norm, if you came to Toronto, we'd have work for you." Jay Firestone and a number of other clients were enthusiastic about the prospect of my relocating.

Ken Atlas and I had discussed this over lunch one day some time earlier. The Montreal office was getting a little too big for me and I was feeling restless. Maybe a move was worth considering. Munching on a curly french fry, Ken looked at me as though I were from another planet, but just listened and nodded. Who was I really kidding? My life in Montreal was set, my family was here, and most important, I still could not imagine moving away from the glorious Montreal Canadiens and the Expos. In the eyes of a Montrealer, Toronto sports franchises were to be despised, particularly the Leafs and the Argos, whom I had grown up hating. I was not yet ready to make a change.

A week later, just before Christmas that year, my mindset shifted sharply. The tax department went out for our annual festive lunch with all the assistants. The conversation was light until it shifted inevitably to language issues. Jean Potvin, a most reasonable federalist and good friend of Pierre Trudeau, opened the discussion, complaining that he could no longer get service in French at the downtown Eaton department store.

The history of Eaton's downtown was a bellwether of the health of the French language in Montreal. For many years through the 1970s, Eaton's was well known for having matronly anglophone women serving customers in a number of departments, few of whom knew enough French to properly serve local customers. The political climate changed in the 70s and Eaton's with it. It gave up the apostrophe and *s* in its name to become Eaton and increased the number of bilingual sales and service representatives across the board. All businesses in Quebec had felt the tremors as the ground shifted and the French language steadily gained ascendancy over the years. Yet here was Jean complaining that perhaps a new era of complacency was once more setting in at the hands of the remaining anglophone masters of business in Quebec. Could it mean that Quebec under a Liberal government was once more slipping backwards? If the phrase *maîtres chez nous* had originated anywhere, it may have begun with frustrated retail-chain shoppers in downtown Montreal who could not be served in their own language.

We batted the point back and forth in the way a group of lawyers debate any proposition. Richard Lewin and I countered that in the face of all the existing French-language legislative protection, we anglophones were the ones living in a language police state. Slowly minority civil rights were being eroded, and a succession of Quebec governments was and would continue to be dedicated to treating us like second-class citizens.

Jean immediately shot back with the words that would change forever the course of history at Heenan Blaikie: "I don't know what you guys are complaining about. You're the best-treated minority in the world."

Jean and Richard continued the debate, but at that moment something inside me snapped. Jean used the words "you guys," but I heard it as "you people." Oppressed minorities have been listening to bigoted majorities in power referring to them as "you people" that want more, that expect too much, that want change to happen quickly, that protest the status quo. It always means the same thing. You people need to know your place in our society. Is that what Jean meant? He must have, because he said it without even needing to think about it. And there was no taking back the words.

Jean was among the most rational, fair-minded Quebecers I knew. Perfectly bilingual, realistic about the challenges our province was and would be facing, both culturally and economically. If Jean Potvin believed in his heart of hearts that we were no more than a "best-treated minority," then that forever defined my identity in his eyes. What did this say about the true nationalists who were very clear in their intent, yet politic enough to understand that the road of oppression of minority rights was paved with bromides to neutralize the masses and obfuscate their true intention: to rid Quebec society of all of us who threatened the survival of Quebec culture, which we formed no part of? Were I to stay in Quebec, my future could never be more than that of a second-class citizen. Like the respected Jewish advisors to the Spanish monarchy in advance of and in the early years of Ferdinand and Isabella, I knew how this story was going to end—if not for me, then for my children or their children. I repeated the story to Sharon that evening, and then I let it percolate while I got back to work to complete the backlog of deals that had to close before year-end.

— • —

On New Year's Day 1989 we put the children to bed and talked late into the evening. The year had begun with a new child on the way, and we were taking stock of the bright future. However, I couldn't shake off Jean's words. Well after midnight Sharon turned to me to ask, "Why are you letting what Jean said bother you so much?"

I sighed. "Sharon, if a man as reasonable as Jean sees us as second class, what kind of future will our children have in this province? What was the point of having so many children if they'll leave us when it's time for university, never to return? Look how close we came to making the decision to leave in 1980."

The big family had originally been Sharon's idea. I was only twenty at the time, but over hamburgers and beer at the St. James Pub one night, she made it pretty clear there would be no more dates with someone who didn't want at least four kids. I'd never really thought about it, but I figured she'd be worth a commitment to four children. I also sized up pretty quickly that there wasn't going to be another date unless I agreed!

And now I was certain that if we didn't leave right away, our dream of a close, mature family living nearby one another—even if rather idealistic—would definitely be impossible. "That's it, we're leaving," I said.

Taken aback, Sharon sat up. "What do you mean, we're leaving?"

"I mean we can't stay here anymore. We need to move to Toronto."

"Just like that? We're moving to Toronto? What about your mother, your partnership, your business, my partnership?"

Though I had not considered a single detail before blurting out that we should move, I began to work out the strategy and the tactics out loud. We talked late into the night. I knew if I did not leave my mother now, our kids would surely do the same to us one day. It was an adjustment we would all make. Many families were doing the regular commute back and forth along the 401. As for work, I decided to speak to Peter Blaikie when the office reopened and give the firm the option to open a Toronto office. If that came together, we could discuss what approach to take for Sharon to transfer her partnership to Toronto.

Sharon never questioned the decision; she was completely supportive. We spent the next day thinking through the details more carefully, knowing we wanted to be settled in Toronto before the next school year began in September. I was adding a lot of pressure to my wife's life, leaving her to coordinate the lives of three children, a pregnancy, a job transfer, the sale of our house, the purchase of a new house, and a move—in short, a complete overhaul of our lives. Once the words were out of my mouth, however, my mind was at ease. It never occurred to me to look back or to question the insanity that I was raining down upon us. I knew one thing for certain: once I walked into Peter Blaikie's office, there would be no turning back.

— • —

My first meeting the next morning was with Michael Prupas. We had been dreaming about taking on the competition in Toronto. We knew that although our reputation was growing across the country and in Los Angeles, the key to any true expansion of our entertainment practice lay in Toronto. Even a storefront entertainment-finance boutique operation was a tempting proposition. We would have to give this considerably more thought over the coming days, but my decision was a door opener. It was also a grand experiment and an opportunity for both of us to spread our wings. I would be the man on the ground while Michael, through his connections, would be assisting in person and vicariously to take us from a regional platform to a truly national one. Toronto might be the first stop, but if we succeeded there, Vancouver would soon be on the horizon.

My visit to Peter's office took place on a characteristically frigid sunny day in early January. A thick blanket of snow covered the suburban landscape around our home, while the usual admixture of slush and patchy black ice dominated downtown streets and sidewalks. While I was normally ice cold under fire, unmoved by the pressures generated by tight deadlines, unreasonable clients, and factors outside my control, I always felt a level of discomfort entering Peter's domain. I could never shake the intimidation factor. Perhaps it was the tall frame, no-nonsense tone, and booming voice, or perhaps it was a chiding I'd taken one day as a second-year associate, when an engagement with Jean left me fifteen minutes late for a meeting with Peter. "Bacal, it's considered bad form to keep the managing partner waiting" was all he had to say in that stern, uncompromising way of his. On this day I showed up on time for our 11 a.m. meeting, and took my seat across from him.

"Peter," I began, "I've decided my future is in Toronto. We've had discussions in the past about the possibility of opening an office there, and if the partners are still interested, I'd be prepared to move to start the operation."

Peter listened calmly. "Norman, have you given any thought to the details of what you're proposing?"

"I've had preliminary discussions with Michael. We're both excited about what this could mean for our practice. As far as I'm concerned, I'd be ready to go over the summer."

Peter nodded. "This is a decision the partners would have to make, so we'll have to vote, but the proposition, as you know, is one we've been considering for years. You may recall that we came really close to merging with Lang Michener in Toronto in the early 1980s. We looked at that deal very carefully then walked away. Why don't the two of you work out a plan, and we'll bring it to the partners to review and consider at our next meeting." He paused, then leaned forward slightly. "What happens if we say no?"

I hadn't actually considered that possibility, so I had no planned response. Instinctively I replied, "Peter, I'm moving to Toronto." Peter's final question drew out of me the essence of my real decision. I was leaving Quebec, regardless. If I had to join another firm to achieve the goal, so be it. If I had to interview in Toronto in order to get a job, I was likely to do better this time around.

The calculus was simple. For stage one I would open a small storefront, no more than four lawyers to start, renting a minimum amount of modestly equipped space. If we were successful, we could unload the space and move. Michael would commute for the first year so that we could blanket the local industry in Toronto and project more strength than we actually had. A number of our partners would be concerned that if Toronto law firms got wind of our presence in Toronto, they would assume that we were now the competition and would find other firms in Montreal to use. To minimize this risk we would fly under the radar, keeping a low profile except in the entertainment and tax niches. Hopefully that would minimize the loss of referral sources from Toronto firms to our partners in Montreal. Stage two would see Roy shopping for a local labour group. We would be frugal and conservative to start and grow only in line with our eventual success.

We had seen Stikeman Elliott adopt the opposite approach years before. They invested capital out of the gate with an accumulation of perceived superstars, created a significant presence immediately, and sowed the seeds of an inter-city rivalry that would last for many years. That approach was inconsistent with our history. We were not a corporate powerhouse, and Toronto-based Lang Michener had serviced most of our Ontario work, so we didn't know if or when we could recover that work. Our instincts and experience pointed at a modest start with a slow build. (The merger with Lang Michener that Peter had referred to had been rejected because Roy and Peter were not prepared to become a small cog in a large firm.)

I had no management experience, but Michael had developed a reputation as a savvy businessman who didn't take silly risks. By taking me into the entertainment group and building what was among the most successful practices of the firm, he had established a good deal of credibility. I had no idea, at age thirty-two with only one year of partnership under my belt, whether my partners were ready to trust me and whether I could garner the respect of the people I would be recruiting to build the Toronto office. I had never had to worry about anything other than gathering new clients, so I was blissfully ignorant of what any of this meant in day-to-day terms. I was an intelligent lawyer with the occasional flash of great creativity. How would that translate into running an operation? In the meantime, I had learned to worry only about the things I could control. Peter was responsible for managing the firm and I had no interest in wresting any of those duties from him.

The presentation to the partners went smoothly. We needed less than 4,000 square feet somewhere in downtown Toronto, not necessarily in the business core. One boardroom, eight or nine offices, and a tiny reception area ought to do it. We would hire two or three senior lawyers, as well as a junior associate and a student. We were unlikely to attract a group to join a brand-new or greenfield operation, so we would need minimal support staff. Between Michael and me, we knew immediate work would be coming from Alliance and Equicap as well as from Atlantis and children's animation specialist Nelvana. All my independent-producer clients would continue to send work, and we assumed there would be referrals from Montreal. The people we hired would also have clients of their own, so it was hard for us to see how this could be a losing proposition.

Peter then summed it up for the group. This was an opportunity we had been considering since discussions had begun with Lang Michener five years earlier. Our downside was small. Peter estimated that a complete failure would cost $50,000 per partner. The real question was whether we were ready to embark on the expansion that we all knew was inevitable if we were to survive. Given the uncertainty of Quebec politics, what was the future of regional Quebec firms over the long run? (Twenty-five years later, with the exception of Lavery, de Billy, none of the significant Montreal firms of the 1980s has survived independently.) The potential for the future could be transformative as long as we were open to expanding and evolving.

Although some partners had expressed reservations about losing referrals from Toronto lawyers who might believe we were now competing with them, the vote was unanimous: the first to anyone's recollection. This was an idea whose time had arrived. It probably didn't hurt our credibility that my practice showed every sign of eclipsing Roy's within the year. Our entertainment practice would become the leading practice of the firm, per capita, for the next dozen years. It was particularly rare for Peter and Roy to agree on anything, so their mutual endorsement of the Toronto expansion sent the right message to any partner who doubted the plan. We had five months to opening day and not a moment to lose.

— • —

Pregnant but still able to fly, Sharon went ahead and began scouting neighbourhoods, while I stepped up my Toronto trips in advance of our opening to spread the word and make sure client support would not fizzle. To the contrary, there was a buzz in the air in the film and television community about our impending move into the marketplace. Michael and I scheduled interviews with potential recruits for this new adventure. We began with the area we knew best and looked at the small pool of candidates with film-finance experience. We sought a combination of youth, expertise, and reputation, and only a half dozen fit the bill, so I spoke with all of them.

Harriett "Hatty" Reisman, practising at McMillan Binch, was the film-lending lawyer for RBC. She was credible and respected. She also knew how to handle Wayne Drury, the hot-tempered RBC vice-president who had been one of Danny Levinson's favourite clients despite their regular shouting matches. A diminutive, thoughtful, and careful lawyer who burned off her stress as a long-distance runner, Hatty was not to be trifled with and was a solid first addition. We also needed, immediately, a commercial lawyer who could be versatile. We had no idea what kind of work outside film finance would walk through the door, but we needed someone with the nerve and skill to take on anything competently.

George Burger was also an ex-Montrealer and an associate at Stikemans' Toronto office. A mere cog in the juggernaut, he was beginning to wonder just how long the partnership track would be over there. At Heenan Blaikie's Toronto start-up, anything would be possible, so if he performed, the wait could be as little as eighteen months. George matched up evenly with Peter Blaikie, inch for inch and pound for pound. Solid features, set jaw, boyish grin, and dominating presence, George appeared to have all the tools. He also came with a recommendation from Calin Rovinescu, a former Stikemans managing partner and an old friend of mine who would one day become the CEO of Air Canada.

Norman Tobias, whose father was a client of Jean Potvin, had an independent tax practice in Toronto and rounded out our plan of entering the market with a couple of niche boutique practices. We now had our starting four, representing an interesting mixture of tax, entertainment, and commercial, some fairly good big-firm pedigree, and a unique blend of skill sets and egos.

Prupas and I shopped for space and had to manage our first identity crisis. Space was available in trendy Yorkville, a little walk-up on Bedford that was a converted home. We would be a stone's throw away from the famous Park Plaza Hotel, at that time the home of the Toronto International Film Festival. Deliberately outside the downtown core, it was kitschy and would play well to our entertainment clientele. We were now in territory for which I had no survival-skill training: hiring lawyers, interviewing administrative staff, and choosing space, furniture, and carpets. What did I know about any of this? After much discussion with our leasing agent, Peter Cook, we finally concluded that anything outside the Toronto core would not leave a lot of room for future growth or for nimble adjustments as opportunities arose in the future. We needed to be in the centre of the legal universe if we wanted to attract the right people long term. So we opted for a 3,800-square-foot sublease in the Toronto-Dominion Centre's Royal Trust Tower (now known as TD North Tower). Architecturally dominant, the three original black towers rising out of the granite plinth were the creation of Ludwig Mies van der Rohe, the internationally renowned architect who had designed the Seagram Building in Manhattan for Phyllis (Bronfman) Lambert a few years before.

—— • ——

Now we needed our law student. We had posted ads in the law school faculties and camped out at a table in the Hilton hotel on Richmond Street to hold interviews well after the major firms had completed their recruiting. I knew what it was like to be among the unchosen, so I was positive there were still some talented prospects out there. Hattie was helping me interview, and we opted for Ken Gordon, a handsome, well-spoken young man. I was always looking for distinguishing features that might provide an insight into character and grace under pressure. Ken had spent a few years in Israel and had voluntarily joined the armed forces, serving as a paratrooper during part of his military service. I don't know how it evolved, but our student would always be known to us as "little" Kenny Gordon, even after he left the practice to become a successful film financier.

After we had interviewed a few students, Adam Kardash sat down and confidently introduced himself, opening with a confession. "I saw your ads in the Osgoode Law Faculty at York University and I have to admit I'm here under false pretences. I'm not applying for a student job because I'm not a law student. I just graduated from journalism at York and I start law school next September. I'm looking for a summer job and I'm intrigued by the entertainment business. So before you throw me out, I just want a summer job in that environment and you don't even have to pay me. You must need someone to empty boxes, make photocopies, and do other joe jobs. I can't do any legal work, I have no training, and, having said all that, I'm sorry to have taken up your time."

Still in his early twenties, Adam had a mop of black curls and a baby face. He looked like a kid. Mind you, so did I. He was a compelling character, so we chatted for a few minutes before moving on to the next scheduled student. At the next break we chuckled about him, admiring his pluck.

A few days later I was back home in Montreal reflecting on Adam, who had left a lingering impression. Here was someone with enough confidence to apply in person for a position he wasn't qualified for in order to pitch us on hiring him. And he had no fear of rejection, the one quality that can't easily be taught. The voice in my head was whispering again. These were the qualities I'd be looking for in my partners of the future.

— • —

I convinced Michael and Hatty to stretch the budget for some temporary summer help. Adam did a competent job that summer and was invited back to stay with the firm through law school. He remained at Heenan Blaikie until we closed the doors in 2014, becoming one of our most productive partners, a member of the Executive Committee, and one of Canada's leading privacy experts.

Adam was the recruiting story for the ages, one that I repeated endlessly for twenty-five years, embellishing it where necessary, driving home the moral to students and young lawyers: "When we recruited you, we saw potential that fit with what Heenan Blaikie was looking for. Young, aggressive men and women have continued to join us to do great things, to begin the journey to an unimaginable destination. I did it, Adam did it, and so can you." That was how the speech began. Someone in that room had the potential to become one of our future leaders and needed to be filled with inspiration. The Heenan Blaikie Toronto brand was born.

— • —

The first half of 1989 was filled with promise and new challenges, but the road was not paved with roses. While I was thrilled with our recent success in production financing, Harold Greenberg, Astral's CEO, was not pleased with the success other producers were now experiencing thanks to the buyback structure he had originally sponsored. While Harold had the biggest heart in the business and would without hesitation extend a hand to lift you up when you were down, you never knew when that same hand was going to slap you across the face.

A few months after I had been named a partner at the firm, Kip Cobbett and Danny Levinson invited me to lunch at the Montefiore Club in downtown Montreal. I appreciated the gesture and assumed we'd be celebrating my ascent to partnership. Kip had risen to a position of authority at Astral, and Danny was still my guardian angel even if he was no longer at the firm. Astral was my oldest client and my deepest relationship. I was proud of my achievements with and for them. Towards the end of lunch Kip reminded me of the days when we began to develop the film-financing structures with Astral. I thought he was travelling down memory lane, when unexpectedly he began to head in an altogether different direction.

"Norman, we feel that all that development work was done for Astral. Yet in the past year we find that many of our competitors are taking advantage by using our structures." By now Danny was looking down and becoming more uncomfortable, shifting around in his seat. "Basically what we're telling you," Kip continued, "is that you can't continue to serve many masters. We no longer believe that you're acting in Astral's best interests."

It was Kip's polished delivery, but it couldn't be Kip. He had come from private practice. He understood that what made good lawyers great were the lessons they learned from one client and imparted to the next. The more diverse our client relationships, the more fertile our imaginations could become. Allowing me to represent Astral and their competitors could only be in Astral's interest, as long as they were not involved in the same transaction, which would be a clear conflict. But denying me the opportunity to represent other companies where Astral had no involvement was a stretch, and both Kip and Danny knew this. It was Kip's mellifluous voice delivering the words, but it was Harold's message. Kip was just the hatchet man, ordered to bring down the axe. This time it was on my neck. The celebration lunch had come to an end and it seemed I had been served up as dessert.

The reality took a few seconds to fully sink in. I had just been fired. There was no playbook for this moment, no graceful exit, no "Thanks for lunch, guys." I lifted my head, feeling sad for Kip and more so for Danny. I was experiencing my first harsh lesson in the unintended consequences of success. The client wanted to own me and my brain, and, when I would not oblige, was left with no option. Danny and Kip showed themselves the door. I felt intense shock and a deep gloom. I was accustomed to success and here was failure glaring at me, failure with my oldest client, who had been handed down to me from Don Johnston, the founder of the firm.

I reported back to Michael, Jean, and Peter Blaikie, who tried to salvage something from a bad situation. But Astral had made a decision and would not reverse course. As long as Heenan Blaikie was going to be representing other film-industry clients, Astral would be taking its entertainment work elsewhere.

The ultimatum got Peter's back up, and I learned once again that the leadership of the firm would support its own, as it had done time after time when faced with a crisis. Rather than picking up the phone to plead with Harold or Kip, Peter's protégé, or offering me up to the wolves, Peter simply told us that the client could go to you-know-where. We were not going to bend over and take it. No single client was worth that kind of compromise. Peter's wisdom proved itself sooner than we had expected.

Shortly after the lunchtime firing, it became clear that Harold Greenberg's ire was directed at Prupas and me rather than at the firm. André Bureau, chairman of the Canadian Radio and Television Commission, had announced his resignation and joined Astral; he would eventually become their chairman. André was also looking for a law firm to associate with as counsel, and Roy convinced him to choose Heenan Blaikie, where André commenced a twenty-five-year relationship. This was a very prestigious addition to the firm. Above all André is a man of great character and class, and his arrival, along with that of his protégé, Lisa de Wilde (now the CEO of TVOntario), sparked the growth of our expertise in the newly emerging world of pay-TV.

— • —

Leadership's support of its partners comprised just one of several facets—the brilliance of the firm's leaders tempered with a refusal to take themselves too seriously; uncompromising standards of legal work; creativity; the drive to excel; the prime importance of people— that, combined with practical joking and tossing footballs in the hallways, had fashioned a powerful regional reputation and attracted a former prime minister. This culture, a rare amalgam of fact, mythology, and aspiration, was what we were going to export and repeat as our formula for success in Toronto.

I also learned a second and even more valuable lesson. From that point forward, any new structure I developed would be owned by Heenan Blaikie, and we would pay for the development out of our own pockets. That decision would allow us to finance the building of the firm over the next dozen years.

— • —

Setting and establishing the brand in Toronto would be central to my role there, though I could not possibly have understood that when I walked into Peter's office that frigid January morning. On July 2, 1989, when we opened our doors, I knew I had to step up immediately with the same nerve that Adam Kardash had demonstrated. Given that we four lawyers in the office held approximately the same seniority, my leadership would have to be subtle. My personality tended, in any event, towards leading from behind, encouraging others to succeed, building alliances to move forward together, and pushing credit outward.

— • —

One member of our support staff was more celebrated than our lawyers. Norman Tobias brought along his assistant, Cathy Smith, a smart woman with bushy blond hair, a throaty voice, and a raucous sense of humour. Norman and Cathy had bonded over their years together and they treated each other as equals. A concerned lawyer brought to my attention that this was not just any Cathy Smith, this was *the* Cathy Smith, the one who had been implicated in the drug overdose that killed comedian John Belushi. Cathy had been part of the Belushi entourage, with a reputation for accessing the drugs that fed the comedian's addiction, and she had served time in a US prison for her involvement in his death. When asked about it, Norman explained to me that he was aware of Cathy's background, and had decided a number of years ago that she deserved a second chance in life. She had done her time, been clean since she left prison, and had been a dedicated assistant. What was more important: the reputational risk to the firm from being associated with a convicted felon or having the firm play a role in her recovery? The answer was easy. Cathy Smith was part of our family. We would discover that clients were intrigued with her and the story of how she had turned her life around.

The only real victim in all of this was Neil Wiener. The Toronto office was small, so each of the assistants would rotate through the switchboard. One day Neil called from Montreal looking for George Burger. Cathy answered.

"Good afternoon. Heenan Blaikie."

"This is Neil Wiener from Montreal. Who am I speaking to?"

"This is Cathy Smith. How are you, Neil?"

"Are you the real Cathy Smith?" he asked teasingly.

"Yes, I'm the real Cathy Smith."

Taking his joking banter one step further, he asked, "The Cathy Smith who killed John Belushi?"

"Yes," she deadpanned.

"Well then, how are you today? Have you killed anyone else recently?"

Neil chuckled as Cathy passed him along to George, to whom he recounted his joke.

"Neil, she is the real Cathy Smith," George said. It took him about five minutes to convince Neil that he wasn't kidding, at which point Neil admitted that he wanted to crawl under his desk and die. The apology would wait until Neil made a trip to Toronto and could grovel in person. As it turned out, this was not a first for Cathy and it hadn't fazed her at all. It seems that Neil was the only one who was traumatized. Cathy graciously accepted his apology, though the rest of us would never let Neil forget the incident.

— • —

The summer passed quickly as we integrated our existing clients and set up for the fall, though the focus was on the Toronto International Film Festival and our opening reception in the second week of September. We boldly chose the courtyard outside of Prego Restaurant, behind the church at the corner of Avenue Road and Bloor Street, daring the weather gods to interfere with our plans. We were betting on a warm, dry, early-September evening. Midway between the Park Plaza and the Four Seasons, we were at the absolute heart of the festival.

Our concept was to bring together, in a unique venue, a diverse mix of people comprising the film community, both local and visiting from around the world; clients from Montreal; Don Johnston's numerous contacts in Toronto; and Toronto clients from our existing practice. Over three hundred people showed up to the party, notably among them Pierre Trudeau with Margot Kidder on his arm, and Albert Reichmann, a guest of Don Johnston. The Reichmann family had recently placed a huge bet on the success of the development of Canary Wharf in London. Various contacts from Los Angeles and long-term clients of the Montreal office were in town for the festival and stopped by to pay their respects, have a drink, and shake hands with Mr. Trudeau. Michael, Sam Berliner, and I had the local film community well represented. David Perlmutter made sure to stop by. He was the firm's most enduring client, with a relationship going back to the early 1970s. He would continue to proudly wave the flag of support for the firm for the next twenty-five years while he and partner Lewis Chesler would crank out made-for-TV movies for two generations.

A warm humid evening worked its magic on the crowd. Guests lingered, and because of the timing and location, many industry types from around the world crashed the party after the early festival screening to catch a glimpse of or exchange a handshake with Trudeau. Heenan Blaikie had arrived in Toronto with a splash.

⸺ • ⸺

Thanks to a random comment by a colleague in 1986, I had begun musing over a new film-finance structure in the first half of 1989, even as we were contemplating the move to Toronto. Martin Scheim, a partner in Stikemans' Montreal tax department, had looked at the buyback structure, which was set up with a US company buying out the investors, and innocently asked why the entire deal was not set up in the United States. It seemed a preposterous notion that a Canadian film should be financed through a US partnership structure, so I dismissed it out of hand.

By 1988 Martin's question was bothering me so much that I put aside my stubborn prejudice to explore it in my spare time. I researched the avenues of American and Canadian tax law that would be at play if we operated our film partnerships out of the United States while having our Canadian investors contribute to a Canadian partnership that would invest in the US operation. One by one I tackled the issues. There was no rush. I was exploring a notion merely to satisfy my intellectual curiosity. Then one day, lightning struck. I had a flash of insight as to how an entire film-investment structure could work. I had discovered a mechanism that was superior to the buyback. The new idea solved some cross-border problems we were encountering with fees paid by US broadcasters on Canadian projects. Even better, the new design would allow the private funding of Canadian films to continue without reliance on a buyback. I felt it was only going to be a matter of months before the Department of Finance eliminated the buyback as an alternative because it had become too popular with investors.

The new structure contained many bugs I needed to work out, but I became certain that by spring 1990 we would once again have a leading-edge technology in film finance. The Heenan Blaikie name had become synonymous with excellent quality. If we said it worked, then it worked, and investors would buy, no questions asked. When it came to film finance, we represented the gold standard.

Jeff Rayman was one of the key sales advisors on the new structure. I worked with him to create a pitch that would explain the deal in under five minutes. That had become our litmus test. If he couldn't explain the structure quickly, it wouldn't sell. The new technology was a generation ahead of its predecessors when it came to efficiency and results, and Jeff understood enough of the high-level concept to explain how this was superior to any film product that had ever touched the market. We originally intended to unveil the new plan in 1990, but the changes to the tax system I was expecting in 1990 arrived in a surprise move in early November 1989. We now had to accelerate the launch date. Miraculously, we closed thirteen deals in seven weeks. The sales poured in and the flow of adrenaline was replaced in Montreal on New Year's Eve with the flow of champagne.

Once the billings were collected on those deals, we reported a record year, and the Toronto operation was officially in the black. My Montreal partners shared in profits from our Toronto venture a mere six months from the time we opened, and we would never look back. For the next twenty-three years Toronto was a net contributor to the firm's overall profit pool, which would always be run as a single pool. My Montreal partners had made a very wise investment in our collective future.

5

SINGLE-MINDED DETERMINATION

In spring 1990 a new source of inspiration entered my life. My son Brian was completing first grade and was keen to take karate lessons. These were the days of the Ninja Turtles, so after a minimal amount of due diligence, we drove down the street to the dojo voted by *Toronto Life* magazine as having the best children's program. It was a late-March evening when we showed up to make inquiries. The storefront window on St. Clair Avenue, just west of Christie Street, allowed for a view of the deep, narrow dojo, mirrored on both walls, teeming with children enthusiastically going through their paces with a number of young group instructors. I had arranged to meet with the owner of the dojo, Cezar Borkowski, and his wife, Marion Manzo. Cezar, a Canadian national champion, was an advanced black belt (I couldn't yet tell what level), and Marion was also a black-belt instructor at the school.

Brian engaged immediately, and the marketing machine that was Northern Karate Schools swallowed him up. Before I knew it, he was enrolled for the next year. Once Cezar and Marion had taken care of the immediate business and ushered him into a white-belt class, they went to work on me. "Wouldn't it be fun to turn this into a father-and-son opportunity to bond?" they asked. I admitted I'd done virtually no exercise since university other than the odd squash game with Ken Atlas, against whom I could never win a match. Perhaps it was time to get into shape and take some martial arts training. A three-month trial seemed like a safe bet.

I started by attending a few evenings of the jam-packed, adult white-belt classes. In the changing room on the first night I tried hopelessly to tie the proper knot in my white belt. Finally a ten-year-old who had just come out of the final children's class of the evening noticed my distress. Despite my embarrassment, I allowed him to give me a hand.

Shortly afterward I switched to Monday and Wednesday lunchtime classes to begin serious training. In those early days the floors were covered in cheap carpet, and within a week the training in bare feet had burned layers of skin off my soles, leaving me bloody and bandaged. I limped badly through that week at the office; it took three months until calluses formed. My general conditioning was appalling, my abdominal strength non-existent. Stretching my tendons and hamstrings at the beginning of class would leave my legs feeling like lead balloons between sessions. I discovered aching, tender muscles in my thighs and hamstrings, while my hips rebelled against the frequency of kicks I was delivering into the pads.

A cross-section of Toronto society attended the adult midday classes. We had bus drivers, housewives, entrepreneurs, bodybuilders, a broad assortment of middle-aged neighbourhood residents, and Mr. Mendoza, a jewellery artisan who owned a store down the street. At age sixty he was the toughest man I had ever met. After smiling his greeting as my sparring partner, he pulled no punches or kicks and left painful welts around my midsection and on the outside of my thighs. Mendoza would often lead the warm-up. He would make us take a partner on our shoulders while we jogged the length of the dojo, or ask us to get into push-up position so that he could kick us in the stomach to see if we'd engaged our abdominal muscles to avoid getting winded. Lord protect anyone who wasn't ready for the Mendoza kick as he screamed "Tighten up!" How could I complain about a man almost twice my age beating on me?

The classes were "all belts," meaning the whites, coloured, and black belts were divided into groups and trained at the same time at different levels. The black belts rotated through, keeping an eye on novices like me and trying their best to show us correct technique. I knew nothing, had never boxed, had no natural grace of movement, and no gift for footwork.

The Monday class was taught by Sensei Claudio, who had the melodic voice of Antonio Banderas. His favourite exercise was to have us pair up and tie our belts together to spar. As a beginner I barely knew how to throw a punch. I quickly learned how to take one!

My progression through the ranks at Northern Karate was slow and painful. While I possessed a natural aggression left over from my teenage years as a football player, I'd shied away from fights my entire life. Observing the grace and skill of the black belts, I was certain that all the training in the world would never get me to that level of expertise or give me confidence that I would ever seriously be able to defend myself. In the meantime I worked on getting in shape, and the classes were a great stress release.

Mondays and Wednesdays at the dojo became fixed in my lunch-time calendar, and I slowly started to feel a little less clumsy. My conditioning was improving as I developed muscular strength, lung capacity, and abdominal tension. I could feel my legs growing stronger and see the muscles bulging in my calves and thighs. Over time as I progressed, the teaching techniques in the lunchtime classes became more refined and advanced. After a few months Cezar took over the Monday classes, and for the next twenty years, it did not matter where I had to travel, on Monday at lunchtime I was at the dojo learning.

The training process focused on both body and mind. I learned how to break fall, how to defend myself from an attacker with a knife or a gun, how to use various weapons, and how to talk my way out of a confrontation. Most important, I learned when to cross the street to avoid a confrontation, which is often the best form of self-defence. Cezar, the true master, taught that avoiding a fight, or talking an adversary out of physical violence, was a matter of mastering self-control rather than responding out of fear. Besides, dislocating an attacker's elbow or seriously injuring him might land you in jail.

Advancing became as much a question of mastering my own fears of failure and injury as developing my physical prowess.

Over the doorway as we entered the dojo, a plaque bore this profound insight (though I paraphrase the English translation slightly):

> *Regardless of the number of years of training,*
> *one will never advance without single-minded determination.*

— • —

Both in and out of the dojo I became preoccupied with the notion of single-minded determination. In the days, weeks, months, and years that followed, whenever the stumbling blocks looked too high, the prospects of success too dim, the road to creating a successful law firm too daunting, I fell back on the determination to hang in, follow the path, and ignore the voices of the skeptics.

This approach also guided me as to the type of people I was looking for to help me advance the dream. I didn't need the smartest, the most gregarious, or the most naturally talented. Though all these qualities would be useful, there was another, more decisive quality within me that I needed to find and refine in others. To succeed in our environment, you had to never give up, never give in; you had to be determined to push through resistance. Some that we hired would be mavericks, others quiet and thoughtful; a few would have winning personalities, and a couple would be outright misfits. Most of all, though, I needed people who would not quit, who were capable of fierce loyalty, who liked the odds better when they were stacked against us. This is what Heenan Blaikie was going to be. I was searching for rare commodities and it took years to accumulate them. But these personalities would become our leaders.

— • —

In those first couple of years, our little office prospered. Norman Tobias's tax practice was steady. George Burger proved himself to be quite resourceful in filling every possible commercial hole, whether working for Jay Firestone at Alliance, assisting on closing the tax financings, or working for Scott Griffin, the one and only Montreal office referral to the Toronto office. Scott was Peter Blaikie's brother-in-law, and his corporation became a source of support to us for many years until he finally sold the company. Don Johnston also sent over a helicopter financing. The first question the client asked was whether we had aircraft-finance experience. Of course George said he did. How complicated could it be? Within a couple of weeks George had plenty of experience. Hatty's financial services practice continued to grow.

I was sitting at the kitchen table one Sunday morning in spring 1990, leafing through *Toronto Life* magazine, which had run a feature on the director of enforcement at the Ontario Securities Commission (OSC). A former associate at McMillan Binch, Joseph Groia had established a reputation for himself as tough, relentless in the pursuit of justice, and prepared to take on abuses of the markets regardless of the power, wealth, or status of those under investigation. An uncompromising idealist, he had likely made some enemies in the highest echelons of Bay Street. He seemed to lead an interesting personal life as well. He made his own wine and was a talented chef, with a particular interest in Italian cuisine. He might be an interesting addition to an upstart Bay Street firm when his term at the Commission came to an end. I still knew very little about the litigation bar in Toronto, but I did know that at some point we would have to build a litigation capacity, if only to serve our existing and prospective clients.

The next day I asked Hatty about Groia, figuring they would have crossed paths as associates at McMillan. She had high praise for him, but she suspected he would be sought after by many firms when he eventually returned to private practice.

Realizing that a Toronto start-up was unlikely to attract someone with his experience, I stopped daydreaming. My elevator pitch to candidates, that they should seize the incredible opportunity to get in on the ground floor and build Toronto's next great law firm, was not yet going to resonate with most senior lawyers. After all, we were only five lawyers with a backing from Montreal, which was both a blessing and a curse. The perception that decision-making in the firm took place only at head office in Montreal was one that would take many years to shake and would scare off some candidates. I had my work cut out for me in selling a distinct Toronto vision of the firm that would bring us out of obscurity. Unless I could create the brand, demonstrate evidence of its success, and sell it — like a Filter Queen — in under five minutes, making a successful pitch to prospective senior recruits was going to be paddling against a strong current.

— • —

Later that year Joe Groia announced he was leaving his seat as direc- tor of enforcement at the OSC, and rumours were circulating that the big firms had been warned by their institutional clients not to engage him. It seems Joe had annoyed many CEOs, particularly among the Bay Street elite, with his no-nonsense approach to enforcement and investigation. It didn't take long for me to get in touch with him, just a few months after I had read all about him in *Toronto Life*. We met for lunch at his favourite haunt in the Royal York Hotel. My pitch was simple. We had a great brand in Montreal and a ground-floor opportunity in Toronto. We needed a lead litigator, and here was a rare opportunity to build a department in the image he desired. We had no major corporate clients to oppose him and few conflicts on briefs he would be interested in attracting.

Hatty had worked with him years earlier, and she and George were strongly supportive. Joe went to visit Peter Blaikie and Roy Heenan in Montreal, as well as the other key litigation partners, and decided to take the plunge. Joe was as much a maverick in private practice as he had been as an enforcer at the OSC. He prided himself on taking on the underdog so, in addition to commercial litigation referrals, he began to develop a reputation for defending the type of people whom he had previously prosecuted. Alleged white-collar criminals, corporate executives caught up in insider trading cases or corporate frauds, or executives otherwise under investigation would call Joe for wise counsel. After all, he understood the inner workings of the other side.

Joe had an extraordinary moral compass, which he shifted from being the protector of the entire system to being a guardian of the notion that even a rogue was entitled to a defence. He had no time for clients who wouldn't take his advice or whom he believed to be untrustworthy, and he had no problem 'firing' them. This allowed us to avoid some of the problems our competitors experienced when bad clients would bring down their lawyers, dragging them into their own regulatory nightmares with the law societies or the courts.

Joe became famous for civility before the courts in Ontario. He was a classic 'character' right out of a high-school English Lit novel, filled with passion, righteousness, and tragic flaws. A man of strong loyalties, he was an ally I always wanted in my corner. If he had a complaint, however, he could be a remarkable adversary. This led to some intense disagreements with particular partners of the firm who occasionally took issue with him on internal matters.

Joe was instrumental in defining and laying the groundwork for our litigation team, which would take ten years to seed, fertilize, and grow into a powerhouse boutique. Over the course of the first few years Joe recruited George Karayannides and Jonathan Stainsby as his two young bucks. Jon had been a professional salmon fisherman who finally left the business to get a law degree. His crusty personality and beard, right out of a Fisherman's Friend lozenge commercial, masked a keen intellect and a soft heart. Sensible and unflappable, George insisted there was a life beyond the law that included drinking good wine.

One day in 1997 Joe surprised me by suggesting we needed some-one in the group more senior than he to serve the wise counsel role. Joe had his eye on Stan Fisher, a former mentor of his at McMillan Binch with an impeccable reputation in the city. Even though he had never worked with us, Stan had directed Joe to consider Heenan Blaikie based solely on our reputation. I was pleasantly surprised that a late-fifties litigator with Stan's pedigree would be interested in us. I met with Stan and we got to know one another a little and exchange life philosophies. He had lost his wife to cancer; now with a new woman in his life he believed it was time for a complete life change by switching firms, platforms, and approach. He impressed me with his wisdom, gained from years of life lessons, about when to be tough and when to yield, and how to advise difficult people who asked for advice they weren't prepared to accept. He had been through the battles of a long career and was ready to impart his knowledge as well as litigate.

Our commercial group would also sprout some shoots with the addition of a few junior commercial lawyers, as well as a senior associate from Torys who had come highly recommended by Danny Levinson. Kip Daechsel added some stability and came with a modest set of client relationships. Danny's referral carried a lot of weight with me. Kip would one day mature to play a critical role in helping to build the firm and to then be among the key protagonists in its demise.

— • —

As a natural by-product of the move, I was the only partner in Toronto for the first couple of years, so I had been invited to sit on the Executive Committee in early 1990. I subsequently joined the first Compensation Committee as a Toronto representative. As a result, I had effectively jumped the queue at the end of my second year of partnership and proudly began to learn first-hand about the mundane challenges of running a law firm. I spent my first year at the Executive Committee meetings listening rather than speaking, unless we were discussing

Toronto. The strain between Peter and Roy permeated the management structure of the firm, which by that time had been tailored to
accommodate the two men. Peter ran the day-to-day as managing
partner, which meant that he was responsible for everything. The
Executive Committee had been created as a venue for Roy to look at
strategy and direction without going head-to-head with Peter, who
would not and could not tolerate Roy having anything to do with managing the firm. The set-up barely worked and my mentor, Jean Potvin,
would often play go-between with Peter and Roy on sensitive issues.

— • —

Roy's dream was to create a national labour platform, and he had
his sights set on a group in Toronto and a leading light in Vancouver. The Toronto initiative had been going on for close to a year.
Brian Burkett, John West, Douglas Gilbert, and Rick Charney had all
developed at Campbell Godfrey (prior to its merger with Faskens)
under their mentor, George Adams, who had left the firm to pursue
other interests in law, and were now leading a group of eight lawyers
ready to make the jump from Faskens. They had planned to leave
the previous year but had been persuaded to stay. Now, a year wiser,
they had been convinced by Roy and the Montreal labour partners
that joining our small Toronto boutique would make them masters
of their own future.

The reputation of the group in the labour community was stellar,
and their clients, which included Air Canada and Canada Post, provided an institutional client base. We had now doubled in size and
garnered a substantial reputation in management-side labour law,
entertainment, and tax. In two-and-a-half short years, though we were
only sixteen lawyers, we had begun to achieve a certain notoriety as
a Toronto boutique.

Brian Burkett, Doug Gilbert, and John West were of equal seniority.
Brian was earnest and well respected, and for many years he never
lost his temper. He had, however, a stubborn streak a mile wide and

a fathom deep. There was no moving Brian off a position once he had taken it. That quality made him a highly determined and formidable labour negotiator. When he believed he was right, he simply never gave in. It also made him a very difficult partner in the world of compromise we call a law firm.

John West, on the other hand, was emotional, with a fiery temper. When John had a reaction, it could be volcanic, but I learned that if I could endure the initial blast of steam, John would calm down and engage in a reasonable discussion. I could have a debate with John and come to a conclusion we both could live with. With Brian, there was rarely a middle ground. The two made an odd couple and eventually John would take half the group and leave for another major firm.

Doug Gilbert was quiet and thoughtful, though seemingly joined at the hip with Brian. Their practices were interconnected and they were close personally. Though Doug could be easier to approach than Brian, they were a single bargaining unit. Divide-and-conquer strategies were never going to work with them. Conversely, their tactic of outnumbering me and trying to wear me down would leave them equally frustrated.

The acquisition of the labour group in Toronto taught me some crucial lessons about growth. We had quickly gone from one group of eight with a single developing philosophy to two groups of eight with divergent outlooks. In the original group, which consisted of the four founders, along with Joe Groia and his small group of litigators, everyone had signed up for long-term growth and development of a new law-firm model. We had an immature client base, largely clients who were looking for a young aggressive firm. We were going to grow alongside the clients. We held ourselves out as a fresh alternative to Bay Street firms. Our new labour partners arrived from Faskens with over fifteen years of goodwill and experience, which were being transported to a new platform. They had been groomed by George Adams, one of Ontario's leading labour lawyers, who had left them to become a judge; they had a mature practice and a great blue-chip reputation in the business community, particularly with companies such as Air Canada and Canada Post. The resulting dichotomy was destined to be a source of long-term frustration: the developing alongside the established; the entrepreneurial beside the institutional; the unproven versus the predictable; those of us who had to be risk-takers juxtaposed with a sure and steady labour practice.

Brian Burkett could never understand why our strategy wasn't geared to taking on more people like him: successful, established, and well known. He thought that we should be waiting patiently for those opportunities—in the guise of lawyers accompanied by solid practices, enormous hours, and a tireless work ethic—and grabbing them as they came by. On paper his strategy was the clear winner, except that those practices and those people would not be lining up to join us. Instead we were looking at lawyers who were developing but not quite there. If they flourished in our environment, the investment would well be worthwhile. Some were younger and showed potential; others were older and could add judgment and credibility. While some would be enormously successful, others would crash and burn.

We were in the early stages of becoming the dominant Canadian law firm in management-side labour law and in entertainment law, two very different practices. I was fond of saying that the labour lawyers paid the rent. The practice was recession-proof and dependable. There was always a steady flow of work, from the mundane to the most sophisticated, for many major Canadian companies and multinationals. At the other end of the spectrum the entertainment group were imaginative risk-takers. If deals didn't close, we didn't get paid. When they did close we were paid handsomely. This represented an entrepreneurial approach for young and growing clients that saw our reputation skyrocket over time. Peter Blaikie, Roy Heenan, and our leadership supported this strategy, which was unique among law firms at the time. I used to joke with Danny Kaufer that while our labour partners toiled in Sherbrooke, Rimouski, Laval, and Sudbury, the entertainment group was hard at work in Los Angeles, London, Paris, and Cannes. Ultimately, labour law provided stability while entertainment would fund our expansion. On a number of occasions

Brian Burkett questioned whether we should limit our growth and stick to boutique areas of practice where we excelled. That was never my dream.

— • —

Bursting at the seams in the Royal Trust Tower thanks to the labour expansion, we required a brand-new space plan. We decided to move to the south tower of the Royal Bank Plaza, at one time the most outstanding landmark of the emerging Toronto skyline. Its gold-tinted windows brightly reflected the sun and played foil to the four black towers to the north. We settled on two-thirds of a floor, which would hold us for another five years, and took an option on the balance of the floor. Once again we had misjudged. On moving day we filled all the offices and exercised our option on the balance almost immediately.

I remember having lunch with Roy shortly before the move. I told him I could easily envision our office going from sixteen to fifty lawyers within another three years. This meant it would take us five years to accomplish what took fourteen years in Montreal. I begged him not to repeat what I'd said for fear our Montreal partners would see that kind of trajectory as reckless.

Our narrative had also changed. We had shifted from an upstart that wove its unique story gradually over time, to two diverse entities under one roof, each with what amounted to its own story. When, if ever, would one catch up with the other? The labour component gave us stability and substance. It also created a market perception that we were becoming dominant in a field that could be perceived as unattractive to transactional lawyers. Our blessing was now our curse and it applied in both directions. Brian continually groused that the high standards demanded of his group could not be met anywhere else in the office. This would eventually change, but never completely.

— • —

Roy had also been speaking to Peter Gall, the dean of labour law in Western Canada. Peter had an enormous reputation as a labour lawyer and thinker. Creative, intense, emotional, and brilliant, Peter had the most dominating work ethic of anyone I had ever met. Peter was half-visionary, half-dreamer. He was well connected with the British Columbia government as well as the opposition and had an array of contacts in diverse areas, from professional sports to private equity. While he was mastering the practice of law, day-to-day practice issues bored him. He had merged his labour boutique of Jordan Gall, where all partners were equal in all respects, with the Blakes corporate machine in Vancouver, and he was regretting the decision. Here was a new opportunity to start another boutique in Vancouver and be part of Roy's dream, to create an integrated national labour practice from Quebec to Victoria. It was too tempting to pass up. Peter saw this as a new opportunity and worked with Joe Weiler to start a new office. He immediately recruited Peter Sheen and Susan Arnold, both of them exceptionally capable, intelligent, and stable, who backed up Peter's flair for bringing clients in the door. They did the work that Peter found mundane. Over the years Peter experimented with various talented consultants as he sought ways to create a greater array of client services out of our law practice.

Peter Gall is a unique personality. He has a brilliant mind, always filled with exciting new ideas, but his business sense is flawed. He jokingly told the story of his venture into an ice cream business with a couple of partners. The business was growing at an accelerated pace, but no one was paying attention to the fact that the more ice cream they sold, the more money they lost. Peter always did much better in law than in any side business ventures.

— • —

Despite our accomplishments, we faced constant challenges in maintaining partner loyalty. While we were growing the national labour platform, Danny Kaufer travelled with Roy to many American Bar

Association events, where he met Roy's numerous contacts. His gregarious personality helped him establish his own deep connections, which turned on the tap of referral work from across North America. It reached the point where Danny referred to those meetings as "shooting fish in a barrel." Roy, however, cast a long shadow, and Danny could not shake the feeling that he was still perceived as Roy's boy, regardless of his own talents. In May 1993 he left the firm, along with his right-hand associate Corrado de Stefano, to become the labour appendage to Montreal's powerhouse commercial firm Phillips & Vineberg.

Set up initially as a haven for Montreal's Jewish lawyers who would not be hired elsewhere, Phillips & Vineberg had become the boutique for the elite businesses and families of Montreal's Jewish community, including the Bronfmans of Seagram's fame. Danny had traded one prestigious boutique for another, but while he had escaped Roy, he was now at a firm that needed him only as a service lawyer. That was not Danny's vision for himself. After a brief sojourn, the prodigal son returned home in 1994. Corrado returned as well and eventually became a partner in the firm. Danny was welcomed home by most with open arms. In fact Danny became our reminder to not take what we were building for granted. He'd had the chance to experience life in another firm and concluded that our environment was preferable.

Danny's story was emblematic of the firm through 2011. We rarely lost partners to another firm, and when we did, some, like Danny, left only to return later. The emotional relationship we had with one another created a connection to Heenan Blaikie that defied all logic. How that sense of connection became ingrained in me, and how I was able to transmit it to the group I would one day build in Toronto, was a secret to the success that for years made us so attractive to lawyers in other firms. I used to joke that we were the "Hotel California" the Eagles sang about. You could check out any time you liked, but you could never leave. While this may have been emblematic of law firms in the 1980s, the loyalty to the HB brand would be unusual as time went on, particularly as law firms expanded and became larger. The movement of partners between firms slowly became the norm in the industry. Similar to professional athletes, over time, partners' loyalty to their firms waned as they began to see themselves more as free agents.

— • —

We chose to build for the future through highly selective recruiting of exceptional young talent. Allen Garson had articled at Goodmans, and then moved on to Robins Appleby, prior to its crash in 1990. For years the fate of that firm served as a reminder to all of us in the legal community of the dangers of expanding too quickly. David Wolfish had been a junior partner who left Robins during the exodus to join a North York real estate boutique. He was the master of banker-side film finance until he died suddenly and tragically after a brief hospitalization in 1997, leaving the entire film industry in shock. I still remember walking with him down slushy Simcoe Street in late February 1989, trying to convince him to join my start-up.

After Allen applied for a position, I called David to ask for a reference. Never one to rely much on the interview process, I preferred the analysis of someone I trusted. David's endorsement of Allen was unqualified. He thought Allen would be a great addition. That was sufficient for my purposes. George Burger led the interview with Allen, which lasted for about an hour. There were four people interviewing Allen in our sparsely furnished boardroom. I stuck my head in the door and chatted with Allen for about five minutes before excusing myself to get back to work. When George came to visit me at the end of the day, we concluded that we should make him an offer. We needed the extra body and we assumed he needed the job.

Allen's version of the story ran somewhat differently. He used to say: "Norm Bacal, the lead partner, made an appearance and, after five minutes, was obviously so unimpressed with me that he didn't bother to stay, so I figured that was that." He may have been shocked when we presented the offer, so he decided to think about it. And he thought and thought and thought, seemingly unable to make up his mind. Weeks became months, until I finally told George that if Allen had this much difficulty making a decision to accept our offer of employment, we had to ask ourselves what kind of lawyer he would be—clearly, the kind who would never decide. George and I finally agreed to give him a one-week ultimatum. In the end Allen managed to string the process out a full six months before finally accepting our offer and starting work. Poor as he would be at making up his mind, he developed an uncanny ability to tease apart and simplify complicated situations for clients without missing any important detail, and getting them to assess the risks with a clear mind. Over time he took on larger transactions and subsequently ran them on his own. He handled many of our investor film-financing structures and eventually took over important relationships that I had brought in with Warner Bros. and Lions Gate Entertainment Corporation. Eventually his talent saw him running the most significant deals that came in to the firm.

—— ◆ ——

Over the next few years we developed a remarkable aura on the university campuses that allowed us to attract students of the highest calibre. We selected against the genius type who ranked at the top of the class and was destined for a research position far from the realm of clients. Students interested in becoming securities lawyers on large transactions or bank-financing attorneys (usually those graduating from the University of Toronto) were more likely to select Goodmans, Davies, Blakes, McCarthys, or Stikemans. We, however, were consistently buried under a mountain of work that necessitated a sink-or-swim approach and required junior lawyers comfortable with that. As well, we expected our lawyers to generate work commensurate with their levels of training and experience. We attracted bright students who thought they might be interested in entertainment law, high achievers in labour law, and others who were drawn to the ground-floor opportunity. Our calling card was our standard of excellence; our mission, to become Canada's next great law firm.

The marketing pitch worked on the likes of Ken Dhaliwal and Jim Russell. Adam Kardash remained with us, graduating from the mailroom to young associate. We picked up Mark Jadd, a junior addition to our tax group, from the castoffs of Robins Appleby. He was another recommended-by-Danny-Kaufer hire who I accepted sight unseen. The final key addition to the group of future stars was a third-year commercial lawyer from Faskens. He was talented enough, but a general lack of confidence made him respectful to the point of obsequiousness. David Steinberg, a.k.a. David Quinton, had spent his late teenage years as a drummer in the Toronto punk rock band The Mods, which had achieved a certain notoriety and groupie following across North America in the 1980s. The contrast between his past and current personae was stark. The son of a well-known cantor and music composer, David was overly serious and seemingly without an ounce of remaining personality. The atmosphere at Faskens had beaten him down, though his legal training had been excellent. He had come well recommended, so we gave him the benefit of the doubt.

With our open approach David recovered, and over the next few months his natural self-assurance, ebullience, and counterculture sensibility returned, along with his humanity. I had released the inner Quinton, who over the years defied every dress code I ever imposed, created a singular client style that would define our entire entertainment group, and developed a unique reputation around the world in the music and film businesses.

No commercial lawyer at HB was exempted from working on our film tax-shelter financings, which were the lifeblood of the office. These were complex deals involving banking, partnership law, film finance, and trust and escrow arrangements. They also necessitated the negotiation of legal opinions involving multiple law firms, including local and major New York and Los Angeles firms, each of them with its own input and approach. The quality of our work product was continually driven to new levels of excellence by the greater legal community. The experience that our junior lawyers gained through these negotiations would serve them well for the rest of their careers. They had to draft and adapt each deal according to the particularities of the situation, taking account of the subtle differences that characterized each one. My role was to push the limits of what was possible, to experiment, and to lead the development of new ideas, continually refining, repackaging, and succeeding.

— • —

I spent the winter vacation of 1991 considering how to replace individual-project financing with a fund concept. The idea was to create a blind pool through which investors could fund a series of projects that met predetermined criteria. The fund's general partner would exercise the discretion to invest if a project met all the financing conditions. The investors would then be able to participate in the profitability of a series of different projects. Our investors didn't seem to care about the artistic attributes of anything they were financing. They appreciated the stability, the commercial safety, the tax rulings, and the possibility of profit if the film or TV show was a hit. In the first five years we had had no hits, but no one seemed deterred.

A fund would also allow us to use one offering document for many financings rather than a new offering document for each and every project. This would be a great project for Allen Garson and Mark Jadd to cut their teeth on.

The key to the success of the fund would be Jeff Rayman's ability to sell it. Jeff was in the process of building Alliance Entertainment's financing arm into an industry giant. After he, Jay Firestone, and I had spent hours debating how this fund would work, Jeff went on the road with a short executive summary of the concept to test its marketability. The economies of scale all around would be enormous. There were also certain tax problems in our individual-funding structure that a fund would correct. If Jeff truly succeeded, he could amass an investor war chest to buy projects, and we would continue to be the firm breaking new ground, thus reinforcing our thought-leadership position in the Canadian film industry.

Out of this intense thought process was born Diversified Media Ventures. Now we needed a professional outside general partner to run the operations: Bernie Abrams, a CA who had worked with Alliance on a number of deals, was about to turn that involvement into a career. Jeff, now deep into the pre-marketing, had soft commitments for tens of millions of dollars, even though we had no formal documentation ready to go.

When the dust settled three years down the road, Jeff had raised over a billion dollars through twelve Diversified Media Venture Funds—but not without continual challenges and variations. Almost once a year new tax changes were announced that directly or indirectly impacted structuring, requiring us to find a way to adjust the product to meet the new criteria.

The funds also gave us the opportunity to visit Hollywood to explain to the US studios how partnering with Canadian producers was in their financial interest. Thanks to a unique partnership of schemers like me and syndicators like Jeff Rayman, a new era in film financing was beginning. Alliance Equicap generated spectacular cash flows for its parent, Alliance Communications Corporation, which had recently gone public, and allowed Robert Lantos the luxury of additional working capital to build his empire. The film and television industry in Canada was about to blossom.

6

BECOMING THE RAIDERS

Michael Prupas and I were realizing our vision for the Toronto office and our entertainment practice. We firmly believed we could capture an entire national platform by sending Arthur Evrensel, at that time a fifth-year associate, to Vancouver to open our practice in the West. By this time Arthur was well trained, and Peter Gall was running a successful labour practice, so entertainment was a very timely complement and growth opportunity. Vancouver was a ripe market, and securing a west-coast position would strengthen our firm brand in Hollywood. Arthur's brother was a successful Vancouver restaurateur, which made it easier to convince Arthur to move. We hoped he'd become a leading entertainment lawyer out west and a fixture in Los Angeles. Was it crazy to entrust the future to a lawyer not yet promoted to partnership? We never stopped to consider the issue. All we saw was potential. Our national entertainment practice was born, and the risk Arthur agreed to take was rewarded with partnership a year ahead of his peers.

The film fund structure allowed Jeff Rayman and me to hunt for product across North America. When we learned that Warner Bros. (WB) was scouting in Canada to produce a *Kung Fu* TV-series sequel to its David Carradine original, we used our Alliance contacts to get an introduction. This project would be a large, lucrative financing. Landing it meant flying down to Burbank to meet Warner Bros.'s global head of film finance, Robert A. (Bob) Fisher, and his team.

Bob's full-time occupation involved finding money to subsidize WB production all over the world by developing creative structures and reducing WB's economic exposure. As a result, he drew on a rich experience with structures throughout Europe, Asia, Australia, and the United States, but had yet to try Canada. Jeff and I were not the first Canadian group he'd met, and I got the sense he was quite skeptical. Could we really offer him a structure that met the needs of the studio to control the financing of a production, while also meeting Canadian legal requirements to qualify the projects as Canadian content? While I had a template worked out, it would need countless adjustments to meet WB's expectations.

The chemistry between Bob, Jeff, and me was immediate. Bob had a steel trap of a mind and an understanding of the leverage that Bugs Bunny and a multi-billion-dollar studio brought to negotiating the best possible deal in the market. He had various requirements and tested us continually by pushing the limits of what was acceptable. My job was to draw the lines in the sand, all of them arbitrary but based on my seven years of finance experience. I had to work creatively with Bob to keep many of the elements of our standard deal while customizing the balance to fit with WB's peculiar standards. One meeting grew into four or five more over the following month as we hammered out the deal. Then I called on Allen Garson to paper the most intricate transaction we had ever conceived.

Jeff sold out the deal very quickly as part of our fund, and our status at Warner Bros. was set. Slowly, over time, Burbank became a home away from home. There was nothing like the scent of blossoms on the studio lot in the middle of February. Occasionally we would have lunch in the commissary, sitting beside film stars on a break from filming. I'd think about my labour partners travelling to Sudbury and other points north and smile, knowing I'd made an awesome career choice.

During that period I spent years nursing pet ideas about alternative financings, turning them into mild obsessions, and then waiting for the chance to follow through on them. In 1986 Peter Hoffman, the American tax expert who participated in my first major tax structure, had been telling me about US syndications of film-marketing funds that took on major studio theatrical releases. In those days all the costs related to making prints, or copies, of a film's master negative, plus television- and newspaper-advertising expenses—commonly known in the industry as P&A expenses—were deductible for tax purposes in the United States, and to take advantage of these deductions, structures were built to raise investor financing. These financings had long since been outlawed in the United States.

In 1993 Jeff Rayman and I began to discuss whether we could design a workable concept for the syndication of a P&A deal in Canada. We concluded that if we partnered with a major US studio under the umbrella of Alliance Entertainment, I could devise a new tax structure with a goal to raise hundreds of millions of dollars to finance the release of slates of well-known films. On the heels of a successful *Kung Fu* series closing, Jeff and I approached Bob Fisher and his newly appointed counsel, David Sagal, about other types of financings I was devising. Outside the practice of law David played a mean saxophone, and his sister was the female star of the *Married with Children* comedy series. Bob and I spent many hours working on the new structure together until we came up with a product that was ready for the market. Jeff Rayman then worked his magic, bringing in the investors. The deal flow and the revenues generated over the next eight years by these new deals and the Canadian film syndications would fund Heenan Blaikie's expansion.

— • —

In January 1993 Michael Prupas managed to secure a few pairs of tickets for Super Bowl XXVII in Pasadena. Michael and I were heading down for our annual Hollywood studio tour, and the trip to the Rose Bowl stadium would kick off the trip. As we flew across the continent on Sunday morning, Michael mentioned to me that our correspondent attorney in LA, Dan Black, was planning to leave his current firm and was considering another firm. Dan radiated calm and quiet class. He had a particular affinity for Canadian projects, having worked for a number of years on the American side of projects produced by Michael's clients.

"Dan wants to know," Michael said, "if we'll continue to refer work to him at the new shop."

Impulsively I responded, "Why don't we open an office in LA?"

Michael looked at me as if I were an alien. "You're joking, right?"

I thought for a second. "No, I'm serious. We've been talking about opening an LA office for a few years, but we never had a real plan. Why don't we see if Dan would like to start a greenfield?"

Without much strategic planning, the idea was born. We had a number of hours on the plane together to work through some of the details. The next morning, after the Dallas Cowboys crushed the Buffalo Bills, Michael pitched Dan. Dan asked for some time to think about it.

It took only a couple of days for Dan to get back to us. "I'm in," he said. He was very enthusiastic. This would be far more complicated for Dan than folding his practice into an existing firm since he would be repeating the experiment I had started in Toronto, putting together an office while carrying on his practice. The first requirement for an office involved recruiting talent. It made sense to look for people who Dan knew and felt comfortable with to start.

Dan suggested that one of his other law partners, who had worked with us in the past, might be interested in leaving his law firm to start up a Heenan Blaikie office. Although we had spoken by phone, I had never previously met Jeff Berkowitz, a tax lawyer who represented the Frank Sinatra estate and who had become a close friend and counsel to Frank Junior. Both Dan and Jeff were New York transplants. Jeff, very proud of his Bronx heritage, was the child of Holocaust survivors and put himself through university driving an ice cream truck. His life passions were his two bulldogs and his golf game. He was the very caricature of a New York Yankees fan from the Bronx, always in your face with the unfiltered truth, a trait that earned him as many supporters as detractors. His tax advice was pragmatic and effective, and his brusque demeanour hid a soft underbelly. Never was there an odder couple than Dan and Jeff. Dan's elegance and polish somehow dovetailed perfectly with Jeff's constant stream of blunt advice, whether solicited or not. This would be a most interesting combination, but they were both enthusiastic, and they planned to bring along Danny Leon, a more junior commercial lawyer from their current firm.

In the course of three days we put the basic concept in place, and Michael and I flew back to Canada to draw up a business plan. We explained to the Executive Committee and then to our partners that we were planning an LA franchise. I had spoken to a few clients with LA operations to see if this was something they would all support. They agreed unanimously that this was a smart and progressive idea. And by that time we had the successful Toronto and Vancouver openings under our belts.

At the partners meeting there was surprisingly little opposition. The fact that we would be the only Canadian firm with a Hollywood address was considered by most partners to be a distinguishing marketing factor for the firm. A number of our competitors had opened in New York or London, and those were markets where we knew we could not compete, so there was a buzz about having a Beverly Hills address that appealed to many of us. Toronto and Vancouver had been profitable out of the starting gate, so it would have been difficult to challenge Michael or me on the business assessment. We had garnered considerable credibility in four short years and managed to keep the values of the new offices consistent with original Heenan Blaikie values. Peter Blaikie finally blessed the project in his inimitable style:

"Bacal, Prupas: it's your necks on the line here."

Once the plan was hatched, Dan and Jeff signed on and then found a number of lawyers prepared to take the risk along with them. We found office space in Beverly Hills 90210, in the magic triangle between Santa Monica Boulevard and Wilshire Boulevard, steps away from Rodeo Drive. The most talked-about aspect of the office was a young recruit hired as a senior associate. A tall, athletic, blond Adonis in the process of developing an interesting music practice, Scott Zolke had been a college quarterback. He was the type who, with the authority of a field general, could rally his teammates on their own two-yard line with a minute to play in the fourth quarter, confidently telling them, "We have them exactly where we want them. Now let's go out and win this one." Divorced and raising his young daughter, he began each day at dawn on his surfboard and played the surfer dude to the hilt—complete with surfer lingo and Hawaiian shirt—until it was time to get serious with clients. There was no one like Scott Zolke anywhere in the annals of Heenan Blaikie.

Over time, Black and Berkowitz filled the office with an assortment of commercial lawyers and litigators, though they preferred hiring senior lawyers, known in the legal industry as "laterals," to recruiting and developing young talent. Berkowitz handled US tax opinions for many Warner Bros. transactions. We needed him on the ground to work with the studio, and he and Bob Fisher developed a strong mutual affection. Berkowitz added great value to the ongoing WB relationship and to a lucrative business enterprise. Once again we had launched successfully, and for ten years LA proved to be a great HB expansion until its utility waned and we finally had to close the office in 2003. The circumstances of our withdrawing from Beverly Hills could have been the subject of a film script.

One of our LA litigators had given some free advice as a favour to some screenwriters looking to get hired by the producers of the *Judge Judy* show. Shortly afterward, the firm was hired by the producers to do other work. The writers were later fired and, in their anger, alleged that we were in a conflict representing both them and later *Judge Judy*'s producers. Our lawyer was doing them a favour for free but that made no difference to the plaintiffs. The insurance company refused to settle as the case seemed so weak. We weren't representing them at the same time and there was never a real conflict. However, the gentlemanly southern lawyer representing the insurer did not play well to the civil jury, which showed little patience or sympathy for the Heenan Blaikie lawyer or the insurance company. The only lesson we took from this was to beware the jury trial in America. It cost us an office.

— • —

In 1993 Peter Blaikie announced that he was leaving the firm, surprising us all with his unexpected departure from the managing partner's chair. While Peter's differences with Roy had been a source of regular frustration, it was his long-time friend and client, Aaron Fish, who had finally convinced him to make the switch from professional business advisor to businessman. Peter was about to take on the role of president and chief operating officer of the public company Unican Security Systems Ltd. He had sat on Unican's board and watched the company grow almost from its inception; now he would be responsible for running the security system empire that Aaron had founded. Peter's last task as managing partner was to recruit Bob Donaldson, a senior addition to our commercial practice in Toronto. Peter's departure ushered in a new era for the firm.

Jean Potvin, my mentor, was a natural to replace Peter. Jean's tax practice had peaked when he was in his mid-forties and he was ready for a new challenge: running a multi-office national firm. Jean's theory of managing conflict was simple. There was no problem that could not be solved over dinner with a good bottle of wine. His charm lowered the temperature in a room and with it the passions that fuelled controversy, particularly in the ego-charged atmosphere that characterizes law firms. He could also be irritatingly chauvinistic in a patrician French manner, with the result that he was not adept at handling women partners. Despite his fishing-town roots in northern Quebec, he carried himself with aristocratic poise, fitting in well with prime ministers, politicians, and other dignitaries. To the staff he was always Maître Potvin, and he was universally respected.

Jean's greatest challenge would come in managing the expectations of our Toronto labour partners. He sat through many dinners listening to their concerns about the rate of growth of our commercial group, which was always either too slow or too fast; about whether Donaldson was a blessing or a curse; about Roy's insistence on trying to exercise control over the national practice and the labour partners' resistance to the hegemony. Jean listened and soldiered on. Not that he could change the situation, but he cared enough to listen.

Jean was seriously bothered by only one problem, which he would have to confront from time to time: Roy Heenan. They had been partners for years and Jean had grown accustomed to Roy's walking into his office to complain about Peter, but I don't think he ever imagined he would become Roy's new target for complaints. If Roy became upset about an initiative Jean was undertaking in management, Jean would hear about it. Roy was never able to limit his criticisms to the idea. Jean received the message each time as a criticism of his leadership and felt that Roy was questioning his abilities as managing partner. Above all, Jean was a proud man. Each reprimand left a wound to his ego. I was never prepared for the late-night calls at home from Jean to advise me that he'd tendered his resignation to Roy. The first call shocked me. All of us perceived Jean as doing an outstanding job. On each occasion Roy would sit down with Jean the following morning to explain himself and to talk Jean back in off the ledge. By the second and third resignations, I had come to understand that the phone calls were simply a way for Jean to vent his frustration.

After the first resignation I developed a new habit in my dealings with Jean, whether in Montreal or Toronto: I made sure to end each encounter with the magic words "Jean, you're doing a great job." We could not afford for Jean to resign; the firm was stable and growing steadily and, more important, no one was better suited for the role. When I started saying this to him, the positive reinforcement was what mattered. Later it became a ritual, then a game, between us. I sensed that he had his eyes on me for succession, so I needed him to know that the job was his, at least for the next ten years. Anyway, based on personal observation, I doubted I would ever want it.

Jean's four years as managing partner saw our Toronto office develop at a rapid pace under his overall leadership. In fact we grew so rapidly that we had to move locations, this time within the Royal Bank Plaza. The design of the new space became a critical issue. Our designer, who had worked with our Montreal partners in planning their conservative look and feel, had to recover from our partners' rejecting her original classic law-firm design. She then polled us by asking a few simple questions, the most memorable being "If you saw yourself as an automobile, what make or model would it be?" The majority response was "Saab," the quirky, upscale Scandinavian brand that didn't resemble any other car in the market. Back she went to the drawing board. For the reception floor she chose multicolour carpeting in yellows, blues, and greys, with rounded green walls and soft, pale wood finishes, set off by the iconic artwork Roy supplied from his personal collection. We represented Canadian modern painting with originals by Jack Bush, a few Group of Sevens, and the odd Riopelle adorning the walls. We more resembled an ad agency than a stodgy law firm.

When Jean visited the new space he was shocked. "You're out of your minds" was all he could muster. He was wrong. When clients walked in the door, they got the immediate impression they were entering a different kind of law firm, unlike any other on Bay Street.

— • —

While I had no official title, I sat on the firm's Executive Committee and Compensation Committee, which Jean Potvin chaired. Since I had no formal management duties, I was in an ideal situation: I had authority without official responsibility. Occasionally Brian Burkett and John West would come by my office to unload their frustrations and concerns. I normally spent most of my time in those meetings listening, which left Brian exasperated because he perceived my silence as passive-aggressive resistance. In his view we were destined to be a second-tier commercial firm, well behind his labour group's standards. At other times he felt Roy was choking the growth of the Montreal practice, since there were no partners with the strength to stand up to Roy.

I was listening, but I wasn't acting on Brian's concerns, particularly when I didn't agree with him. While he tended to be insular and overprotective of his group, he was providing outstanding client service. Some of his worries were real and his fears were occasionally realized. His group was slowly growing as Rick Charney was developing a local independent practice. Rick, admittedly curmudgeonly, was very concerned about firm expenses and the finances of the firm, but overall was becoming a very solid partner. Future stars John Craig and Tim Lawson were beginning their careers.

Joe Groia was building the litigation group as Jon Stainsby and George Karayannides (who became known as George K) were beginning to mature, while Stan Fisher was playing the role of wise counsel. Meanwhile, the cracks in the brotherhood of partnership were beginning to show. There was no love lost between the labour group and the litigators at the senior levels. The labour group had thrown up a barrier in terms of access to their key clients, which was a source of frustration to the litigators. While my style may have bordered on the passive, Joe Groia's was full-blown aggressive. The labour lawyers did not like Joe's client base, which included clients accused of white-collar crime. They were particularly unhappy that Joe was representing John Felderhof, the former vice-chairman of Bre-X, on securities-commission–related charges; they were concerned about their blue-chip clients' opinion of a firm that would represent this type of clientele. Joe believed the labour group was too insular and only interested in their own success, and he let that be known. Tension levels between Joe and especially Rick Charney, a man of equally strong character, grew over the years. The relationship between the two would eventually sour and stink like three-day-old milk left by the back door.

The rift was also symptomatic of a growing division within the labour group that had joined us a few years earlier. Rick formed part of the group that left at the end of 1996 with John West. The departure of partners to another firm was a rare occurrence for us, so when a small group announced they were leaving at the same time, we were left somewhat in shock. Was this departure a sign of internal problems that would lead to other defections? Were we about to face a crisis of confidence? I spent a considerable amount of time working with the remaining group on the message to clients and to our local partners: our labour practice and our firm were not adversely affected by the departure and we would continue to deliver the high-quality service for which we were well known. In fact, we lost very little business and our partners became comfortable that the labour practice was quickly adapting to the departure. In hindsight the breakup of the labour group was inevitable and allowed for new direction and growth of the remaining practice. I learned that sometimes departures are a healthy component of a law firm's development.

Managing a law firm calls for an ability to manage difficult person-alities. For four years I observed Potvin at work. He was a master. He taught me the value of listening. We were more successful than most firms in avoiding partner departures, particularly as times changed in the 1990s. Before that time it was rare for partners to leave their firms. I can recall one situation in Montreal in the 1980s when a partner was asked to relocate because he had an affair with another partner's wife. Beyond those extreme situations partners simply stuck it out where they started, regardless of whether they were happy. All that changed as the legal world matured and firms got bigger and more impersonal. Partners started to move regularly when they saw better opportunities elsewhere. Without that phenomenon I would not have been able to build a firm.

The magic we relied on, and that I would have to master, consisted of keeping the relationships personal. We had to make these difficult men and women feel valued and loved and attached to a culture that was the foundation on which we built the firm. As in a strong marriage we had to learn to tolerate one another, particularly when someone said or did something that was perceived as hurtful or disrespectful. We also had to learn to say we were sorry. The Groia-Charney feud taught me that on rare occasions the breakdowns could not be fixed. In those cases it was best to deal with the problem and, if necessary, encourage those who did not fit to leave and move on. This whole philosophy would be an important priority in defining the type of work environment we were creating, particularly in Toronto.

— • —

Discipline and single-minded determination had been my guideposts for unprecedented success, both in and out of the dojo. My karate training regimen had increased to three lunchtimes weekly, and my appointment book would not allow for interference with my training. I may have set the record at the club for the slowest progress from white belt through to yellow, orange, and then green. It took well over a year to transform my uncoordinated performances into something resembling the beginnings of basic proficiency. Along the way I suffered bruises and muscle strains, a nasty sprained ankle that had me on crutches for a week, and the odd back spasm. After breaking a rib it took many years to overcome my fear of sparring and my involuntary habit of closing my eyes anytime a punch was aimed in the direction of my head. There were many moments when it would have been easy to justify giving up.

By summer 1994 I was part of a small group ready to grade for the *shodan*, or first degree black belt. I still had not completely overcome my fear of, and distaste for, sparring, but I had no choice if I wanted to advance. As part of my pre-grading, Sensei Marion was running a sparring drill designed to test the limits of our endurance. It began with an advanced black belt attacking me. After a couple of minutes, a second one entered the fray. Now I was defending myself from two attackers simultaneously, trying to arrange my body position so they could not attack from different directions. I surprised myself by remaining on my feet. By the time Marion sent in the third black belt, I was exhausted and almost ready to give up, but I fought hard. I understood this was not a test of skill so much as a test of my spirit and determination. Finally they overwhelmed me and Marion called them off. I had survived.

To achieve black-belt status, one had to demonstrate a proficiency in self-defence, grappling, sparring, and a series of moves, or *kata*, as well as skill with various weapons. Cezar also insisted that we train our minds to overcome our internal resistance resulting from fear. To do that he introduced a challenge involving breaking boards with our bare fists. I had seen demonstrations on television, with martial arts masters shattering blocks of concrete or ice with the sides of their bare hands. The term *karate* means empty, or open, hand, so a karate chop is a blow with an open hand. To break a block, the mind and spirit must be focused. We had spent over four years practising technique, first into the air, next into pads, and then into the human body (albeit while slightly pulling our punches). Now Cezar, who had by this time had the ceremonial title of *Kyoshi* bestowed upon him by the masters in Okinawa, was convincing us that we could succeed with one-inch-thick pine planks. The technique remained the same, but the mind had to accept that the board would snap on impact. Cezar expected us to execute a perfect punch on a horizontal plane that would penetrate and snap the barrier.

I was third in line. We had to put our focus, or *kime*, on a spot six inches behind the board, which was the real target. The goal was to explode to that focal point and the board would snap on the way through. I took my turn, convincing myself that the board was not really there. Cezar had two boards in place, each an inch thick, extended in front of his chest one behind the other. The first board had already been broken by the student ahead of me in line, and the second had not. My fist had to pass through the two-inch barrier. I reminded myself: "Transfer the rotation of the hips into the explosion of the arm and the twist of the closed fist, just as you've done thousands of times. And release the energy and breath with a loud *kiyai*."

Snap! I didn't quite understand it, but there it was—the board sliced into two pieces. Jubilation!

It was never my goal to earn the shodan. For the first year after I began to wear the black belt, I felt unworthy. I had no idea of the responsibility that came with wearing the belt in the dojo. Suddenly I was a sensei. I had unknowingly crossed over to management, and my lunchtime training sessions were no longer a simple diversion from work. I was now a teacher as well as a student. I watched others far more accomplished than I and began to wonder whether Kyoshi had made a mistake. Over the next couple of years, though, I grew into the belt as my skill set continued to improve—and with it my confidence. These feelings of adjustment foreshadowed what I would be going through in my work life in 1997, when I would be suddenly taking on responsibilities as managing partner—a role for which I had little training or experience.

— • —

Meanwhile, Heenan Blaikie was on a run. The entertainment deals multiplied. Arthur Evrensel had developed a fine relationship with MGM and the television division of Sony Pictures Entertainment, and Michael Prupas and Sam Berliner in Montreal were in touch with numerous independent producers. Jeff Rayman and I continued to work with WB, financing the release of a series of their movies across North America. During the period from 1994 to 2001 we were involved in financing hundreds of films for various studios, including *Mars Attacks!*, *Murder at 1600*, *Jack Frost*, *You've Got Mail*, and *The 6th Day*. The HB franchise for film finance had traversed the continent, and our structuring expertise was now recognized as leading edge. If our name was on the product, investors understood that the deals were built to endure.

By the end of 2001, the sun was setting on our film tax-shelter business. While we had participated in financing hundreds of films shot in Canada, which created thousands of jobs and helped build a domestic industry, none of the films had generated any profit for the investors. That's not to say that the film studios and distributors did not do well, but once they got through covering all their expenses and fees, there was rarely any profit left over for the investors. Over the years the investors had come to understand that while they might hope for a profit, picking a highly successful film was no different from buying a lottery ticket.

Incredibly, our winning number did finally come up. It was a last-minute $250,000 investment in a small independent picture. Tom Hanks and his wife, Rita Wilson, were involved, and the producers came looking to defray their costs. The film was obscure, written by a Canadian, and the investment so small that I almost said no. To make it work we had to package it with a film from another studio, called *Harvard Man*. (If you ever have the chance to see *Harvard Man* on video, don't.)

A couple of years passed and my partner Steven Lewis came into my office to ask me if I had been following the success of *My Big Fat Greek Wedding*. Who hadn't been? It was quickly becoming the most successful independently released film of all time. The box office was in excess of $300 million. But what did that have to do with us?

"Norm, you tax-sheltered the picture," Steven said. "I did all the work. It was the other picture in the package with *Harvard Man*."

I'd had no idea. It was time to take a more careful look at how the investors were doing. I checked the distribution reports and, sure enough, it didn't seem to matter how well the film performed at the box office, the movie was not making any money. We did a little independent checking and discovered that some of the other profit participants were threatening court action. There was no way this film could not be making money. I thought about it and concluded we had to litigate. While we did not expect the amount owed to change the lives of any of our investors, I was more concerned about another factor. If Revenue Canada got wind of the fact that a hugely successful movie was not returning a profit, they might assert the position that this entire investment scheme was a fraud on the tax department. We could not take that risk. At the very least, we had to demonstrate that we were prepared to exercise our rights to get paid what ought to have been owed.

Ultimately, we litigated and settled on terms that cannot be disclosed. Our investors ended up with a cash distribution. And the file taught me a lot about Hollywood accounting. It also reinforced a lesson that Jeff Rayman and I took away from our meeting a few years earlier with Tom Pollock, the former head of Universal Studios. We were investigating the possibility of an investment deal between one of Canada's largest pension funds and a major Hollywood studio. We had asked Tom to educate us about the secret of picking successful films based on the script or treatment. Tom had agreed to see us for fifteen minutes but was so intrigued with our proposal that he sat with us for two hours.

"Don't ask me," he told us. "I'm the guy that refused to put money into *Forrest Gump*. I never thought that movie would work. Everyone in Hollywood passed on it. Instead I picked what I thought would be a great Kevin Costner picture. We spent two hundred million dollars on *Waterworld*. It was an economic disaster. All I can tell you gentlemen is one thing. Nobody knows what will work." I came away from the meeting understanding that building a law firm by picking successful lawyers might be considerably easier than picking a successful movie based on a script.

— • —

While our tax group was solid, Bob Donaldson, the senior commercial lawyer Peter had hired just prior to his departure, was instrumental in helping us build two of our departments. For a number of years we had been interested in Bill Orr, a well-known securities lawyer in the city, who had risen through the system at Fraser & Beatty. Bob's arrival at the firm created an interesting opportunity to build a strong commercial department, and Bill could be an important next step for us. He was becoming one of the leading lawyers in advising independent committees of boards of directors on their duties in the event of takeover bids, whether friendly or hostile. Bill had grown unhappy with his firm's development. Bob Donaldson, and later Stan Fisher and Joe Groia, had got him excited about what we were building at HB. Signing on with HB turned out to be a perfect career move, since Bill readily bought into the notion of helping to build a securities group in the office. Later he brought in his good friend and younger partner Lisa Davis to add to the expertise of the group.

I had also been trying to build our reputation in corporate restructuring. We had Ken Kraft, a solid young lawyer, but we needed a bigger name in the community. I was pleasantly surprised that Bob's presence, bolstered by Bill, allowed me to land Barry Goldberg, an old childhood friend of mine, who had grown up in the Osler system and had developed a reputation as one of the up-and-coming stars of the insolvency bar. Barry represented American vulture capitalists and wanted an aggressive platform.

I felt that we were becoming like the Oakland Raiders, an NFL team that dressed in black uniforms and were counterculture to the league's staid franchises. They were the pirates, the newcomer expansion team that, under John Madden's leadership, had won a Super Bowl. We were similarly young and brash, with an admixture of grey-haired wisdom, but ready to take on any opponent to fight for any client. Barry's recruitment was ideal. It made a statement to the market that we were now able to attract commercial lawyers with strong reputations. More important, our strategy of building slowly with strong young talent on the litigation side with people like Wendy Berman, Ian Godfrey, and Ken Kraft from Torys was starting to pay off. We were beginning to add senior leadership to grow the practices. Barry's role as a mentor to Ken was expected to be a boon to Ken's career. Barry also added needed profile to the practice, and he paired well with our Montreal expert in the field, my old pal Ken Atlas, who was building a reputation in Montreal as an expert in bank-syndicated financings and restructurings. Calls were now coming in from lawyers at other firms who were interested in possibly joining us. The Heenan Blaikie aura was spreading across the legal market.

book II

LEADING
A FIRM
1997–2012

7

TRIALS OF **LEADERSHIP**

The year had concluded and 1996 proved to be the most successful the firm had ever experienced. All cylinders were firing, and many partners were now earning more than they had ever imagined possible. A unique trait of lawyers is that after admitting their lives have turned out far better than they'd ever dreamed, most will start wondering why they're not doing even better.

Sitting in Compensation Committee meetings since 1990, I learned much about most of the firm's partners, including their practices, whom they worked well with, whom they resented, and what drove them. I also learned to listen. For most partners the process of talking about themselves and bragging about their accomplishments was difficult. An outsider would never expect to hear that lawyers had difficulty promoting themselves, but for most partners this was a very trying experience. Like the shoemaker who wore tattered shoes, they might be wonderful advocates for clients but had little sense of how to best advocate for themselves. A few were driven more by work challenges than by money, though many defined themselves by what they earned or where they stood on the status ladder. Everyone respected the process. Committee membership terms were staggered, with the composition of the committee changing every three years, and, now that I had served my sixth year, it was time to get off. The compensation process, which took two months to complete every year, involved considerable time and effort and was emotionally draining. Sitting in the room also cost money. To protect the integrity of the system, committee members would always deliberately take a little less than would have been expected had they been non-members.

We were midway through 1997 and Jean, now in his early fifties, went for his routine annual physical. He was a jogger, kept in good shape, lived well, ate healthy food, and had settled into the managing partner role with grace and acknowledged skill. Unfortunately, something unusual showed up in his blood work. After being sent for additional tests, he was diagnosed with a malignancy, but the doctors could not determine the source. Though Jean was prepared to fight, it would take months to figure out exactly what he was fighting and the correct protocols to deal with it. Jean concluded that there was not enough room in his life to continue running the firm, now in five cities, while treating a yet-to-be-determined form of cancer. Something had to give.

I got the call a few days later. Jean explained that it was time to put his career on hold and fight a more important battle. I could feel the shock setting in, first personally and then professionally. This was not the grand plan. Jean, my mentor and friend, was supposed to be running the firm for the indefinite future—or forever, as far as I was concerned. He had mentioned once that the day would come when it would be my turn, but that day was still beyond any foreseeable horizon. I was only forty-one, without any management experience. There wasn't much about being managing partner that appealed to me and, frankly, my previous experience didn't qualify me for the job.

If, though, it was my turn, the moment had arrived with some irony. Perhaps it was related to my age, but I felt I had reached the zenith of my career a little too early. If tax-oriented film finance had been an Olympic sport, then I might have qualified to be Canada's representative. I was recognized as a leading expert in my field world-wide, but I was starting to feel there was more to life than film finance.

I had even begun to wonder if HB was a stepping stone to something else. I believed strongly that at the appropriate moment the light would flash on and the little voice that drove me to Toronto would once more guide me. For now my career was on a high-level coast, but I needed a new challenge. Managing the firm, however, was not on the list.

The issue of Jean's illness and resulting leave of absence urgently made its way to the National Management and Executive committees. Any internal search would have to start with an inventory of our best business people, not necessarily our best lawyers or best administrators. The discussion was interesting, but it became clear that this was a job no one in the room wanted. I flashed back to a discussion I'd had with Georges Audet, one of my mentors and a solid Montreal litigation partner, who had left a few years earlier to join the bench. At one of our cocktail parties in Montreal he was telling Jean and me that law firms had advanced to the point where the firm's strongest business leader needed to be running the organization. That comment weighed on me.

We decided that Jean would lead a small search committee to take stock of the potential candidates and appoint someone on an interim basis, which would allow the partners time to decide on a more perma-nent solution. We needed a quick decision to maintain stability, since most of the partners were still not aware that Jean was ill or that he'd stepped down from the managing partner role. The word would be out shortly and the firm needed a plan. Jean called and asked me to consider taking on the managing partner role. My initial inclination was to decline. When I got home I told Sharon about the dilemma.

— • —

"Who am I to take on this role? What evidence is there that I could suc-ceed? Administration isn't my strong suit," I ranted. "I'm a dreamer and a schemer, and while I might have been a builder, I'm not the one who pays attention to detail." She listened intently but let me continue. "My communication style is cryptic and I speak quietly … unless I have a microphone in my hand."

Sharon chuckled. "You don't have to remind me of your penchant for making speeches to any audience."

"Okay," I countered, "but I'm not naturally socially adept. I hate cocktail parties and small talk, and that would be part of the job. I may be likeable, but I wouldn't describe myself as a natural people person."

"You also hate conflict. You like to sweep things under the carpet. I'm not sure if that's an asset or a liability in this job," she said half-jokingly.

"Besides, the function's always been a Montreal position."

"But you have the Montreal background and your French is decent."

I sighed. "Except I'm not socially comfortable in French. And the administration for the firm is run entirely out of Montreal, so how much time would I have to spend there just to deal with mundane matters, which, to begin with, are my short suit? There are so many reasons to say no."

"What did you tell Jean?"

"That I'd think about it. I'm just not sure what to do."

Sharon smiled a reassuring smile. "Look, Norm, you already know there's no one better qualified. I trust you'll make the right decision for you, and whatever it is, I'll support it."

Although I'd built a career out of never saying no to an opportunity, this one had come along ten years too early. But I had an idea. I called Jean back and told him I was worried that Montreal partners and administrators needed someone there on the ground full-time. So why not name two co-managing partners to share the job for now? I would take on half, and undoubtedly someone could be found in the Montreal office for the other half. We'd work this way on an interim basis until January 1998, at which point we could all re-evaluate. This arrangement would minimize my Montreal commute, and during the period of Jean's crash course for us on running a law firm, we would have four hands and two heads.

The attendant risks had not yet dawned on me: that I and my mystery co-manager might not agree on important issues; that our personalities might not be a good fit; that this would increase the perception of a struggle between smaller Toronto and big-brother Montreal; that partners would play us off against one another like children and parents; and that no one would know who was in charge, because we wouldn't know who was in charge either. Besides, shared positions rarely worked out in organizations.

But we would experiment. If things didn't go smoothly, we could make adjustments, or the Executive Committee would ask one or both of us to step aside. After all, this was an interim appointment. We would figure out the long-term arrangement later.

My decision created some additional work for the Executive Committee, since they now needed to find a Montreal candidate. This had to be done quickly and tactfully, so that those not chosen would not feel any sense of rejection. No doubt there were a few partners who may have felt they were next in line, though it seemed fairly evident from a political perspective that the Montreal candidate would have to be a francophone for the sake of linguistic balance.

Michael Prupas had shown an interest, but my selection would sound the death knell for his aspirations, at least for now. In every practical sense, two anglos could not run the firm. Ironically, Michael was going through the same soul-searching as I was, and when he didn't land the job, he began to make plans to leave the practice of law and begin a career as a film and television producer. Guy Tremblay, one of our labour partners, had the support of both Jean and Roy. Dependable, francophone, confident, solid on his feet, and a great labour lawyer, Guy Tremblay was trusted by all. There was rarely a question as to where he stood on any issue. Ten years my senior, he was the right vintage. Though he was a partner when I joined the firm as a student in 1980, he was the partner whom I knew the least about. I called Danny Kaufer for a reference. "Norm, I'll tell you one thing about Guy—the only thing you need to know. You can trust him." That was good enough for me.

To say that the partners could not have chosen two more polar opposites may be an overstatement, but not by much. Guy was the prototypical extrovert: he sported garish ties and was defined by his noisy bold-coloured striped socks that would only become stylish around 2013. Guy's fashion sense allowed him to beat the trend by a number of years. He could be loud, brash, quick with a joke, and always seemed to be laughing hard. Guy was passionate about life, art, and his golf game, in no particular order. On the golf course he was the type who would regale clients with stories, and if he was having a good round he made sure everyone knew.

Roy had been Guy's best man and walked him down the aisle for his second marriage, to Renate, the love of his life (though his precious Shatzi, a little white Yorkie, would eventually rank a very close second). Roy was his mentor and his idol. Guy recognized and forgave all the shortcomings of the great man, respecting that without Heenan there was no Heenan Blaikie, at least in Montreal. Amusing, occasionally misperceived as a clown, Guy was fast to react and always emotive, so there was never any question about what he was thinking. Many wondered whether he was serious enough for the job. This was the outward Guy, the only part I had ever seen in the past.

As I wrote earlier, I have always been a textbook introvert. I generally keep my opinions to myself until I'm thoroughly prepared to share them, and even then, I share only with those I trust. I've been told I remind people of the Egyptian Sphinx—tough to read, quiet, always preferring to listen rather than speak. I'm also known to be calm, steady as she goes. You could set your stern to my compass. As I've mentioned, I always prefer to lead from the rear and to move the chess pieces around the board without being observed. I am a natural strategist and my great challenge lies in communicating to others the path I plan to take to get from starting point to goal. But put me in front of a microphone or at a speaking engagement, or task me with recruiting a lawyer, and another person emerges. When I explained all this to some recent acquaintances after a speaking engagement, they were shocked to hear of my introvert tendencies. I suppose that over the years I learned how to compensate, projecting an infectious enthusiasm whenever it was called for.

Looking at Guy and me, a handicapper might not have given very good odds for our marriage as co-managing partners to succeed beyond the interim period. We did, however, share one common world view. Neither of us ever took ourselves too seriously, so we had no problem leaving our egos at the door when it was time for a critical discussion. The fact that we didn't know each other well enough to have preconceived notions about one another was also an advantage, since we were both working with blank slates.

We had our first meeting to discuss the ground rules, and given that neither of us had any idea how to do the job, we couldn't be giving advice to one another. We were midway through 1997 and the immediate objective was to survive the year. For the first few months we were able to rely on Jean's wise advice and direction, but as his chemotherapy advanced, he became far less available. We decided to split some of the responsibilities according to our respective talents.

Guy was an excellent organizer and had a talent for dealing with details. His background was in employment, so he was a natural to deal with the Montreal administrative staff. I couldn't think of anything that interested me less. At the other end of the spectrum, Guy did not know one end of a financial statement from another, had never paid attention to the financials, and did not have a great facility with numbers. He was a labour lawyer after all. I was the tax lawyer, living my life for numbers. Nothing was more exciting to me than checking the bank line of credit each morning, planning six-month cash flows, and focusing on various ratios that analyzed our financial performance. I was appointed the 'numbers guy' and would work with our CFO to set up brand-new systems over time. Guy took primary responsibility for the Quebec business, while I would cover Toronto, Vancouver, and Los Angeles, as I had been doing informally since inception.

This was an arranged marriage and we were strangers. We were going to have to learn to decode one another and to accommodate each other's idiosyncrasies and irritating habits. I tended to be quiet and pensive, while he would react visibly and occasionally emotionally. Guy often had no idea what I was thinking and learned to pull it out of me until I learned to become more open. For my part, I sometimes had to wait for Guy's first-reaction thunderclaps and lightning bolts to pass, like a summer storm, before we could have a constructive discussion.

— • —

For the next six months we took stock, meeting with our administrative staff, learning about the nuts and bolts of our operation, having discussions with our COO and CFO, and spending much more time listening than speaking. Fortunately, the slower pace of summertime allowed two novices to ease into the learning process.

There were going to be challenges running a firm with what amounted to a three-headed monster. Based on what Jean Potvin had experienced, I was wary of Roy and his potential criticism of me. My fears were not well founded, but not because I was beyond reproach. Being in Toronto provided me with five hundred kilometres of insulation. Guy and Roy already had an established relationship, so when Roy was upset it was convenient for him to walk down the hall and unload on Guy. Unlike Jean, Guy understood not to take any of this personally. He knew Roy from the inside and instinctively knew how to manage the situation and outlast his onslaughts. On many occasions he sat, listened, and then ignored. When Roy had a valid point and was not simply venting, Guy and I would discuss the issue, form our own conclusion, and then get on the phone with Roy, in a calm moment, to work out a solution.

I soon learned that Roy didn't like Guy or me talking about bad news, not because he had any problem hearing it, but because he worried that it would be distracting to the partners. "Norm," he'd say, "we don't want to scare the partners. Be careful about how you put the news to them, because some will blow it all out of proportion and suddenly the sky is falling, and instead of practising law, everyone is worrying about a crisis that they've manufactured. I've seen how this has destroyed other firms, so let's just keep everything in perspective and deal with it."

Cynics, including Peter Blaikie in his day, might have concluded that this translated to "Put a positive spin on all news. We can't trust them to handle the truth. They may be lawyers capable of dealing with the most sophisticated client problems, but they can't be left to deal with their own."

The first six months passed quickly as Guy and I prepared to lead our first partner retreat the following January. In most firms there would have been a formal process to conclude the 'interim' nature of the arrangement and officially install us for a term as the new national co-managing partners. That wasn't the way things were done at HB. Instead, Roy and the partners ignored the issue altogether. Over time it became obvious to all that the experiment was working, and everyone assumed that this was the new status quo. We both, however, disliked the title of co-managing partners, so after a few months the 'co' disappeared and we were referred to as simply the managing partners.

— • —

Looking back, there was no particular moment when I formally decided to accept this position on a permanent basis. Guy and I slipped into the roles, and once it became obvious that we were a good fit, it never occurred to either of us to take a step backwards. I began at a walk and eventually I started running. The momentum carried me all the way to the end of 2012.

While Jean was managing partner I remember thinking that my own practice could flourish because I didn't have to spend a moment worrying about the well-being of the firm. That was Jean's job. Now it was becoming mine. My responsibility was to allow partners to sleep at night secure in the knowledge that I was on top of everything. Over time I discovered that this didn't feel like a burden, as I might have expected. Instead I felt empowered by the trust my partners had placed in me. Over the days, months, and years, that trust grew as I became more experienced.

Neither Guy nor I recognized Jean's true brilliance in managing his own succession until after the firm collapsed. Apparently he had told each of us that we were qualified to replace him as the sole managing partner of the firm. He allowed me to come to the conclusion that I needed help in Montreal, and he told Guy that politically Toronto had to be represented in the leadership, so Guy would have to work with me. We each came to the job believing that Jean had the confidence to trust us to run the entire operation.

Much as I had worried about administrative duties, Guy gravitated towards them. I enjoyed finance, strategy, and growth ideas. We learned to cover one another's weaknesses, and slowly a partnership between us emerged. We had two heads, but we wore one hat. My reticence gradually melted away and I started to enjoy the challenge of being a managing partner.

— • —

The origins of Heenan Blaikie as a small firm were tied to principles of frugality and caution. The partners borrowed minimally from the bank and withdrew earnings only as cash flow permitted. As we grew, the capital to finance the expansion had to come from somewhere, so the partners decided to delay taking out previous years' surplus earnings rather than have the firm or the partners borrow from the bank to support expansion. Essentially a portion of our earnings had become our capital investment in the firm, and Jean Potvin could never project from year to year when it might be possible to distribute those earnings.

My first order of business was to change the system to make it more like every other professional services firm. We were the dinosaurs. The system may have been fine for a static firm that managed its cash carefully, but it no longer made sense for us. There were now all kinds of unfair biases built into the system. Older partners might have considerable earnings tied up while new partners would have no investment at all in the firm. The existing system did not provide the equity to continue recruiting new partners, who ought to be assisting in financing the business.

With the assistance of our new managing director, Danielle Chagnon, and our accountants, I sat down and designed a system that would call for partners to contribute capital, which they would be free to borrow from the firm's bankers. This became part of a new social contract that saw earnings for the year distributed completely within six months of year end, which was common among firms. It took us almost a year to implement the idea because we had to fully work out the new system and then explain it. Those partners who came from elsewhere couldn't figure out what had taken us so long, but this entailed a considerable change for the more senior partners.

Within a couple of years, the firm had established roots in Toronto, and my own reputation in the film-finance business had grown. Sharon and I had settled into a routine with our four very young children and were slowly integrating into the local community. Sharon was also establishing herself as a partner at Coopers & Lybrand's North York office. We had a subscription to *The Globe and Mail*, and from time to time Sharon and I followed the scandals they reported on in the business community. I watched with horror the endless coverage of the Lang Michener debacle, which revolved around the improprieties of their immigration law partner, Martin Pilzmaker, who had gone astray and later committed suicide.

One day Sharon made the only request I can ever recall concerning my professional career.

"Norm, I don't care what opportunities present themselves. Whatever you do, please don't get involved with anything that might report your name in a negative story above the fold in *The Globe and Mail*."

It was unimaginable to me how that might happen. From time to time over the years prospective clients approached me with questionable tax schemes, and I always kept Sharon's warning in the back of my head. It was an excellent guidepost, because there were many opportunities to get the firm involved in aggressive tax planning that was quite lucrative but, to my mind, would eventually put the firm's reputation at risk. Richard Lewin had rejected these schemes while I was still in Montreal and my job was to do the same in Toronto. No amount of legal fees was worth risking the franchise value of our name and the reputation we were building.

After I took on the role of co-managing partner, Sharon gave me another excellent piece of advice. She told me it was fundamentally important to spend time every day walking the halls. "People need to see you, need to hear from you personally. It's not enough to tell people your door is open. You won't ever get a sense of what's happening on the ground unless you're present and engaged." I discovered over the years that there were few activities more challenging to build into the schedule or more vital to the role than doing just that.

Managing partners tend to lead a cloistered life. Between endless meetings, phone calls, and whatever practice they maintain, they have few free moments. Many lawyers will not want to waste your time with their individual concerns and will only approach when the problem has become serious, and, typically, more difficult to solve; others will find the office of the managing partner to be intimidating and will avoid you at all costs. (That was how I'd felt about Peter Blaikie.) In a corporate setting it would be equivalent to a meeting with the CEO. Consequently, the managing partner is easily pushed out of the daily information loop. You may have a hand on the daily cash position, you may see reports on your departments, and you may know about new and prospective clients or those who refuse to pay significant bills, but otherwise leadership can be lonely and remote from what is happening 'out there.'

Walking the halls gave me a sense of the pulse of the firm. Saying hello and stopping to chat with support staff said more to them about their importance to the organization than staff appreciation days. When the managing partner drops unannounced into an associate's office just to chat and catch up on what's new, that is going to give her a boost. If we were building an organization where people mattered, then the tone had to be set at the top. I noticed on these walks that as I passed a lawyer's office I might remember a word of praise about her from a partner, or a compliment from a client that had reached my office. It meant a lot to the associate to know that the news had travelled to my desk. On more than a few occasions I would pass a doorway and remember an illness in the lawyer's family, the death of a loved one, or any one of an assortment of joys and sorrows that I had completely forgotten about until that moment. Heading back out the doorway, I would quietly thank Sharon for her sage advice about walking the halls.

— • —

While I had taken on this new role, I continued to run my film-finance practice at full tilt, though the latest government changes, which introduced tax credits for production services on foreign films shot in Canada, were impacting the flow of our business. These changes were designed to end the schemes that I had developed. The government decided to fund these productions directly through the tax system.

I was fairly certain that our run of over a dozen years of tax-shelter finance in the film business had come to an end. In a certain sense I was relieved. We had an incredible 1996, supported by the fees from these financings, but the competition between the tax promoters was directly out of *Mad* magazine's "Spy vs. Spy" cartoon.

There were three major syndicators. The first was Alliance Equicap, which was run by Jeff Rayman, and for which I was the brain supplying the technology. We spent days, weeks, and months together in California wooing the studios to produce in Canada. Our largest source of competition was Grosvenor Park. Don Starr was the face of the company while Bradley Sherman was the brain working out the evolving structures. We each held onto our industrial secrets while trying to supplant each other as providers of product to the various Hollywood studios. Try as they might, they were never able to advance with any company in the Warner Bros. or MGM families. For a few years they serviced Sony Pictures Entertainment until we made a breakthrough, which was very satisfying. Similarly, it didn't matter how many meetings we took with the Walt Disney Company or Viacom. There was no breaking the Grosvenor lock on those relationships. We fought for product and we fought for investors, though in reality there was more than enough of both to satisfy all of us. The third entrant in the market, Monarch Films Inc., was based in Vancouver. None of us took them very seriously, though they had a good relationship with Universal Studios.

After the federal government announced that they would make changes to create tax credits, which replaced our tax financings, we all packed it in to move on. Don Starr decided he preferred London and moved out there to take advantage of the UK's unique tax structuring for film. Grosvenor Park disbanded. Jeff Rayman became a financier of the new tax credits and Brad was bored, looking for something new. I had a law firm to run.

The Monarch principals also withdrew. However, their lawyer, Rob Strother, convinced by former Monarch employee Paul Darc that there might be a new Canadian scheme in the works—despite the fact that the government had seemingly replaced our financings with a tax credit—went to work with Paul, and the decision would eventually land Rob in hot water with Monarch. The company sued him all the way to the Supreme Court of Canada for having failed in his fiduciary obligations to advise them he was working on a new plan without them. But that is a story for another day.

I began to hear rumours about a new tax plan out of Vancouver, but I was absolutely convinced that Revenue Canada would never reopen the door to us. It did not matter how many times I heard the story, or how many times Jeff Rayman asked me to investigate. It was preposterous. I was sure that Darc and Strother would never get the advance tax ruling necessary to relaunch a syndication business, and I was not going to waste a single moment thinking about it. I was that certain.

In fall 1998 I got a call from Tom Malanga, who ran financing at MGM. Tom was one of Arthur Evrensel's best contacts.

"Norman," he said, "I've just been approached by Rob Strother and Paul Darc. They tell me they have a tax ruling and want me to send my new productions in Canada to them."

He paused and I swallowed hard. This was unbelievable.

"Now, Norman, MGM would like to take advantage of this opportunity, but we've always preferred dealing with Arthur, you, and Jeff Rayman. So if you tell me you have your own deal, I'll pass on the other proposal for now."

It was moment-of-truth time. How could I have been so stubborn! I answered Tom in the only way I knew how.

"Tom, I can assure you we're working on our own structure, and now that a ruling has been issued, we should have our own in time to manage all of your upcoming productions. As it happens I'm headed out to LA. Why don't we meet to discuss it in a couple of days?"

We ended the call and I exhaled. The only thing that I hadn't been bluffing about was the trip to LA. I was heading to the airport in Toronto and planned to have dinner with my LA partners, Dan Black and Jeff Berkowitz.

I immediately picked up the phone and called Mark Jadd.

"Mark, they got the ruling."

"What do you mean?"

"I'm telling you. Malanga just called me. Darc is pitching him on a production services deal. Call your contact at Rulings and find out anything you can."

"Norm, you know these rulings are confidential, at least until CRA publishes a redacted version in six months. But let me speak to Alan Nelson—he's my contact—and I'll see what I can find out. Call me tonight when you land in LA."

That was a start, and I felt confident Mark could get enough information so that I could begin my work. I had a lifetime fantasy about working out a deal on the back of a cocktail napkin and tonight might be my night.

I landed in Los Angeles and called Mark immediately. Alan Nelson could not reveal any information about the deal. All he told Mark was to look at one particular subparagraph of the *Income Tax Act*. I did not have to look. I knew exactly what it said. The provision was burned into my brain. Mark and I were working on a journal article explaining how it worked. While tax shelters were no longer permitted to finance 100 percent of the Canadian costs of making a film, that paragraph left the door open to financing just short of 20 percent of the costs. Now all I had to figure out was how to invent a deal that was attractive enough to studios, lucrative enough for investors, and still left enough money for lawyers, accountants, bankers, and salespeople to make this all worthwhile.

After dinner I made my way to the bar in the famous Beverly Hilton hotel, tucked into the magic triangle where Wilshire and Santa Monica Boulevards intersect. The Polo Lounge had once played host to some of the most important get-togethers in Hollywood history, and the bar had served drinks to many film stars, agents, and high-powered lawyers over the years. Tonight it was just me, a pile of cocktail napkins, and a pen. I didn't even have a calculator. The blondes and brunettes at the bar were trying to make eye contact. After all, they too had to make a living. They gave up quickly, though—I assume they could see I was consumed by my own figures.

I worked on an assortment of permutations and combinations for almost three hours. It was probably three in the morning Toronto time when I knew I had it: the next deal along with the offer I knew we would be able to make to MGM. I could barely restrain my excitement, though I knew there was not much point trying to call Mark at that hour.

At 6:30 a.m. we got on the phone. It took about three minutes to explain the deal to Mark. I left him with a simple instruction: start working on our ruling application. I would get Malanga to authorize us to use one of MGM's pictures as the named production for the ruling. How much more authentic could we be about our intentions?

After finishing with Mark I called Jeff Rayman. I told him we had to sit down to plan the marketing campaign and some of the key features of what we were still in the process of inventing. I was then going to visit Bob Fisher at WB to let the studio know we were all back in business. Within a matter of twelve hours I expected we would line up at least $300 million of product. And this was just the first day! This run would take us through to the end of 2001.

Guy and Norm

8

PULLING TOGETHER
THROUGH CRISIS

Heenan Blaikie culture made up an important part of what we were selling in our recruiting on the street, and it wasn't just marketing hype. We encouraged respect for one another. We did not tolerate destructive behaviour. We were edgy lawyers with difficult personalities, but nothing demonstrated respect more than our showing genuine interest in people. The firm was not yet nirvana and we had a long way to go before we could get there, but we were on the right path. The social experiment that was Heenan Blaikie Toronto was also developing. We had created an environment where lawyers celebrated working together, where we encouraged one another to bring in new business, where everyone loved to come to work in the morning. Associates and support staff had a role to play in improving day-to-day functions. It was early 1998 and the firm was humming. Little did I suspect that I was sitting on a stick of dynamite that might detonate at any moment.

I was reviewing some paperwork in my office one day when one of my articling students knocked tentatively at the door.

"Norm," he said, "do you mind? Bill Orr suggested I come speak to you directly."

I could tell from his tone that the meeting was going to be serious, and I automatically straightened in my chair and asked him to take a seat. I wasn't sure what to make of the tension in his face.

Nick[3] fidgeted for a second and then plunged in. "I recently attended a meeting of the board of directors of Company A with one of our senior corporate partners, Oscar. Oscar is a member of the board of this company. The board had been discussing strategy about a plan to open a business unit in Europe and was looking to do the same in Ontario." He stopped and seemed hesitant.

"Okay," I said and nodded encouragingly. "And?"

"Well ..." Nick looked nervous. "Oscar has also attended board meetings as a director of Company B, a public company and also a client of the firm, which seems to me to be involved in a similar and possibly identical business undertaking."

Nick hesitated. He now had my undivided attention. "I see."

"And Oscar takes me around to all these meetings to take notes. I don't pretend to know enough of the details of the two businesses to assess whether this is a problem, but I remember from my corporate law classes in law school that a director has to act in the best interest of the company and can't be involved in competing businesses. That would be a breach of his fiduciary obligation. From my view I think maybe these two companies are competing. And since Oscar is on the board of both companies, there might be a problem here."

"Thanks, Nick. Bill was right to send you here and I'm going to look into it."

Looking relieved, Nick left the office. I closed my door and collapsed into the soft blue leather swivel chair behind my desk.

Nick had hit the nail on the head of the potential legal problem. A director of a company has a number of duties. He must act loyally to the company and he cannot use a corporate opportunity for the benefit

---

[3] Names have been changed or disguised in this recounting.

of any other person. It would be improper for Oscar to have any association with a competing company. Sitting on the boards of two competing companies at the same time exposed him to lawsuits from either or both companies. Because he was a partner in our law firm, it exposed us as well. As I began to assess the issues, my brain was running like an out-of-control freight train. Perhaps Oscar had cleared the matter with the two clients, or maybe Nick was mistaken about the overlap in the businesses. In either of those cases there would be no problem. But for now I had to assume there was no reasonable explanation, which meant we were headed down a convoluted road. If fiduciary breaches had occurred, then they might well be multiple, applying to Oscar both as a director and as a lawyer. There might also be an assortment of consequential obligations related to the firm that fell squarely in my lap. This was not a time to be relying on my own counsel, so my first task was to gather my own experts internally.

I convened Bill Orr, our corporate board expert and a man with experience advising CEOs on managing crises, along with Joe Groia and Stan Fisher, our wise counsel, to run through the story as I understood it and to advise me on next steps. After a preliminary discussion, I sent Joe and Stan to talk to Oscar and get his version of the story as quickly as possible.

My next call was to Guy Tremblay in Montreal to explain the situation. As co-managing partners, we were responsible for dealing with any problem, and this was the first test of the thesis that my concerns were Guy's and vice versa.

It did not take a vivid imagination to work out the worst-case scenario. If Oscar had no client authorization, the firm might be facing a lawsuit from either or both clients. We would have to notify our insurers. We didn't yet know whether they even covered this type of claim. Did we have to report this to the Law Society of Upper Canada? If so, when? This was all new to both of us.

Joe Groia and Stan Fisher reported back a few days later. First, they said, although Nick's story was accurate, Oscar didn't believe he had done anything wrong. Joe was particularly incensed and disappointed.

From Joe's perspective, Oscar was way over the line, and putting aside any moral judgments or legal analysis, Joe felt betrayed and hurt. Joe could sometimes be accused of hyperbole, so I questioned Stan for quite awhile about his perspective. Stan was equally perplexed and alarmed at all the potential implications. This was not going to end well. The only question was how bad it was about to become.

We had a potential firm crisis on our hands, the proportions of which we still couldn't gauge. Would the firm be caught up in the grinder of negative media coverage for weeks or months on end? What steps did we now have to take to protect the firm and hold the partners together in a growing storm? We had no manual to follow and I did not have years of experience to fall back on. Nor had I built up the internal political capital that comes from leading partners through past battles together. My leadership skills were about to be tested for the first time.

— • —

Living through crises in the film business had played to my nature, which was to remain level-headed in all situations, and those experiences taught me lessons that would serve me well later in my career. When faced with unpredictable setbacks, I would not react immediately. I learned to step back, remove myself from the surrounding panic, and assess the situation. I would go to a quiet place that was physically away from the hurly-burly or, at the very least, migrate to that quiet place in my head. I had to project calm. I came to understand that passage of time was a great healer, allowing people to adjust to a new reality.

Above all else, I learned that unless someone actually was dying, no one was dying. Most business problems revolve around money, which is fungible. Your family is not fungible. Having or lacking money may affect your lifestyle but does not need to affect your level of happiness. I perceived a life rule at play here: in one year's time, today's crisis would be a distant memory. People generally find a way to move on from a crisis, and those who can't are miserable and get left behind.

But in the meantime, my life was about to become very difficult. I had to navigate a developing crisis that could prove highly troublesome to the firm, particularly if the media were to swoop in and make it the focus of the next news cycle. Negative media attention to rogue partners and how their firms dealt with them had almost ruined Lang Michener years before and, more recently, Blakes.

After briefing Guy, I put together a small working team of four. Bill Orr was a thoughtful, calming influence throughout. Stan Fisher also provided counsel, and Joe Groia, having completed just the first stage of investigation, would lead a team to carefully establish all the facts. We sat down together and outlined all the potential issues, divided up the responsibilities, and set up a process to meet and update daily.

At that point, information about the situation was on a need-to-know basis within the firm. Aside from the working team based in Toronto and Guy, Roy, Nick the student, and Oscar, no one had an inkling of a problem. We would need to advise the Executive Committee, but what about the partners generally? What were the risks that the story would leak out before we were prepared? This type of story, once it became gossip, would take on a life of its own, with innuendo and supposition quickly replacing fact. Advising the partners at large would increase the risk that the story would make it to the street through an assistant overhearing a fragment of conversation, or through an offhand comment made in an elevator by any one of an expanding group of individuals. While lawyers are bound by confidentiality concerning client matters, they can often be the worst gossips about internal matters. Still worse would be partners hearing about it from lawyers in other firms or in a newspaper article. Until we felt we had learned enough through our own investigation, we would have to wait before we allowed the information bubble to expand.

There was a risk though, however careful we were, that the story might leak out before the investigation was complete. Bill Orr recommended public relations experts to help me deal with the media, partners, lawyers, staff, and clients. I had to be prepared. We would also need to retain an independent law firm to advise us on Law Society issues. We could not risk making a decision that might be seen as motivated by subjective factors, which would leave us open to criticism and public chastisement by the Law Society. Our litigators also needed to begin preparing the notice to our insurers. The need-to-know group was already expanding.

Finally, we needed a plan to approach the two clients, who had both been extremely loyal to Oscar up to this point. Perhaps we had blown this entire matter way out of proportion. Going to either or both of them behind Oscar's back might be the worst approach.

Managing Oscar was also a problem that had to be handled carefully. We needed his co-operation, and he could not see that there was a problem at all. There was an inevitable growing tension between us, and I asked him to take a leave while we sorted out the mess.

This was crisis management time, and I might have benefited from a graduate course in law firm leadership when I took the managing partner job. Instead I had to rely on basic skills I had developed from many years of transactions: break the complicated problem into its tiny components; delegate to small, expert teams the pieces of the problem they could handle; and have them report back to me, while I quarterbacked the overall operation.

On the advice of counsel, we informed the relevant authorities at the Law Society of the situation and let them determine whether there had been any impropriety. Both clients had to be informed as well, and we concluded it was best to involve Oscar in that process. Now the partners had to be advised, quickly. I also understood that any rush to judgment or any move to sanction Oscar would be premature and would likely create the very media problem we needed to avoid.

Guy and I called an urgent partners meeting by teleconference in our boardrooms in Montreal, Toronto, Quebec, and Vancouver. Between our various offices we were now over sixty partners. We expected virtually all of them to attend. I would run the meeting. We had two objectives. The first was to convey information that would be shocking to many. I could not see how we could relate what we knew so far without raising the spectre of a crisis. My inner voice was telling me not to sugar-coat the problems or downplay the issues. Any attempt to make the situation look less serious than it was would be perceived as weakness on my part. The only way to proceed was to face the matter head-on and wrestle it to the ground. But that approach risked having partners leave the meeting feeling agitated and uneasy. Once the story emerged in the media, the firm would become a target of both sympathy and derision. I had no doubt that some partners would want to see Oscar's immediate execution or, at the very least, his immediate dismissal. We could not afford to have the partners leave this meeting without a plan for going forward, though the plan, inevitably, would not appeal to everyone.

The second objective was to project strength, calm, and control. Lawyers have much in common with wolf packs. The leader must rise above all, regularly fighting off challengers and pretenders. If partners smell weakness or blood, they will eat you alive. Many battles have to be fought successfully before partners will trust you without question, and I had not even started to build up that kind of trust in my good judgment. If I flinched, my management career was over. If I projected uncertainty, I would be overrun by the crowd of second-guessers. I had to present a well-thought-out, methodical plan. Often the greatest critics become the strongest supporters. Converting them is all about how their objections and concerns are handled: anticipating them, listening to them, taking them seriously, responding to them, and overcoming them. This was applicable as much to convincing partners as it had been to selling Filter Queen vacuum cleaners so many years before.

While this was technically a problem for the entire firm, it was a Toronto-centric issue, so I had carriage with Guy's support. Executive Committee members had been briefed earlier and were prepared for what was to come. Roy naturally favoured an approach that would have us avoid acting precipitously and leaping to conclusions about Oscar, his future, or any others involved. He always favoured a slow and measured approach. Let some time pass and benefit from the perspective of a little distance and careful reflection. The Executive Committee agreed. Some partners would view that approach as unacceptable, since their personal instincts, honed by their own client experience, would tell them that quick and decisive action was called for.

The meeting began, and as I laid out the story in as much detail as I understood, I tried to read the faces of my partners sitting around the table in Toronto. I could see initial shock being replaced with disgust and finally anger. Many were taken aback by a situation that could swiftly affect them all as we navigated this minefield. Step by step I led them through a plan, calmly outlining the various steps that we were about to take to protect the firm and its reputation and that would consume me over the next few months.

First, we would be approaching the two clients and were reporting to the Law Society as well as to our insurers. I would be exclusively responsible for dealing with the media outside Quebec; if the story made its way into the French-language press, Guy would handle the communications on that end. My next step would be to hire the media consultants recommended by Bill Orr to help us prepare the story and key messages and to give us some specific training, as I was more or less unskilled at the moment. The partners asked many questions but none that we had failed to consider. Chief among them had to do with Oscar's future, and some partners were urging immediate and harsh reprisal.

I understood, however, the repercussions their approach could have. Any hasty action to sanction Oscar would eliminate him as an agent for solving the problem between the clients. It would also move the story from oblivion to the front pages of every business paper. While Oscar had been sent on leave for the time being, I told the partners that we needed to be circumspect and slow to judge, and that preserving the firm's name and reputation had to remain paramount in these considerations. The meeting ended with most partners grumbling, and somewhat dazed, though it was clear to them that Guy and I were in control of the situation.

The next morning Guy and I began to execute the plan.

For months I waited, but the media calls never came. For reasons I'll never understand, the two clients, while very upset, both calmed down and never took action against the firm. Perhaps Oscar was able to work some magic behind the scenes. After an extended leave of absence, Oscar eventually resigned from the firm, and the Law Society eventually decided to let the matter drop. The strategy of letting time run its course had worked in our favour.

The firm did, however, suffer internal repercussions. Slowly and over time a number of the lawyers who worked in Oscar's group left as well. In the same period, and quite coincidentally, we experienced a few other departures. Barry Goldberg, our insolvency star, decided that he preferred to become an investment banker and left to make his fortune. Elizabeth McGuinness, now the most senior member of the entertainment group, decided that captaining her husband's charter sailboat, *The Life of Riley*, was far superior to practising law and bade us farewell.

It had come to the point where I was afraid to come to work in the morning for fear that another partner would be announcing a resignation. Outwardly I steeled myself, continuing to walk the halls, projecting an optimism that I did not feel, knowing the entire workforce was scrutinizing me for clues as to the health of the enterprise.

We had few senior commercial partners left in Toronto. Aside from Kip Daechsel and the members of the entertainment group, many had depended on Oscar's ability to generate work and had to leave to find new employment. The dust eventually settled and, slowly, partners began to forget and move on. The trauma we endured pulled us together. I knew that I had survived the tsunami, with the firm somewhat battered, but still intact with its reputation undiminished. Partners in Quebec and Vancouver, who might have called this a Toronto problem that didn't involve them, instead tied themselves closer to us.

— • —

I hadn't the slightest idea how we were going to rebuild the commercial group. The demise of this group was both a blessing and a curse for our labour partners. Brian Burkett and Doug Gilbert had no confidence in the abilities of many of our commercial partners. Beyond that, they had never trusted leadership: not me, not Potvin, and not Roy. Brian was torn between berating me for hiring a lawyer who was doomed to falter and reaming me out for building a commercial group so frail that it could collapse like the little pigs' house. He chose both. He wondered aloud, and continued to wonder for the next five years, whether it might be wiser to give up on perpetuating a second-rate commercial practice. We could change the plan and become a series of thriving and federated boutiques specializing in practices where we were strong, like labour and entertainment. That would be lucrative enough and satisfying for Brian, but it wasn't my dream. While I had no right to impose my will on any partner, I would just as soon have quit as abandon the quest to build a very special, high-functioning, full-service firm. We would have to rebuild the commercial group from square one.

Even in the darkest days of 1998 and 1999 when we shed partners and associates, when our corporate ranks thinned, when I would have to take a deep breath before walking through the office door every morning waiting for the next anvil to drop, I had to project to my partners a vision of the future that saw us building a first-rate commercial law firm. It was far from easy; Jean Potvin was now in the advanced stages of dying, as was my father. By the end of 1998 both men who had played such important roles in my life would be gone.

— • —

During this time, my father was fading fast. Both he and my father-in-law had malignant kidneys diagnosed and removed in the early 1990s, but my father's cancer spread to his lungs a few years later, and he began an aggressive form of chemotherapy in this period that would ultimately fail. Meanwhile, he was turning sixty-five and this would likely be his last birthday. I'm generally unimaginative at giving gifts, but this time I managed to hit on something special.

Dad was crazy about bridge. For many years until I left Montreal, we played together and had won a series of events as partners. While I had basically given up the game to raise a family, bridge remained my father's passion. A high-school buddy of mine, Jordan Cohen, was a contract bridge expert and told me that some of the world's best players made a living playing with amateurs for a fee at US tournaments. He gave me Eric Rodwell's contact information at a time when Eric was among the top five ranked players in the world. When I called and explained my father's situation, he graciously agreed to play with him at a tournament in Chicago. Over the course of the weekend they won one event and did reasonably well in a couple of others. Dad returned home, unable to stop telling everyone he knew about the tournament. The adventure connected us in a way that we hadn't connected in years, and I still get a lump in my throat recalling the delight in his voice each time he recounted his experience of a lifetime.

My father was an overachiever and far from a perfect man. His business dream had collapsed on his shoulders in his mid-forties, but he had hunkered down, repaid his debts, and lived an honourable life. He believed in service to the community and helped build the YM-YWHA in Laval, going on to become the Y's Montreal metropolitan president. He loved me deeply and always served as one of my role models. In the final year of his life, my father taught me more about living than in the rest of our lives combined. Once he had accepted his fate, he showed a unique grace in making amends with anyone from his past he could reach out to. He embraced the time he had left and displayed no fear of death. He died in mid-August 1998.

I spoke my last words to Jean from my father's home in Montreal in late July 1998 as I was finishing a visit. Jean put on a good show, pretending that he would return to work in a few months. But I had talked to his friends in the Montreal office, who told me that his hair had turned snow-white and that his face was etched with lines, signs of a proud man in the final stage of his life. "Goodbye, my friend,"

I said in farewell, knowing that we were at the end of our journey together. I hung up and felt warm tears streaming down my cheeks. His funeral took place just one week after my father passed away.

— • —

Life was throwing me a diet of curveballs, yet I knew I could not show vulnerability. Thankfully I had Sharon in my corner, propping me up. Every member of the firm drew strength from my cues. I kept reminding myself that when dark clouds settled over an organization, the job of the leader is to stick his or her head above the clouds and chart a course for the horizon. Above the clouds it's always bright and sunny. Tough periods pass.

In hindsight, had Guy and I disagreed over how to lead the firm through our first crisis, or had we shown any weakness or uncertainty, the problem might have overwhelmed us. Our ranks in the commercial group in Toronto thinned but nobody panicked. Guy and I projected a unity and a faith in the future, which we didn't allow our partners to question. While I couldn't yet appreciate it, I learned from this experience that every challenge I had to face, or defeat I suffered, gave me new perspective for the future, made me a better leader, and taught me that maintaining a positive outlook was an enormously powerful tool.

History, however, does tend to repeat itself, and in 2012 we would have to confront a similar problem. The circumstances would differ, but once again we would be dealing with a partner who had acted outside the bounds of what the firm could tolerate, and we would be challenged to pull together. And once again, brand-new leaders of the firm would be facing a challenge of leadership. We would not fare nearly as well the second time around, but as Heenan Blaikie approached the millennium, we had no inkling of what lay ahead. Instead we were focused on expansion, and the future looked enticing.

9

MARCEL

In December 1997 Guy was approached by his former law school class-mate Marcel Aubut, the well-known Quebec City entrepreneur, who had managed his own law firm in Quebec City for many years and was looking to merge it with a Montreal firm. He was considering us because we had a national platform, a solid street reputation, and a former prime minister on our roster. Marcel was a public figure in Quebec, but still relatively unknown outside the province other than in the hockey world. So while this was a major recruitment opportunity in Quebec, I thought it might be of less importance in Toronto and Vancouver.

Larger than life, Marcel had a passion for sports that kept him in the spotlight in the French-speaking community. He realized his dream of bringing a professional sports franchise to Quebec's capital with the Nordiques, a WHA team later admitted to the NHL. Marcel knew every Quebec politician and understood how the game was played both in and out of the arena. He was also relentless when it came to getting business. No one felt neutral about Marcel. He was either loved or despised by players, fans, business people, and lawyers. The road was littered with bodies of those whom Marcel had steamrollered after he decided they stood in the way of his dreams or objectives. Marcel had had a preliminary conversation with Jean Potvin a couple of years earlier that had gone nowhere. There was zero chemistry between Jean's Robert Redford–like elegance and Marcel's rough-and-tumble approach.

Guy had begun a process of introducing Marcel to various Montreal members of our Executive Committee. It may have been Michael Prupas's wife, Betty, who thought this was not a good idea. I told Guy at the time, "Our wives are often right, even when we ignore them."

During the course of our discussions with Marcel, Guy had me fly in from Toronto to meet them both at the Beaver Club, in the Queen Elizabeth Hotel. As I walked in, I reflected on the irony of how my career had advanced since that day many years ago when I had received a death threat from Jean in front of that same building after I'd gingerly contradicted him in front of a client.

The Beaver Club had a reputation as the place where the establishment made its deals in Montreal. In the days when that city, dominated by anglo business leaders, was the seat of corporate power and finance in Canada, the restaurant was a popular lunch and dinner venue where the corporate elite went to muse about the future and plan their acquisitions and financings. The venerable setting was adjusting to a new reality—one in which two francophones and a native-anglo Jew who had abandoned the province could now meet together over a meal to plan a joint enterprise.

Marcel struck me immediately as charming and passionate. He was looking for a home that would accept his Quebec City partners, to whom he maintained an undying loyalty that would tug at him once more twenty years later. He also needed a firm that could adapt to a very large personality. I admit that while I had arrived with little immediate interest in expanding the firm eastward, I left intrigued— even though as a diehard Canadiens fan, I'd grown up with a deep hatred of the Nordiques, particularly in light of the famous Good Friday playoff brawl between the two teams in 1984.

Short, stout, always in need of losing sixty pounds, and definitely not what one would ever classify as handsome, Marcel nevertheless radiated an oddly attractive energy that I've rarely observed in anyone else. He might have forgotten to tuck in his shirt, but his eyes glowed when he had a new idea, and when that happened, he was unstoppable. Still, he'd been used to having his own way with his firm for many years, so fitting into another organization would be a challenge for him, or as the French would say, *un défi*.

I subsequently conducted limited due diligence and discovered that some of his players—like the Stastny brothers, whom he brought to Quebec from their native Czechoslovakia—had seen him as a father figure, while others saw him as an ogre. He could present as a jovial man of the world, or as a difficult person with no manners and less civility. There was no doubt in my mind that these contradictions drove him to great things. The question was whether the firm and its reputation would be buoyed or sunk by his energy, ruthless drive, and determination.

— • —

Guy initiated a process that would spark a national debate within the firm, with opinion divided across the country. Was this a move that would solely benefit Quebec, with the other offices bearing the reputational risk? The only thing we all agreed on was that Marcel would be a tiger, but how much of the firm's administrative resources were now going to be dedicated to managing a regional office in Quebec City along with our plan to grow an office in Sherbrooke? What were our long-term strategic objectives?

Heenan Blaikie was facing in microcosm the same questions being raised in the country as a whole relating to Quebec's status and role in the federation. I couldn't make up my mind about where I stood. A number of partners felt strongly that we should pass on the opportunity, while others felt we had to seize it. On the eve of the vote at the partners meeting called by Guy, I was no closer to deciding.

We held the meeting by conference call; partners from across the country expressed their views. Guy gave everyone his or her due, and I decided to listen carefully and wait. The partnership seemed quite evenly split and the balance could have tipped in either direction, though a close vote was undesirable. Close votes were frowned upon, since they worked against consensus building and were regarded as tantamount to rejection of the proposition being voted on. Without a clear show of Toronto support, we also risked a split on linguistic grounds, which would be untenable for the long-term good. I felt and had expressed to Guy that this was still a bit of a crapshoot.

My turn to speak finally came and I stood up. "I've listened carefully to the discussion this evening, to the supporters and to those who've expressed concerns about Marcel and his larger-than-life personality, with all its attendant pluses and minuses, and whether it's suited to this firm. I've heard these same concerns expressed to me by others outside the firm, and I've also heard the accolades of third parties in the course of my own due diligence. We're at an important crossroads as a firm."

I paused briefly as I formulated the thrust of my argument in my head. "We've been successful so far in laying the foundation for our national dream. Adding an office in Quebec's capital city can't possibly be a bad idea, and the lawyers seem like decent people. The office is obviously run with discipline. Adding a sparkplug like Marcel in Montreal will fill a major hole in our commercial practice."

I looked up to see many heads nodding. Encouraged, I continued. "We've earned recognition for litigation, labour, and entertainment, but our reputation still needs to be built in the commercial market. Maybe Marcel isn't the solution, but when faced with challenges, the man has demonstrated a rare ability to rise to the occasion. There are no perfect decisions in life, only those that in hindsight were brilliant and obvious. We never have all the information necessary to make a completely informed decision. On balance, though, I support bringing Marcel and his partners in. When I compare the risk with the opportunity, I believe that this is a risk we have to take."

I sat down, Guy called the vote, and the Yes side won handily. While I had been recognized as the leader in Toronto by virtue of my status, this was a landmark moment in my influencing group opinion, particularly in Montreal where I was a prodigal son who had not returned home.

— • —

In hindsight, was this a good decision? Over the years Marcel proved to be a tireless business promoter, the likes of which I've never seen before or since. He was completely driven to succeed at any endeavour and at virtually any cost. There was no prospective client he was shy about approaching for new work. His energy and drive helped build the careers of Marie-Josée Hogue, a developing leader of our litigation group who now sits on the Quebec Court of Appeal, and Eric Levy, a future star Montreal securities lawyer, both of whom went on to take over important files that Marcel marched in the door. They became anchors of our office. Marcel was an instant catalyst for growth.

Coincidentally Eric Maldoff joined us from Martineau Walker (now Faskens) in the fall of 1998, and between him and Marcel, we had made significant strides in building our Montreal commercial practice.

A number of years after he joined the firm, Marcel took responsibility for having a partner retreat in Quebec City during the heart of Carnaval season. It was "Quebec City 2000" and I still have the navy-blue sweatshirt attesting to it. Normally our corporate retreats were set up to combine downtime to relax and get to know one another socially with business meetings to discuss strategic objectives of the firm. For this particular retreat Marcel had programmed every moment of the retreat from the minute our feet set down in Quebec City to the moment we left. The schedule and related logistics ran with military precision—typical for Marcel. Our administrators told us that he had his finger on every last detail, from arrangements to transport lawyers from the airport right through each and every routine for the entire weekend. While he could have delegated authority, it was critical to him that he approve every decision.

The retreat was perfect, but we all knew it was the 'Marcel Show.' Pre-programmed alarms woke us up in the morning, and we were hounded through our waking hours to get to our activities on time. Every aspect of the day, from morning until 10 p.m., when partners filled the bar, was organized, and an abundance of staff and volunteers had been drilled in their responsibilities. Our managing director, Danielle Chagnon, confessed to me later that Marcel had overseen every detail of the entire weekend, making it his mission to create the greatest retreat in the history of the firm—which it was. The evening dinner included a performance from a revivalist church group and other incredible entertainment. It was designed as the show to out-do all shows. No cost was spared and no detail ignored. Guy Tremblay and I, as co-managing partners, had to approve the cost overruns afterward; we chalked up the additional expense to a learning experience. Achieving perfection was Marcel's strength—but it was also his glaring weakness. He was completely oblivious to the consumption of resources necessary to accomplish his goals. After the retreat ended, our support staff was worn to the bone but had to go back to their regular nine-to-five jobs on Monday morning. If you happened to be working for him, he wielded a very heavy whip. On the other hand he was equally likely to send gifts to the key staff as a thank you.

This was the first of three Quebec City retreats orchestrated by Marcel, each one striving to outdo the last, though nothing exceeded a special client reception in Quebec City to celebrate an office move. Only Marcel could arrange for the arrival of a motorcycle cavalcade inside an internal venue, to 'wow' the crowd. Cost was never an issue (until it was time for Guy to approve the bills!).

Marcel needed to do everything in a big way and that included his business expense account. When it came to serving contacts, clients, and prospective clients all over the world there was no limit to Marcel's largesse. In some cases this might include getting tickets for professional or Olympic sporting events, Formula 1 races, or Céline Dion concerts in Las Vegas. Marcel tapped into every possible connection to deliver favours, no matter the cost. He could achieve the impossible with a goal of providing the best service on the face of the earth. All this came at a cost to the firm and Guy was responsible for managing the costs. Marcel's annual expenses were usually at least double that of any other partner in the firm. While this upset many partners we all had to agree that Marcel was incomparable in turning these relationships into business for the firm.

Marcel could be equally demanding of client loyalty. If he felt one of our financial institution clients was not sending enough work, he would follow up with countless calls to their general counsel. I recall one beleaguered GC calling to tell me, "I've never gotten better service from lawyers than what Marcel has his team deliver to me. But what do I have to do to get him to stop calling me so relentlessly?"

"That's simple," I answered. "Just send us more work!" The GC laughed and sent over a few more files.

Marcel was a great believer in teamwork—as long as he was in charge of the team, a condition that he simply took for granted. He positioned himself as the key contact with many of his clients. That presented issues where other senior partners of the firm had relationships with the same clients, particularly the large institutions. One partner finally left the firm to join a competitor, believing that his own relationship with the client would be better served far away from Marcel's reach. Marcel was not at all unhappy, though he was a little surprised, when the other partner left. It would never have occurred to him that he was the source of the problem.

The negatives were generally outweighed by Marcel's overwhelming enthusiasm. On countless occasions he threw all his energy behind convincing partners to back initiatives he thought were important for the firm. In the end there was not a day in his history with Heenan Blaikie when I could say he was anything but completely loyal. He was a man who absolutely needed his organization to succeed. This would serve us well in our final year of survival—though not well enough.

— • —

I still remember vividly when Marcel approached Roy, Guy, and me at a partner retreat in Vancouver in January 2008 to seek permission to run for the presidency of the Canadian Olympic Committee (COC). That was vintage Marcel political brilliance. He could simply have advised us that he was planning to do this. We would never have demurred. Yet he went out of his way to ask permission, which made us collaborators in the venture. My heart immediately went out to the woman who believed she was next in line for the position. If Marcel, whose only credentials were in professional, not Olympic, sports, was going to throw his hat in the ring, I was beyond certain that he would mount a political campaign the likes of which the COC had never seen before. Marcel never took on a fight that he didn't expect to win. His meticulous preparations and coast-to-coast lobbying assured his victory and was the first step in launching the COC to new levels of recognition in corporate Canada. Was it coincidental that Canadian athletic performance under his leadership increased dramatically?

For a man with such incredible instincts to succeed, Marcel was also dominated by his impulses and his need for approval and love. He needed to be the centre of attention, recognized by all as the most important person in the room, and his ego fed on keeping score of his many accomplishments and insuring that others recognized his importance. He understood at a cerebral level that a man in his position should not be taking the slightest risk with female support staff or associates, especially since he knew a misconstrued comment or touch could taint a successful career. I could not begin to speculate on how his behaviour may have been perceived by those who worked for him when he was president of the Canadian Olympic Committee. His resignation from that position in 2015 may have been construed by some as a day of reckoning, but for those of us who knew the man well, it was simply a very sad day.

10

MATURING TO **GREATNESS**

Roy, Guy, and I were determined to expand nationally as one unified partnership, without division. We wanted to celebrate group rather than individual success, and we wanted a name brand that spoke of class, excellence, and innovation. We were now in our tenth year in Toronto, and as we approached the year 2000 we were beginning to plan the next phase of our development. We had offices in Vancouver, Ottawa, Trois-Rivières, Sherbrooke, Quebec City, and Beverly Hills. It was easy to talk about teamwork and unity (every firm does), but realization of that goal was complicated to execute. To do so, we had to align our systems and actions with our espoused values.

I believed we were running the legal equivalent of a mutual fund. In some years particular practice sectors would have stronger years and cover weaker performance in slower sectors. Over the years the peaks would cover the troughs. That philosophy was aligned with compensation, where we took a long view. No one was punished for a subpar year or overly rewarded for a single outstanding year.

The national platform was built on a single compensation pot. While we analyzed the performance of practice groups, we did not keep profit pool statistics on an office-by-office basis. By adopting that approach, we felt that individual offices would be encouraged to bring in files that could be serviced anywhere in the network, without fear that local statistics would come before any other performance measures. Rather than have partners hoard work locally, we encouraged them to involve lawyers with the best expertise from any office in the country, as if they worked down the hall. In this way clients would receive the best and most efficient service. This could only work if we avoided focus tied primarily to office performance.

By 1999 our Vancouver office had evolved into a labour law, litigation, and entertainment boutique powered by Peter Gall and Arthur Evrensel. We slowly built a commercial presence as well. A number of our Vancouver partners began their careers in Calgary and had very good contacts in that market. Guy Tremblay and I had many discussions about the need to expand to Calgary. If we were going to be a true national firm, then we would have to take steps to create an oil and gas practice. The slump in the oil cycle had come to an end, and we had no strategy.

In early January 2000 John Legge, one of our litigators, and Rod Kirkham, a partner in our commercial group, sat down with Guy to discuss an idea they were mulling over concerning the opening of an office in Calgary. Shortly afterward I was out in Vancouver and we met to follow up on the idea. John got the ball rolling.

"Norm, my former partner in Calgary, John James, was appointed a judge and he hates it. He'd like to go back into practice, and I think I can talk him into joining us and starting a small office."

Rod jumped in. "And I know Rod Ferguson, a securities lawyer, who's really unhappy at his current firm. He's not an oil and gas lawyer, but a number of his clients are in the business."

They had captured my attention. "Guys," I told them, "this is worth exploring. You know we've been talking about this at the Executive Committee for awhile. I have no idea whether these two are the right fit, but I'll tell you one thing. I'm not prepared to support this unless the two of you tell me you'll make the Calgary initiative a priority. It's going to take a lot of work to get an office off the ground in the first few years."

"We've thought about that," John said. "We both have a number of buddies at the mid-level in their firms, and we think they'd jump at the prospect of building a Heenan Blaikie office. This firm isn't like any other in the market, and the autonomy you guys give to the smaller offices will be very attractive in Calgary."

Guy and I brought this information back to the Executive Committee. We understood that Calgary would be a brave move. This would be the first office that was not immediately self-sufficient. It would take a number of years to build an energy practice, but we were planning for the long-term prosperity of the firm. Starting without a bona fide energy lawyer was a risk. Who could guess how long it would take before a Calgary office was truly successful? We could easily have talked ourselves out of it and there were a number of partners who were doubtful. On the other hand, we had a consistent track record of successful office openings.

The internal review, a broad survey of partners, and the final decision to go ahead were concluded in under eight weeks. In February 2000 we opened in Calgary. Legge and Kirkham convinced their old buddy Robb Beeman to help build the litigation practice, and the office was born. Was this decision borne of thorough diligence, an outside consultant's market study, or a detailed analysis? That was not how we operated. Instinct told us we had to be in Calgary and guts had us push the green light. How did we know at inception whether we were making a good decision or a bad one? Like Beverly Hills, we didn't. But we had the confidence to jump first and make corrections later.

The first couple of years in Calgary were slow. We were on the ground looking for opportunities when we learned that a mid-size firm was in advanced discussions to join Code Hunter, a forerunner to Gowlings' Calgary office. Guy and I put all other matters aside to meet with leaders of the firm and explore whether we might represent a better opportunity for them. They decided to move ahead with the other deal. In the course of due diligence, Mike Black and Mitch Shier, two of their oil and gas lawyers, caught our eye. Mitch was not ready to join a start-up, so Peter Gall, John Legge, and I invited Mike to play golf with us in Palm Springs over a January weekend. We spent a couple of days getting to know Mike and pitching him on coming over to lead the expansion of the Heenan Blaikie oil and gas practice.

On the second day, as we were standing on a tee box, John turned to Mike and asked, "Do you really want to be the guy at the bottom of the totem pole where you are, or do you have a greater vision for what you could build with us in Calgary?"

It wasn't long before Mike became the first step in building Calgary into a key market for us. It would take many months of courting to convince Mitch Shier to accept the risk of joining the young boutique we were building. Once Mitch joined, we had enough critical mass to attract a team of commercial lawyers to support the deal flow.

— • —

The final tent pole in the development of the office was a senior recruit suggested by Mike Black. For a number of years Mike had worked for one of Calgary's larger oil companies whose senior in-house counsel was a fellow named Jim Pasieka. Jim sat on the boards of a number of junior companies and had strong relationships with some of the biggest oil and gas financiers, though he would be coming with just a few potential client opportunities. Guy and I decided to back Mike's judgment, and we hired Jim in one of the great coups in our history. Within five years the office would transform from questionable beginnings to one of the more lucrative practices in the city. We might not have generated an institutional practice, but we had access to entrepreneurial investors who continually bought assets, consolidated them, spun them out, and then restarted the entire cycle.

My trips to Calgary and to all the smaller offices were consistently special. In as little as two days I could connect with all the partners and most of the associates. I would generally spend the first morning stopping by the offices of our associates and head of personnel and chatting with staff. This way I'd begin to get a feel for the lay of the land, learning about key office and business issues from the people at ground level. There are no secrets in a small office. One simple technique worked consistently: I listened. As I visited lawyers one after another, I used the knowledge gleaned from one lawyer to make further inquiries of the others. If there was a serious problem, the associates assumed I knew about it, so it was easy to get their perspectives on how various issues affected them. The associates were a rich source of intelligence, allowing me within a couple of hours to grasp every key issue affecting the office. The next day-and-a-half I could spend talking about these issues with the partners to address the underlying problems, or to embrace the successes or positive morale that the associates reported.

I had also taken Jean Potvin's lessons to heart: most problems could be openly addressed by the time the second bottle of wine arrived at dinner.

Some might say we were lucky in Calgary. We started an office in order to have a basic presence there and a beachhead from which to grow. A number of partners were skeptical. They felt strongly that unless we had a first-rate energy practice from the start we were wasting our time. Guy and I understood that was not practical. We were fortunate to find the talent to fulfill the dream and build a solid reputation in the city in as little as ten years. But we were also confident that our fresh approach to the practice of law and the way we treated one another would continue to attract unhappy lawyers from our competitors.

— ❈ —

Most great professional sport franchises rely on strong farm systems to develop talent and then supplement that homegrown talent with free agents. The legendary teams produced by dynasty franchises like the St. Louis Cardinals, Green Bay Packers, and Montreal Canadiens were all built on refreshing pools of young players who were brought up through the system, trained in the ideals and objectives of the organization, and formed into a close-knit fraternity in which the torch passed naturally from one generation to the next.

Growing up I watched the Canadiens and their brilliant general manager, Sam Pollock. He built a farm system loaded with young talent and made sure the tradition and rich history of hockey's most storied franchise was passed down from the elders to the juniors. The club invested in training skills and the values of the organization. Each year Sam would make one or two shrewd trades towards the end of the season to bring in experienced veterans to fill weaknesses and add to the leadership. The team's coaches also came up through the organization. Even Scotty Bowman, among the most successful coaches in the history of hockey, was trained in the Canadiens system before coaching for a few years in St. Louis and returning to Montreal.

In a similar way we began to benefit in the Toronto office. The first generation of young recruits, who had arrived in 1990, were maturing. The core of our entertainment group was now being led by David Steinberg along with Jim Russell and Ken Dhaliwal, who were stepping up and enjoying success as talented entertainment lawyers. Arthur Evrensel, who had moved to Vancouver as a young associate to start a practice, was now one of the leading entertainment lawyers in western Canada.

Other great examples of our internal talent development included Tim Lawson and John Craig in the labour group; Adam Kardash, who had been asked to develop our technology practice; Allen Garson, who was maturing into a solid commercial lawyer; and Mark Jadd in tax. They all went on to become leaders of the firm. Meanwhile Jon Stainsby and George K were maturing in the Toronto litigation group. In Montreal Marie-Josée Hogue was pegged as the future lead litigator while Manon Thivierge, a protégé of Jean Potvin, led the tax group there. Eric Levy was our rising securities superstar in Montreal. Carl Belanger was another budding commercial star. All these partners would figure in the firm's rapid ascent. (Ironically, they would all have key roles to play in the year of our demise.) There were countless examples of young partners ascending through the ranks in every office across the country.

The build-from-within also required that we recruit senior talent willing to make the lateral move from other firms to Heenan Blaikie. One of my responsibilities was to ferret out these individuals and convince them we were different. I hunted for laterals who had extensive client relationships or who fit into niche practice areas we were trying to develop. Over time I found litigators, securities lawyers, and commercial lawyers; when we identified natural resources as a priority, I searched for mining and oil and gas lawyers in Toronto and Calgary while Guy did the same in Quebec.

My key preoccupation over the years was to continue ongoing dialogue with new laterals. I made sure they integrated well into practice groups, reinforced what was important to the organization and how they could contribute to its development, and weeded out the ones who didn't fit. Whether they joined us in Sherbrooke, Ottawa, or Victoria, the lifeline of our firm was based on a successful integration of laterals. The first year was the period during which we lived together, deciding whether to marry. Some laterals were made to wait longer if there were any lingering doubts. They too would be evaluating whether they could align with our spirit and philosophy. We were not for everyone, and conversely everyone was not for us. Once we achieved alignment, the laterals would be completely integrated into the partnership and treated as equals. This allowed us to preserve our values over the years. In the same way that we managed without a formal detailed partnership agreement, the contractual arrangements with laterals never ran more than two pages. They came in on a handshake and an understanding that if they liked the work environment and the ability to grow their practices the way they saw fit, we would integrate them quickly and they would integrate until they became us. That process usually took a year or two. If not, they would leave.

—— • ——

Our growth was still predicated on making valuable senior additions. While the quest for a senior mergers and acquisitions (M&A) lawyer in Toronto continued, we became aware that one of Toronto's prominent litigators might be available. David Roebuck had run his own litigation boutique for many years, having shunned the big law firms since leaving Faskens early in his career. He was now at a crossroads. His firm, Roebuck Garbig & Perschy, was no bigger than the three names on the door. As one of Toronto's most respected senior litigators, he was attracting significant briefs but could only play a counsel role, since most of the cases required a battalion of lawyers to completely service the client.

David knew that making a move to a larger firm would be more lucrative. He was also aware that it could cost him autonomy and would likely result in conflicts. He would have to turn away briefs from potential clients wanting to sue existing clients of the firm, which would cost him business. Stan Freedman, one of our commercial partners recruited a few years earlier, had worked with David while providing commercial support for litigation clients. He had spoken highly of our firm to David and began the process of recruitment.

By the time David and I finally had lunch, a number of our litigators had already met with him. I was immediately drawn to his open approach and steady demeanour. We talked about life and family, and I laid out the vision of what we were trying to achieve in Toronto. I told him we were not driven by the immediate need to build a full-scale corporate presence, and even in the rosiest of dreams, we did not believe we could achieve such a goal before David's retirement. Retirement was an issue for him, as he still had a young family and had no interest in moving to a firm that would insist he unload his practice at age sixty-five. Heenan Blaikie had no retirement policy, in part because we still saw ourselves as a young firm, with no more than a handful of partners who were even close to reaching their golden years.

I was able to sell David on the firm's supple nature; he would be free to operate his practice as he saw fit. I also sensed he could be an excellent mentor and leader for those of our younger litigators who needed some direction after Joe Groia left at the end of 1999 to open his own boutique with two of our promising talents, Wendy Berman and Lara Jackson. After realizing that Heenan Blaikie was a better career platform for them, the two women returned to the firm a short time later and became integral to David's practice.

David brought along rich relationships with several real estate families with substantial litigation issues. He also teamed with Edward Greenspan, one of Toronto's leading criminal attorneys, to provide commercial litigation backup for Eddie's white-collar trials. David's claim to fame was an uncanny ability to cross-examine witnesses. He prided himself on being able to make even the most straightforward person seem unsure and outright dishonest, shaking the tree of credibility at every opportunity.

— • —

In 1986 the Canadiens were winning an improbable Stanley Cup, defeating the Calgary Flames in a year when teams with more talent fell by the wayside. The Canadiens had a knack of seizing unexpected opportunities and riding them to championships. They pulled off the same miracle in 1971, defeating a far more talented Boston Bruins team led by Phil Esposito and Bobby Orr. Nothing better describes how we emulated the Canadiens' approach than the story of how we landed Teva Pharmaceutical Industries, Israel's most prestigious public company and the world's largest generic drug manufacturer, as a client.

We had identified patent litigation as an area for future growth, but we had no idea where to begin. Jean Potvin had failed to negotiate the acquisition of an IP (intellectual property) firm in Ottawa a few years earlier. I had recruited Andrea Rush, a brilliant copyright and trademark lawyer, from Gowlings to begin an IP practice in Toronto, but otherwise we had no expertise.

Paul Rouleau, a great commercial litigator, who now sits on the Ontario Court of Appeal, had joined us a few years earlier when I merged sixteen lawyers from Genest Murray, a labour and litigation boutique led by John Murray, into the Toronto office in 2000. Paul walked into my office one day to explain that Teva was looking for additional Canadian litigation counsel. Teva's regular counsel was Blake Cassels, or Blakes, as they were known on the street. Blakes is among one of the more powerful commercial law firms in the country, forming part of the "Seven Sisters," the nickname for the reputedly most successful Toronto commercial law firms. The seven may have actually numbered eight or nine, and how they came to be known as sisters is one of Toronto's best-guarded secrets. The name was less ostentatious than that of the "Magic Circle" firms in London, England, though equally irritating to the firms not recognized as being in the elite. Since Blakes also acted for some of Teva's competitors, Teva wanted other firms available as backups in the event of conflicts. One of Teva's contacts knew and liked Paul and asked him whether we might be prepared to take on one of their drug patent infringement cases.

Normally I would say yes to any new file but there was one problem. We had no expertise whatsoever in patent litigation. This was not a trifling gap we could fill by teaching ourselves the issues. Rather it seemed to be insurmountable. We were being asked to take on a technical drug case though we had not an ounce of scientific expertise. We had no patent agents and little experience before the federal courts, where these cases were heard.

After much debate we decided to take the case as a learning experience and swallow a significant cost for the steep learning curve, which we could not charge back to the client. The more reasonable approach would have been to direct Teva to a firm that had patent expertise, but that wasn't in our DNA. Our problem was that even if we took this litigation, it was difficult to imagine how we could get a second or third case without investing in building a practice. That would be costly, and without a regular client to support the expenditure it didn't make much sense. Notwithstanding all the logic suggesting this was a bad idea, I told Paul to accept the case from Teva. Was it instinct or short-sightedness, audacity or foolishness motivating the decision?

Paul took the brief and brought in Andrea Rush and Jon Stainsby. Jon had great litigation instincts but zero technical knowledge, and only Andrea understood how the federal courts worked. As an experienced litigator who understood strategy, Paul was supervising, although he was in over his head in this case. Shortly into the process, it became clear that there were too many cooks in the kitchen. As Andrea put it, Jon was going to have to crack the books and take this over; otherwise, he would never succeed. She was right, and Jon stepped up to the challenge.

We were a year into the case and still far from a trial date when lightning struck. The brass at Teva called Paul to advise us that Blakes had just fired them as a client. There were simply too many conflicts with their lucrative brand pharmaceutical clients. We had a couple of weeks to put a team together to meet Teva's key people and their US counsel in New York to explain why we should replace Blakes, in whole or in part. As we sat in my office to discuss strategy, we realized this was comical. We were a firm with no patent expertise, one year into a case that had not yet been tried. With no courtroom experience in drug cases, we were being invited to bid. What was it about this scenario that made sense? Nothing.

We put together a bid, though we expected to be blown out of the water by either Lang Michener, which had a developed patent group, or Bennett Jones, which had great oil and gas patent expertise that ought to be transferable.

As head of our litigation group, David Roebuck agreed to make the trip with Jon Stainsby and me to Manhattan. I always enjoy a good fight, and with nothing to lose, I liked the odds. Off to New York we trundled, short on experience and long on a sense of humour. While I had no experience with the Teva people, I did understand Israelis. Aggressive and full of nerve, they don't suffer fools gladly, or indeed at all. They understand how to make a point by twisting a knife between your ribs, and they also understand family and loyalty. At the very least, I had a sense of how to build an approach to win.

We introduced ourselves: David Roebuck as the head of litigation, with pedigree and poise in the courtroom; Jon Stainsby as the litigator on the case who knew some of the key Teva people; and me as the managing partner. After we went through the basics of our presentation, which we knew would impress no one, it was my turn to speak. My strategy was simple. We had no experience, no conflicting clients (the only positive we could offer), and no specialized expertise, so I did what only an Israeli company could understand: with a heavy dose of nerve, I turned it back to them.

"I'll build a practice to support your work," I said. "It'll take me a few years. Since you have a better sense than I do of how to build such a team, including knowing the experts to hire in Canada, I'm making the following proposition: You'll direct me as to the talent I need to hire to build a practice to serve your needs. I'll go shopping to get it. To do that, I need a commitment from you of $3.5 million in work in the first year. If you can deliver on that commitment, I'll hire everyone necessary to support the work in short order. We'll give priority to your files and I will *never* conflict out your files. This practice will exist to serve *you*."

This was a big package, audacious, with nothing to lose and no middle ground.

A few days later, to our great surprise, Teva offered us half its work for at least $3.5 million and accepted the partnership I offered. The first condition was that we hire Henry Bertossi. Henry ran all of Teva's commercial files, and with Teva's departure from Blakes, he had to decide whether to follow them to one of their new homes. Teva had offered the other half of its work to Bennett Jones. No doubt that firm would be after Henry as well. My grand quest to build a pharmaceutical patent practice where none existed previously had led us to our first bona fide Seven Sisters commercial lawyer.

My brain was already focusing beyond the hiring of Henry (in my mind a *fait accompli*, though I had never met the man) to the day when

Teva would be our largest client and a key component in developing an IP powerhouse under our roof. If I could pull this off, we would be on the road to transforming the firm—but I had no idea then that Jon Stainsby, a commercial litigator with no IP experience, would actually become one of Canada's top patent litigation lawyers, eventually leading a highly rated team of forty professionals. From a single opportunity we became a household name in Canadian pharma IP.

— • —

I was immediately struck by Henry Bertossi's earnestness in our first encounter. I sensed immediately that he was not driven by ego. He seemed cautious and sensible as he queried me on the economic status, background, and history of the firm. More than anyone I had interviewed previously, though, he was interested in the culture, how we approached decision-making, and what we considered valuable.

We had a series of at least five meetings. At each one he would arrive with his pad of yellow foolscap paper filled with due diligence questions. In accordance with our firm's tradition of recruiting laterals, he was introduced to partners, first in the commercial group, then in the office at large, and finally he went to Montreal to meet members of our Executive Committee as well as local commercial and other partners interested in meeting him. He also wanted to take his measure of Guy Tremblay and the distinctions in approach, if any, between Montreal and Toronto. It took Henry a few months to satisfy himself that HB was the right place for him, since Bennett Jones was pursuing him as well. I had to keep reminding myself in the course of our discussions that I was the more senior lawyer, perhaps because his bald head and deliberate, soulful approach made him seem older than his years.

Courting Henry was the easy part; having the firm agree that we could import a partner from Blakes and pay him what he was currently earning there was the greater internal challenge. I had positioned his recruitment as a game changer for us. We had spent years in the corporate wilderness, with little reputation outside the corporate mid-market. Now, though, we could finally begin to recruit partners who would gradually elevate our commercial reputation and status. We were also in the surprising position of being able to launch a new practice group that would be profitable from inception. I was hoping that with Teva as an anchor client, we could build expertise in a bur-geoning sector of the economy. The explosion of health care services, medical devices, and drug technology in North America could become one of our drivers and carry us along rather than leave us in its wake. We had the opportunity of a lifetime dropped into our laps. Were we bold enough to seize it?

While no one was opposed, a few partners in Toronto raised their hands to ask whether this type of move preferred the newcomer to the incumbents, who had spent years working to bring the firm to where it was right now. The question was valid in a vacuum. There would always be tension around sensitive compensation issues. Was it worth risking cultural values around compensation to land newcomers with great economic prospects? This had to be weighed against the need to develop the IP practice area and the reputational value it would bring to the firm. Most important, we would have to bet that the firm's profitability would increase as a result of such an acquisition and that all incomes would rise as a consequence. If this happened, I would be a hero. If not, I would wear the goat horns. It never occurred to me to worry about being wrong.

The deal eventually moved ahead and Henry joined us in April 2003. Shortly afterward, Bill Mayo was easily pried away from the boutique where he also worked on Teva files. The two new additions joined with Jon Stainsby and Teva's legal group in Toronto and Phil-adelphia to build the larger team, manage the new files, and begin a rich relationship. We had no trouble meeting first-year targets, and the group grew methodically. Bill built a team around him of science nerds, such as Lesley Caswell, who were expert at drug patents. Jon recruited into his litigation group young lawyers like Mark Davis, whom we hired away from Ogilvy, as well as Andrew Skodyn and

Neil Fineberg to round out a solid litigation team. His team refused to lose cases, which made Jon a client favourite, while Henry took care of the commercial work.

For years we had been trying to build our securities group in Toronto beyond Bill Orr's board advisory practice, without much success. This had been a source of frustration for me and for Bill, who probably felt he was letting me down by not adding to the group, beyond the recruitment of Lisa Davis, who followed him from Fraser Beatty. The other changes in the firm had created a positive buzz on the street, and opportunity finally knocked again following on the heels of Henry Bertossi's arrival at the firm. A couple of securities lawyers at Aird & Berlis were considering a move and their head-hunter, Lorene Nagata, suggested they speak to me. Word on the street was that Heenan Blaikie, having built a national presence, was an interesting place to practise law, and Bill Orr had developed a great reputation as a securities lawyer. Kevin Rooney, the more senior of the pair, was looking for a broader platform and a vision for the future he was not convinced his firm possessed. He was attracted to the mentorship opportunity that working with Bill Orr might present in relation to corporate governance. Sonia Yung projected a no-nonsense, practical approach to the world. Their client base was self-sufficient, anchored by the Sprott group of funds and independent investment bank Cormark.

Their profile was in my wheelhouse: they were young and ready to build. They might have chosen another firm to slide into a larger practice, but I presented them with the chance to paint the future as they saw fit. I challenged them to build an entire department in their image. Internally, I pitched hard to get approval from the Executive Committee and the local Toronto partners. This was the opportunity to build that I'd been waiting for years to see, and a second chance might not come around. My instincts all said go, so I pushed the throttle hard to close the deal.

Kevin and Sonia joined us and shortly afterward, to their surprise, Bill Orr left to join Faskens. It was rare for us to lose a partner

to another law firm, but this was not a shock given the unique circumstances of Bill's life. Part of the reason for the departure may
have been his frustration with his own inability to recruit, but the
more likely reason was personal. Bill had fallen in love with and
eventually married Manon Jolicoeur, the head of our Montreal real
estate group. The logistics of managing a young family and practice
in Toronto and a marriage to a partner in Montreal led Bill to conclude it might be time to put some space between his personal and
professional lives. Kevin was greatly concerned, since Bill had been
a determining factor in his decision to come on board. Kevin and
Sonia quickly shook off the surprise and resolved to build from the
ground up. They benefited from one of our outstanding young lawyers, Corey MacKinnon, whom they groomed and developed into a
star. Within a short period the shock of Bill's departure wore off and
the work was flowing in the door. We went back to the well to build,
adding a number of new partners and senior associates from Aird
& Berlis over the next twelve months. I began to feel guilty that we
were over-raiding a particular firm, and we finally self-imposed an
embargo. While I wanted to grow, I did not want to severely harm
any competitor's business in the process.

Over the next few years the department took on a life of its own
as Kevin and Sonia began the slow process of rounding into leaders
of an outstanding practice. If there was a defining moment for our
commercial group, it was the arrival of the two securities lawyers.

— • —

Looking back, why did they take the risk and join us instead of going
to a more established firm? Lorene Nagata, who was their advisor,
explained to me many years later that the business opportunity was
a small part of the decision. More important were the values that I
was talking about during the recruitment and which were reinforced
in discussions with many of my partners. We were a place where
everyone had a desire to come to work in the morning and where we

actually cared about the partners, the associates, and their support staff. This was the attraction and our marketing edge.

The recruit and integration of the many lateral partners over that growth spurt self-selected against people who were looking to make as much money as possible and in favour of those whose long-term vision was already aligned with ours. That consistency of vision made the ultimate integration go smoothly.

— • —

Our roll through the decade continued as we built success on top of success. Our franchise was finally growing, and our reputation began to precede us. The street was buzzing about Heenan Blaikie, and it was all positive. I counted on that momentum in making continued strategic acquisitions of laterals from other firms.

All these new additions might have upset the balance of an established firm. Some firms, like Goodman & Carr, which failed in 2007, expanded quickly through aggressive recruitment of laterals, but never really integrated them. There was a tight group of incumbents who were at the centre of decision-making, but many of the newcomers were treated as if they were outside contractors, recruited with the sole view of increasing firm revenues. They never felt part of the firm and were the first to leave when they perceived tough times coming.

How did we manage the growth for so many years without upsetting the balance? We imposed a division of labour. My role was to consider the areas of the firm that needed bolstering, particularly in Toronto; to ferret out the talent; and to present the opportunities to the partners. Unlike other firms, I did not seize the authority to make the decisions. I could attempt to add my influence, but the ultimate decision to hire lateral partners was only made after a series of meetings between the candidate and a considerable number of partners. In the end, the partners, not the managing partners and not the Executive Committee, made the screening decisions. If the local partners were not prepared to support a hire, we ended up passing on the candidate.

Most did not make the cut, whether for reasons of insufficiency of the practice or, more likely, for perceived incompatibility. The more successful we became, the higher the bar was raised. David Steinberg attended recruiting meetings to impose his "no assholes" rule. One or two fooled us, but did not stay for long.

It was equally important for us to integrate newcomers quickly into the social fabric of the firm. Many partners went out of their way to take new laterals to lunch or out for drinks to begin the process of inculcating our values. The candidates had heard all about the special HB culture during the recruiting process. As one of them put it to me subsequently, "I really thought you guys were overselling the culture; that it couldn't possibly be as important as you were holding out. Now that I'm here I can't get over the reception I've received." The telling words always followed at the end of the conversation. "My last firm was nothing like this. I like being here." It was as simple as that!

Many business leaders and CEOs would not have accepted a world in which their stakeholders had a veto over the CEOs plans. If I had judged myself by the number of times that particular initiatives I explored were rejected, I would have resigned many years before the end of my term. Instead I developed a thick skin and came to understand that our process was an important part of our culture.

—— • ——

When we began our tour of duty as managing partners, Guy and I were both able to combine running our legal practices with operating and leading the firm. As my devotion to firm expansion and strategic growth took up more of my time and energy, I had to shift into a counsel role with clients and transfer the daily management of my practice to Allen Garson and Mark Jadd. I continued to live by a few precious guidelines of my own and the discipline that Sharon imposed on our lives. My weeks were filled with travel to our offices around North America and to clients in Los Angeles, plus business development trips. I was on the road most of the year, but I came home to the family every Friday for the weekend.

Sharon also insisted on family dinner every night at 6:30 p.m. If I was in town I was expected to be at the dinner table, where family came first. Work could always be resumed after the kids were in bed. She felt that every hour spent with our four children in their early years would save us ten hours of therapy when they became young adults. As a result we formed a very strong and close family unit. If I was going to speak to others about the virtues of building a personal life and a career, I had to set an example to all our younger lawyers about the importance of family.

I also made a habit of rarely travelling on a Monday. For years Monday and Wednesday karate classes were sacrosanct. Cezar, who had progressed to eighth degree black belt (and would later attain the ceremonial title of *hanshi* when he attained his ninth *dan*), taught the Monday classes, which were burned into my schedule. Over the years I progressed to *sandan* or third degree black belt, but as my skills improved, my right knee slowly degenerated with arthritis. My knee, like my career, naturally wore down to the bone as a product of my success. By 2012, as my term as leader at HB was coming to an end, so did my life at the dojo.

11

JEAN CHRÉTIEN

The winds of political change that had been blowing through Ottawa for a couple of years led to increasing speculation in 2003 that Jean Chrétien would soon step down as prime minister. He had announced well over a year earlier that he intended to resign in December 2003, but the political infighting in the Liberal party, spurred by the persistent attempts by Paul Martin's supporters to unseat the prime minister earlier as leader of the party, was continually feeding the news cycle. The press were making lunch and dinner over the daily political intrigue, and it was only a matter of time before the prime minister would end his political career.

Roy Heenan had been maintaining a dialogue with Chrétien going back to 1979, when he had first joined the firm as counsel during the six-month period when Joe Clark was prime minister. Chrétien's popularity had plummeted in the previous year as a result of three factors. First, the decision not to follow the US into Iraq was controversial at the time and not well received by many Canadians. Second, Liberal party infighting was unflattering to all those involved. Third and most important, the Canadian press had had enough of him after ten years; they wanted new blood and the media criticized the prime minister at every turn. It was time for him to step down and get on with his life.

Roy advised the Executive Committee in September 2003 that he would pursue the initiative to bring Mr. Chrétien back and soon became convinced that he would be joining us when he stepped down. Unfortunately for us, the first news to break in the legal media after Chrétien's resignation was that he had accepted a counsel role at Bennett Jones (BJ). The move struck most of the legal community as odd, in that the firm's headquarters were in Calgary, in the Conservative Party heartland and not a location where one would expect a prominent Liberal to add much value. BJ's Ottawa office was no more than a cubbyhole, with only a couple of staff operating out of the tiny downtown premises. One of the BJ partners, however, had been a close advisor of the prime minister and managed to persuade both sides that there was a value to the relationship beyond the apparent contradiction. Shortly after that, we learned that Chrétien had also made an arrangement with Montreal-based Desjardins Ducharme. It seemed inconceivable that he could be working for multiple firms simultaneously, but Desjardins had an interesting practice in Africa, led by Jacques Bouchard. Bouchard had a history with Chrétien, who was passionate about participating in projects that would assist in the development of French-African nations.

When Roy finally explained to Guy Tremblay and me how this three-way arrangement was to work, Guy and I scratched our heads. Was this really a wise move?

Roy had a long history of being a dog with a bone when it came to his pet ideas. It didn't matter whether it was a particular legal argument, a course of action that needed to be taken, or a reaction to negative media coverage (particularly as it related to his role as a director of the CBC). Once Roy had made up his mind, he could not be moved off his point. Ever. Roy's memory sometimes functioned like a tape recorder. When reacting to any type of criticism in a meeting with partners, he would revert to a pre-recorded diatribe in his brain, using the same words to make the same points verbatim, over and over again, for decades. It was as if we were pressing a button in his head to replay the speech.

Guy and I discussed Chrétien's proposal. We noted that we were the only firm of the three with an established office in Ottawa. Having recently recruited Ron Caza, a champion of minority language rights, to lead our local litigation practice, we were also the only major firm in Ottawa with complete bilingual capacity. Being able to surround Chrétien with people he could socialize with daily in either language was a feature only we could offer. In our estimation, "the firm of Trudeau," as he would call us, had the best chance of becoming "the firm of Chrétien." If we let events unfold, Guy and I believed that within a couple of years we would be Chrétien's exclusive professional home.

All of this publicity about three law firms and an additional consulting arrangement that Mr. Chrétien had agreed to with Power Corporation of Canada created an internal maelstrom. Reaction among partners ranged from embarrassment, to anger, to cold neutrality. Many in Toronto thought it was not a good idea. Some thought it smacked of insanity. The litany of complaints piled up: "How could we come in third place?" "This is unprecedented; what kind of crazy arrangement would it be?" "How is Chrétien going to divide his loyalties, and won't this create unmanageable conflicts?" "The whole country hates him, George Bush hates him, my mother hates him ... how can he possibly generate any business for us?" And then there was the infamous sponsorship scandal that plagued him through his last few years in office, followed by the federal inquiry led by Justice Gomery in the early years of Mr. Chrétien's relationship with the firm. The former prime minister would famously quip that only a Canadian scandal could have "no money stolen, no deaths, and no sex." Comments like that did not make our partners feel any better. Faced with the criticisms from the vocal minority, even partners who supported management's approach were concerned. After a series of positive steps to build the brand, some were worried that we were making a significant misstep.

I responded in my trademark cryptic style: "I learned through our relationship with Mr. Trudeau. When you have the opportunity to hire a head of state, you don't ask questions, you simply take it. I have no idea how we're going to utilize him just yet, but I'm convinced we'll be better off for it."

The goodwill that Mr. Trudeau created when he joined us was immeasurable, yet he too had been reviled in many quarters when he left office. And we had observed an interesting phenomenon: with each passing year after he left office, Mr. Trudeau seemed to become a little wiser in the eyes of others, thus adding to the reputation he would leave for posterity. Outside the country he was regarded with the high respect commensurate with being a former head of state. He also had access to CEOs in the private sector, government contacts, and insights on foreign affairs that clients wanted to hear about. With all this in mind, Guy, Roy, and I knew we had to weather the storm of criticism and soldier on.

Then I crossed my fingers and hoped for the best. In most cases that type of business approach usually fails, so we immediately created a "Team Chrétien," whose primary responsibility was to find opportunities in our client network to put Mr. Chrétien to work. He had no intention of sitting back to write his memoirs, or spending time meeting former cronies to talk about the good old days. He made it clear to Guy and me that he wanted to create value for the firm, and he insisted that we find work that would suit his unique talents.

As much as he was a leader and had spent his career travelling the world and dealing with presidents, prime ministers, royalty, and international icons, Mr. Chrétien was always a man of the people with a great sense of humour. He loved to address the staff and young lawyers informally.

"You know," he'd say with his gravelly, French-Canadian inflection, "when I was a boy, it was just after the war and Louis St. Laurent was visiting Shawinigan. My father took me out on the street with the crowd. I asked my father why he was pushing me to the edge of the curb as the procession was nearing. 'Son,' he said, 'when you have the rare opportunity to shake hands with the prime minister of Canada, you take it.'"

At that point the former prime minister would pause for effect and look a young lawyer in the eyes, waiting with a devilish smile for the hand to be extended to shake his own.

We were not long into the relationship with Mr. Chrétien, when Desjardins's Jacques Bouchard approached Guy. Jacques believed that he would be able to access the former prime minister much more easily as well as enhance his own credibility in Africa if he could operate from our national platform. The continent might be rife with military strife and untrustworthy dictators, but a number of international firms saw it as an area of the world that would generate enormous amounts of legal work. Mr. Chrétien saw the potential for economic development leading to greater prosperity and improved social conditions. Jacques saw dollar signs. And he saw Mr. Chrétien, with his high-level contacts in many African countries, as an ally in building a successful practice.

In March 2005 Jacques left Desjardins, and as a result Mr. Chrétien terminated his relationship with that firm. Now he was dealing with only two firms. A year later, Mr. Chrétien and Bennett Jones parted ways. The former prime minister had become very comfortable in our Ottawa office on a daily basis, with a visit to Montreal once a week. Our gambit had paid off. We were now exclusive.

The relationship that Guy Tremblay and I had with Jean Chrétien was unlike anything we had previously experienced. Guy was assigned the task of negotiating and periodically renegotiating his contract, particularly after the relationship became exclusive. Unlike Mr. Trudeau, who did not want to be either paid or beholden, Jean Chrétien came to Heenan Blaikie to work and to earn some income. After thirty years in politics and no family fortune, the eighteenth of nineteen children had entered the phase in his life where it was time to make some serious money through multiple consulting sources. He remained an advisor to Power Corporation and the Desmarais family (to whom he was related through the marriage of his daughter). Kip Daechsel, one of our Toronto commercial lawyers, arranged a number of fascinating international mediations for him to handle. This turned into a very profitable relationship for the two men and enhanced Kip's reputation within the firm.

Mr. Chrétien occasionally told us that his wife, Aline, wanted him to slow down, take it easy, and enjoy his retirement from politics. It may have fooled others in the firm, but Guy and I were certain he would never give up the chase, irresistibly attracted as he was to solving conflicts. There was still considerable tread on the tires, and we continued to roll along, benefiting from his acumen.

Fortune was smiling on our leadership. Over the next seven years Mr. Chrétien proved to be one of the best and most lucrative additions to the firm. As with Pierre Trudeau, the more time that passed after he left office, the wiser he became in the eyes of the public. In particular his decision not to join the United States in the war with Iraq—reviled at the time he left office—was, with the benefit of hindsight, applauded by a growing number of Canadians. As the Chrétien brand improved over time, so did the firm's reputation through its association with him. One of the turning points may have been his response to Mr. Justice Gomery's public assertion that golf balls embossed with the prime minister's signature were "small town cheap." The day he appeared at the Commission of Inquiry into the Sponsorship Program and Advertising Activities, Mr. Chrétien pulled out a sleeve of balls embossed with the name of the judge's former law firm, much to the delight of a national audience.

A few months after Mr. Chrétien joined us, the Toronto Argonauts made a Grey Cup appearance under the leadership of Doug Flutie, one of the most accomplished CFL quarterbacks of all time. The game was to be played in Lansdowne Park in Ottawa. I bought a pair of tickets and drove to the Canadian championship with my son Phillip, who was nineteen at the time. At halftime we headed under the grandstand for a hot dog, and there was a huge noisy crowd, backed up and surrounding someone. There was Mr. Chrétien with no security, holding court, chatting up the fans, and having the time of his life. I pushed Phillip forward through the crowd to shake hands. Later I explained why.

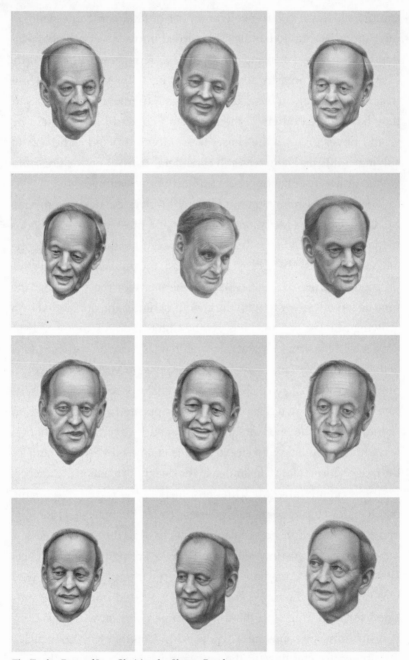

The Twelve Faces of Jean Chrétien, by Sharon Bacal

Jean Chrétien, 2009
Charcoal on paper,
by Sharon Bacal

Jean Chrétien visiting Sharon
in her studio

12

WINDS OF **CHANGE**

We were a firm that, remarkably, attracted two former prime ministers. While this certainly distinguished our brand, it was only one of the elements that made us unique. Partner compensation is the most challenging and most important process for professional services firms to manage. In all law firms, compensation of partners is a central concern. At HB compensation had also taken on a fundamental role in reinforcing the values of the firm.

Professional services firms have differing approaches to disclosure of compensation information. In some firms no partner knows what any other partner earns. At the other end of the spectrum sat firms like ours where every partner knew how much every other partner in the firm earned each year. Other firms lie somewhere on the spectrum of partial disclosure. Full disclosure creates transparency, which supports the perception that the process is fair. Complete transparency, however, does have its drawbacks, particularly as firms become larger and most partners have no idea about the contributions of partners in other departments or cities. There is no way most partners can determine whether the results are justified. Ultimately, they must trust in the wisdom and fairness of the committee they have appointed. Many partners benchmark themselves against partners they know, or rely on internal gossip, to make their own evaluations about colleagues. Most are less concerned about how much they earn in absolute dollars. They are driven more by what they earn compared to the "bastard down the hall," who is being paid too much, in their opinion. And none of them believe that they are that "bastard down the hall!"

The six-member Compensation Committee in our firm included the managing partners. I had been there since its inception, originally as the Toronto representative, while Guy had joined as a Montreal representative in 1995. Robb Beeman, the calming face of the Calgary office, had been the western Canada representative for a number of years. David Steinberg often complained about the number of hours he was spending between compensation meetings, mentoring young lawyers, listening to concerns of more senior associates of various departments, and doing the hundred other things that great partners do. He was the paradigm of the virtues that originally defined the firm. With his connections in the entertainment business across North America, he was emerging as one of the leading entertainment lawyers in the country. He served for six years on the firm's Compensation Committee, gaining an insider's knowledge of every aspect of the firm from one end of the country to the other.

We heard lawyers from across the country advocating their positions, providing positive feedback on their colleagues, seeking a favourable ranking for themselves and sometimes for others. Overall, we would achieve our annual goal of leaving partners slightly unhappy about the amount of money they were earning. This was as important a feature of our firm as anything else we aspired to. There was not a single one of us in the upper range of the grid who did not believe he or she could be making more money at another firm. The social contract we had accepted had us paying a price for the freedom to practice in a way that suited our particular personalities, and for the pleasure we found in working together. For years it was known as the Heenan Tax. That difference varied from year to year, depending on the economy and the premium work generated. But to put things in perspective: we were all earning more money than we had dreamed imaginable when we were growing up. We earned a very good income by professional standards. We were the fortunate few working Canadians who might be able to retire one day. There might be more to be earned elsewhere, but to what end and at what cost?

For those of us who were brought up in the firm, this philosophy was tied to a reverse snobbery about the larger, more profitable firms. We couldn't see ourselves fitting into another major firm with constricting rules and general unhappiness. Our quirky acceptance of one another and the genuine mutual respect we all shared came with an overall loss of efficiency. We were not going to save every possible dollar; we would spend a little more to make sure our support staff felt they belonged and were important. We still valued lawyers who wanted to build and to teach our younger lawyers how to do just that. We would not be reliant on large institutions to feed our young talent. Instead we had them experiment, be brave, fail occasionally, and push in new directions. There was an economic cost to this approach, but overall, partners and laterals who were finally having some fun with their careers understood that the cost was worth the outcome. For years our high-performing partners (with few exceptions) knew they could earn more elsewhere, but refused to consider the alternative. Young partners like Adam Kardash and Eric Levy and more senior people like Kevin Rooney, Sonia Yung, Allen Garson, Manon Thivierge, and Marie-Josée Hogue would never consider another firm. The centripetal force that held us together was our unique philosophy, financed by the Heenan Tax.

When it comes to compensation of partners, most experts believe that the process is more important than the results. HB was no different in that regard. Partners needed to feel comfortable entering the compensation room. We were an intimidating sight. Six lawyers sitting around a boardroom table with mountains of data for current and past years strewn across the table, making for piles of history on each partner, department, and city. Partners were required to prepare an annual memo telling their story. In hindsight, I would say David Steinberg played an essential and critical role in keeping the visits from becoming emotional or confrontational. As much as partners were strong personalities, when they entered the room, most felt at a disadvantage. By putting them more at ease, David ensured that the process felt fair and unintimidating to everyone who walked in that room. The size of the partnership grew every year, as the firm grew, making the process longer and more complicated. When I joined the Compensation Committee in 1991 we were fewer than thirty partners. By 2000 that number had tripled and would become over two hundred in the next ten years, when the firm reached well over five hundred lawyers.

The time would come in 2012 and 2013, as the composition of the Compensation Committee changed, when the process lost its rounded corners, and the hard edges and lack of respect the committee showed to numerous partners became factors in the erosion of those critical cultural values holding us together.

— • —

We had built a firm of swashbuckling entrepreneurs who dreamed big dreams and felt they knew how to manage risk. The firm was dominated by strong personalities like Roy, Peter Gall, Marcel Aubut, Mike Black, and Jim Pasieka in Calgary, David Stratas, and John Murray— all forces of nature. Beneath them we had built a disciplined business tempered with risk-taking. We had succeeded in large part because of the time Guy and I invested in managing the personalities, while never sacrificing the culture of entrepreneurship, respect, and fun. Tension between partners sometimes arose from the perception that if the big personalities wanted their way over an issue, they would get it. While Peter Gall and Roy were well loved by those around them, and the lapses that came with their special personalities forgiven, those more distant were far less forgiving. Marcel was also an unstoppable force, very committed to the firm and loyal to his team, but not one to accept opposition, whether from outsiders or his own partners. Marcel could handle resistance to a plan like a German tank rolling through the Maginot Line.

Yet some partners were asking, as we became larger, whether it made sense for the firm to evolve into a more institutional format, with more rules, or whether we should continue as an organization whose core was based on aggressive risk-taking and whose specialty was catering to unique personalities. These questions evolved into a formal review of our governance. The process took a year, involving hundreds of hours of input. It resulted in a governance report that outlined the powers of the partners and the firm's various committees and regulated terms of service, including imposing limits on the length of time any person could serve in the future as chair and as managing partner. The first step had been taken to define a more institutional firm, adding a little more precision to our structures, while still drawing on our history of insisting on partner ownership and participation.

The builders of the firm were mavericks, freethinkers, and dreamers, not really suited to functioning in an institutional environment. We were still very much "the cult of personality" that Henry Bertossi, the head of the Governance Committee, would aptly label us. Perhaps the next generation waiting to inherit the edifice would be more attuned to sensible rules of governance. Henry and his co-chair, Michel Poirier, believed that. Roy Heenan, Peter Gall, Marcel Aubut, and Calgary leaders Mike Black and Jim Pasieka were not, however, cut from that cloth.

As part of this governance review, the seeds had been planted to bring about a complete changeover in leadership by the end of 2012. We had given ourselves more than five years to get the house in order. This was supposed to allow Guy and me ample time to arrange the transition and assure the partners that they would not be subjected to the life servitude of unchanged leadership. As we would learn much later, the thoughtful process that had been started by this review of our structures and by our new governance policies, though well intentioned, was an early shovel driven into the graveyard earth. While Guy and I were now facing retirement dates, the difficult questions about who would replace us and whether we would perpetuate our three-headed system of leadership were left for future discussion.

There were a couple of fatal flaws in the new system that we had not factored into the analysis. First, we left it to Roy Heenan's good judgment to decide the appropriate time for him to retire from the position of chair. Second, the system involved Guy and me stepping down from our co-managing partner roles at the same time. We hadn't done any forward thinking about how a leadership transition would work. We simply proceeded as though that would be a problem for a different group at a later date. We also hadn't really thought about how a more structured governance approach might impact our continued evolution. As Roy aptly put it, "Will all these new rules destroy the special nature of the firm?"

As we entered the final phase of management of the firm by Norm and Guy, inexorably a vocal minority of partners grew tired of the perception that a Star Chamber ran Heenan Blaikie. We still had to decide on a paradigm: would it be a firm driven by dreamers, with a liberal approach to risk-taking, or a more disciplined platform for an incoming management group that would replace Guy and me? We were soon to find out.

— • —

The world economy was on a wild run and the real estate market in 2007, particularly the housing market in the United States, had been spiralling upward. Business was booming and law firm profits were being carried along with the wave of prosperity that swept North America. Our lease in the iconic Royal Bank Plaza would soon expire, and I could not come to terms with our landlords. I had a nagging feeling the bubble was about to burst, ending the era of accelerated economic growth, yet the rents they were asking were considerably higher than what we had been paying. If our rents were going to increase for the next fifteen years, our partners preferred a new environment. We negotiated a lease in the brand-new Bay Adelaide Centre, where we were the first tenant to move in. I hoped the build-out design, expertly managed by George K, would define our future. The building, all green-tinted glass and steel, was state of the art. Our boardroom complex on the twenty-ninth floor was designed to impress guests with its open concept. The view of the east of Toronto and the lake was breathtaking, especially on the evening of our opening reception in fall 2008, when over five hundred clients joined us to celebrate. Our space reflected a new confidence in the future of the firm and defined the successful image we had of ourselves.

During the course of the lease negotiations I thought an economic correction was in order, but none of us could predict the house of cards on which US bankers had built the foundation for the world economy. A combination of unbridled greed, unregulated financial instruments, and deceit ignited a chain reaction that threatened to destroy banks in the United States and around the world. As the guillotine was about to drop on the financial markets in mid-2008, the entire banking system in the United States was in critical condition. Those of our practices that relied on US sources of business were suddenly major question marks. Would US credit be frozen, and if so, for how long? How many industries would be affected? Could we expect financings of energy and mining transactions to be put on hold indefinitely? Would there ever be a new normal and what would it look like? These were the questions that Guy and I and every other law-firm leader were contemplating. The impact hit hard just after we moved in, during the fourth quarter of what was otherwise a very strong year, so the effects of the crisis on our 2008 results were muted.

We had lived for years in a business where expenses rose by 6 to 8 percent annually. Most of our costs were fixed: salaries and benefits, rent, and technology expenditures represented the lion's share of the costs. Costs increased as our junior lawyers became more senior. Normally we compensated either by increasing the hourly rates that we passed along to clients or by working harder. We were an inflation-driven business, but only the thickest of heads could not see the new writing on the wall. There would be huge pressure from surviving clients to become more efficient and lower our fees. The only question was whether this situation would be temporary or permanent.

We found out the answer faster than we expected. A revolution in client reaction had begun at major corporations in the United States. The goal was to control legal spending, open it to competitive bidding, and monitor it closely. The trend swiftly made its way to Canada. A new level of competitiveness had spread through the legal profession. We did not yet understand the implications, but the winds of change had swept through the industry. Many areas of law were beginning to commoditize, becoming less and less profitable. The need to establish areas where we were delivering value was now critical, and paramount among our concerns.

— • —

Searching for lateral partners who could add value never ceased. We sold ourselves as an environment where lawyers could not only thrive but also have some fun. By 2009 we had developed a reputation, most notably in Toronto, for attracting senior lawyers from other firms who were looking for a refreshing environment to continue building their practices. The great challenge for lateral recruitment was integration, and our ability to recruit, retain, and convert new laterals to the Heenan Blaikie philosophy was far above the industry average. After our successful recruiting of Kevin Rooney and Sonia Yung, we persuaded corporate governance expert Jeff Barnes to join us. Meanwhile we were developing a mining group, led by industry veteran Steve Vaughan. We had also managed to build a litigation boutique, which was highly unusual for a big law firm. David Roebuck was the core of our securities litigation group. David Stratas, another lateral who had developed into one of the finest administrative litigators in the country, was building a young team of future stars.

The commercial and litigation teams complemented one another, and no one was more representative of the crossover strength between the two teams than Subrata Bhattacharjee. I had given "Soobee," as David Steinberg nicknamed him, a budget to travel the world and develop an expertise in competition law. He made the investment over many years and was acquiring a reputation as a Canadian expert, chasing after prospective clients with Don Johnston in Europe, Japan, and South Korea. We were building niches that were enhancing our reputation in leading areas of the law.

When we recruited, we tried as best we could to convey who we were through the lengthy interview process, so potential hires could assess whether their values and ours aligned before making the decision to join us. I remember a few very accomplished lawyers who met with us no more than once or twice, at which point it had become clear they had different priorities. A few were only interested in how much money they could earn and for what period we would guarantee their earnings. My first rule of thumb was that there would be no guarantees. If you wanted to become one of us, then you had to agree to be treated like the rest of us. A number of American firms collapsed under the weight of untenable commitments made to lateral partners. As Brian Burkett aptly put it, "Why would we favour the newcomer over the incumbents who had built the firm?"

During the recruiting process, Barnes, a senior M&A lawyer in Toronto, remarked about the consistency between our Toronto and Montreal leaders in terms of their vision for the firm, their approach to the business, and the growth objectives. We had achieved a like-minded approach that many national firms were having trouble achieving, and ours traversed the cultural differences between Quebec and the rest of Canada. We were selling a vision of ourselves that had become appealing to successful lawyers across the country.

In 2000 the premium value in our business model was largely dependent on film and television finance. The latter represented as much as 10 percent of our revenues but constituted a practice area subject to the whim of government policy. The risk in that practice was that it could be ended at any time without notice, which is exactly what happened in 2002. The government decided to eliminate any tax advantage to private finance, and our lucrative practice came to a crashing halt.

— • —

To protect ourselves we embarked on expansion. By growing numerous practice areas and offices, in seven years we were able to increase our profitability while reducing our reliance on tax-based financings to less than 2 percent. The government may have shut one door, but they had left a few windows open to allow me to architect a scheme in the mining industry. The revenues generated from the big deals in the resource sector and from the major pieces of litigation handled by our two largest offices were adding to our growing reputation. Our pharma group was expanding, maturing, and winning cases as Jon Stainsby evolved from an unknown commercial litigator into one of the best pharma litigation lawyers in the country. Roy was able to convince Michel Bastarache, who had retired from the Supreme Court of Canada, to join Mr. Chrétien as counsel in our Ottawa office, and I landed John Morden, the retired associate chief justice of Ontario, as litigation counsel in Toronto. For all his legal genius, John was among the most humble gentlemen I had ever met, and a paragon as a role model and mentor for our young developing litigators. Our salary negotiations were out of *The Twilight Zone*, with him insisting on less money than I offered, and me reluctantly accepting on condition that if I felt he was being underpaid at the end of the year, I could force him to accept more.

After the 2008 financial market crash we set environmental expertise as a strategic objective. I had been researching the environmental law market for six months when I received a call concerning a litigator at Oslers who was looking to leave. Born in Egypt, the son of a judge, Ahab Abdel-Aziz was educated in Canada and was unlike any candidate I'd ever encountered. He was shaped like a statue of Buddha, with a short goatee, a wry sense of humour, and a brilliant mind. Ahab had great environmental expertise, as did his senior associate Lynn Mitchell, who joined Ahab as part of the package. Together they created the foundation of our practice.

Ahab brought with him a couple of key clients, among them the general counsel of Atomic Energy of Canada Limited, the Crown corporation that builds nuclear reactors around the world. Ahab also brought a whole new level of expertise in nuclear builds, refurbishing, financing, and regulation, along with a client that would be involved with considerable litigation issues for the next five years. Ahab also played a significant role in Heenan Blaikie's ongoing development as we eventually shifted our strategic intentions from domestic opportunities to international aspirations.

——— • ———

To be successful as a leader you have to take some chances and you have to make decisions without having full information. You do the best you can with the information you collect. At best, one in every four decisions will be wrong. If your batting average is better than that, you are probably not making enough decisions. Philip Rodney, the managing partner of Burness Paull, the most successful law firm in Scotland, expresses this as the "rule of 75 percent." We always had an eye for the future, and when opportunities like establishing Calgary and Beverly Hills offices or building a pharma practice and a mining practice from scratch presented themselves, we made decisions quickly. We were nimble and prepared to make adjustments, though sometimes that was not enough. We knew that we were going to make mistakes on occasion. I believe that my growth as a leader was the result of what I learned from, and how I adjusted to, the setbacks and the failures along the way.

We believed in an ongoing evolution of our firm and of the practice of law. To me, standing pat means falling back. I used to express this same thought in different terms: we are sharks in the water—our survival is dependent on perpetual movement.

We were prepared to make decisions that a third of our partners may have vocally expressed concerns about from time to time. If our partnership had required unanimity or near unanimity to make decisions, we would have failed as an organization. As leaders we understood we could not please everyone, nor allow them to paralyze the growth of the business. Remarkably we lost very few partners to other firms during this period of intense growth.

Finally, like a good husband and wife, Guy and I had our battles in private with the doors shut. To the public we always presented a united front. We had each other's backs at all times.

Guy and I also figured out that we could not do it all ourselves and that there were limitations to our skill sets. We engaged professional coaches to assist our promising attorneys with practice management, marketing, and life balance issues long before it became fashionable for law firms to do so. Professionals, like Susan Harris in Toronto and Lucie Rousseau in Montreal, were instrumental in working with talented associates and partners, and later with a number of our practice groups, in order to bring out their best qualities and help shape them as leaders.

— • —

As a final postscript, the period between 2000 and 2010 represented our striking evolution as an organization from wannabes to one of the more respected brands in the Canadian legal market. The additions we made, the building of Calgary, the gambit into pharmaceuticals, and the development of our talent were all paying dividends at the same time. Our leadership was on a hot streak: we had made a series of great decisions. We managed the firm with direction. But the 75-percent rule was lurking in the background, and it was only a matter of time until we made some mistakes. As fate would have it, the law of averages caught up with us, and in a critical period—just as we were headed for a preplanned change of leadership.

— • —

Not every lateral recruit worked out. We added Ivor Hughes's intellectual property boutique just before the 2008 financial crash. We had been expecting a major growth spurt by Teva that was put on hold. Ivor also expected to be able to attract other generic pharmaceutical companies. For a number of reasons, including potential business conflicts with Teva, now our largest client, this did not materialize either. When Ivor announced that he was making the move, his major client, Apotex, decided not to follow him. We were expecting this to happen since Teva and Apotex were rivals in the generic drug business, but we had every expectation of integrating Ivor's group into expanded Teva matters. I was a proponent of this move, but suffice it to say that by 2011 the initiative had proved to be a failure. There was not enough work, and we had failed to factor into our analysis that the approach of Ivor's group to Apotex matters differed from our team's approach to Teva. We were trying to mix oil and water, and little integration was possible. Would a more thorough diligence into the manner in which Ivor's group practised have caught the disparity? That was a valuable lesson for the future. We dealt with the inevitable housecleaning of professionals who didn't have enough work to keep themselves busy, and many blamed me for what proved in hindsight to be a poor business decision.

I also supported the addition of an insolvency lawyer with a significant financial institution as a client. After the lawyer joined us, the client refused to send work to the firm. It took a couple of years before the lawyer was finally asked to leave.

These experiences served as harsh reminders that if we took enough risks, every once in awhile there would be a failure. The 75-percent rule was coming home to roost. After a long period of successful risk-taking, several errors in judgment were piling up just as Guy's term and my own as managing partners were winding down. Though they were few in number over the years, I was to learn that no one forgets the missteps. While everyone shared the success, the mistakes in the last couple of years I wore on my own, like a stained necktie. Regardless of how well Ahab worked out, other initiatives in my final years as managing partner were beginning to stink, and the foul odour clung to me. These errors would be the first steps on my road to perdition.

13

OUR **INTERNATIONAL** EXPANSION

Despite all the growth the firm had experienced, in 2008 Guy and I saw the future as tied to international expansion of our operations— not that we had any precise idea how to achieve that goal. But as local competition intensified, we saw limits to the size and scope of the domestic market. Canada had become a nation that would rise and fall with the strength of natural resource commodity markets. We were developing an expertise in oil and gas and mining that we believed could be applied to markets from South America to China, Africa, and the Middle East. We hadn't reached the point where we thought the firm should be practising foreign law in local markets, but we knew we had to begin the process of experimentation, if only to keep pace with competitors who were operating in New York, London, and Hong Kong. There was no question in our minds that two categories of Canadian firms would emerge: the few that would remain purely regional, and the rest that would be opening offices in China, Europe, Asia, and perhaps even Africa. We could not sit idle on the sidelines if we hoped to thrive in the future.

In the province of Quebec this meant seeking foreign markets that could use French-Canadian expertise, so French-speaking Africa was a natural target. As mentioned earlier, Guy had recruited Jacques Bouchard, believing he was the ideal person to expand the firm's presence in Africa, using Jean Chrétien and his network of political relations across the continent as assets. Jacques had cultivated contacts across French-Africa, including in many countries where the rule of law was not recognized. Dictators led many of them. Mr. Chrétien's interest was in improving conditions in those countries, and his contacts in Africa were useful to Jacques in opening doors for businesses looking for relationships with the governments, which were essential as a starting point for development. Our oil and gas expertise in Calgary was exportable to Africa, so Jacques began working regularly with Mike Black on potential financings. Some of these files would result in intriguing legal mandates; others would result in success fees tied to connecting projects with clients.

Mr. Chrétien had already worked on some fascinating and lucrative mediations with Kip Daechsel in Europe. While Africa was the next step in our international expansion, we recognized that it did not operate in the same manner as Western Europe. Many partners were concerned about whether there were sufficient controls in place to monitor the type of work, and whether we might be representing unsavoury characters, or worse still, dictatorial regimes that oppressed their citizens.

Jacques was a master politician; he understood that to survive he needed friends in high places in the firm. His strongest relationship was with Guy, who travelled occasionally on business development trips to Africa. Jacques was also wise enough to keep Roy, Marcel Aubut, and me in his sphere of influence.

From the beginning Jacques delivered a successful practice. Africa may seem a mysterious continent to Westerners, but Jacques seemed quite at home there. As his practice grew, he took one of our young commercial lawyers, Poupak Bahamin, under his wing; she accompanied him on travel to Paris and then to various Africa countries. Jacques's practice was earning him a growing ranking within our compensation system.

Jacques was not the only one creating international work and a global reputation for the firm. Pierre-Marc Johnson, for a brief time premier of Quebec, was among the most revered and respected counsel in the firm. He was born into a political family: his father was a former nationalist premier (whose name could not be mentioned in my house while growing up without a scowl appearing on my father's face) and his brother was the head of the Quebec Liberal Party. Pierre-Marc had been the Parti Québécois leader who slowly but surely became more centrist in his views after leaving politics. A medical doctor and lawyer by profession, he was among the world's leading environmental experts. He represented Quebec in negotiating various free trade agreements, assisting our partner Paul Lalonde in developing his own reputation as an international trade expert. Don Johnston had returned to the firm as counsel after serving ten years as secretary-general of the Organisation for Economic Co-operation and Development (OECD) out of Paris, so the two former politicians gave the firm credibility around the world. Pierre-Marc also happened to represent every attribute of the best of what the firm had to offer. While some partners may have been concerned about our international aspirations, having counsel the likes of Chrétien, Johnston, and Johnson created a seal of approval for the firm in many countries around the world.

— • —

Paris, the City of Light. The birthplace of modern European civilization. There is no city in the world like Paris and no people in the world like the Parisians. There are also no lawyers in the world like the French: heroic when they succeed, and never responsible when they fail. Haughty, smart, and cultured, they are born with the genetically ingrained assumption that the British are unfair and North Americans are inferior beings. Sharon's advice about Paris still rings in my ears: "Stay away from Paris unless we're going on vacation. You're going to regret it." Paris would become Guy's Achilles heel and would plague my final two years as managing partner.

The concept seemed simple enough. Jacques Bouchard was doing an enormous amount of work in Africa and the commute was wreaking havoc on his life. Many African diplomats and businessmen treated Paris as a home away from home, and the trip there was manageable in and out of Africa. So we concluded it would make sense to station Jacques and his family there on a temporary basis. The practice grew; the results were exciting. Poupak Bahamin had become a partner in Jacques's practice and was considering relocating her family to one of the African jurisdictions. Guy and Jean Chrétien were figuring in the business initiatives, and Jacques was working regularly with Lucie Bourthoumieux, a Parisian lawyer with many ties to African countries where Jacques did not have his own excellent contacts. We decided that Lucie would be a timely addition to our team. The costs of taking over her sole office were not significant. The public relations value of announcing that we now had an international office based in Paris looked smart, so we moved ahead with Lucie.

As time passed and Jacques's practice continued to grow, he was in touch with another Parisian, Jean-François Mercadier, who represented a group of over a dozen lawyers that had merged into Norton Rose a number of years prior. Jean-François was feeling unloved in a firm that was transforming itself into a global powerhouse and where the influence of Paris was waning. His group had a considerable mining component, so there was a strategic alignment with our vision.

We had learned that a one-lawyer office in Paris was not a long-term formula for success, so the question was whether we were prepared to commit to a permanent presence in Europe with strong ties to Africa. This would give us a real base to evaluate all future opportunities. The world was becoming smaller, and law firms had to adapt to this new reality. Large American and UK firms were expanding their reach as global brands around the world. They were in the process of swallowing the major Australian firms, who were quickly deciding whether they could survive without an international presence.

Industry experts were all predicting that Canada would be next, and firms here would shortly be confronted with large international firms wanting to swallow them up as well.

Against this backdrop Guy and I led the discussion with our Executive Committee. Was this a chance to discover, in advance of this tide, whether we could continue to build a global brand of our own, one office at a time? We had done it in Calgary, and we had run a successful branch in Beverly Hills for ten years until changing economic factors led us to close it. We had experience to build upon. Were we brave enough to continue experimenting?

The Executive Committee sent me along with Guy, Marcel, and Jacques to meet with Jean-François's Parisian team to see if a deal should be done. We arrived for our meeting a day early to give us time to exchange views and strategy. The sun was setting on a warm late-spring evening as we dined in an outdoor bistro near the famous George V, one of Paris's most expensive hotels.

We were sipping wine as Guy mused, "Jean-François has an excellent reputation as a commercial lawyer."

"His group have worked together for many years," Jacques chipped in, "and I've seen them on a few deals. He's a very classy guy."

"Expanding from a single lawyer to a full office on the other side of the Atlantic is a challenge the likes of which we've never faced," I reminded them. "While the group is small by our standards, we'll be looking at different accounting and tax rules and technological challenges for the set-up and maintenance."

Guy leaned back and said thoughtfully, "There are also regulatory restrictions imposed by the Paris bar."

"True," I said. "But we faced similar issues when we started LA, so we have experience with long-distance offices. The difference here is psychological. We're crossing an ocean if we do this deal."

Marcel looked at Jacques. "If you believe in this and you're prepared to use all your energy to make this work, then I think it's a good idea. This is all tied to how well you'll all do together in Africa. I'm counting on you, Jacques."

We met Jean-François's team and discovered the tight-knit group of five partners represented various practices, including international arbitration, European private equity, and M&A across Europe and the Caribbean, in addition to the mining practice in Africa and the Middle East. We got comfortable with their expertise, credibility, philosophy, and suitability, but we learned the proportion of mining relative to their overall practice was beneath the threshold we were expecting.

We returned home, where Guy and I pondered the options. This was not going to be quite the Afrocentric deal we were expecting. On the other hand the base looked solid, the lawyers impressive, and this would still be an interesting beachhead for us. What was the future of our firm to be? That was the existential question. We had pioneered a vision that had taken us from a strong regional player to a national power with a stellar reputation. The brand was now well known nationally and was beginning to develop a reputation in several of our global practices due to the work of our counsel and through our natural resource practices. We had learned from many years of experience that feet on the ground was a recipe for success. We had carefully monitored our serial office openings, sent over people to instill cultural values, and continued to grow. We had never failed in a new office venture.

As I saw it, the future was international growth and perhaps inevitable merger. Our preference for now was to follow our model, which tied new initiatives to growing strengths. Opportunity had come knocking; if we passed it up, it might be a long time before the next chance presented itself. If we seized the moment, we would be growing, making inevitable mistakes, and learning from them. We would have a much better sense of what the future of these expansions might be. Once we had taken this step, it would signal our intentions to the world, and it might drive other opportunities towards us.

The Heenan Blaikie future that I envisioned had us opening offices around the globe, though I had no idea yet how we would accomplish the vision. I knew one thing: we needed to become the kind of exciting player in the international arena that would attract a broader array of Canadian companies looking to expand their own brands. This would also allow us to sell a story in recruiting that would continue to evolve and be compelling to young lawyers. We had opened in Beverly Hills and then in Calgary based on guts and instinct, and we could do it again—as long as we set near-term modest goals and pursued the strategy at the core of our historic development: aggressiveness combined with financial prudence, fearlessness, and vision. We would undoubtedly make mistakes in Paris, but it would become a training ground for us and it would help us formulate a long-term approach to international expansion. We needed to take a first step in order to learn and continue to grow. Assuming Jacques was prepared to put his shoulder into making this a success, Guy and I decided we were prepared to push the initiative along.

We returned to the Executive Committee and shared the vision. Convincing partners to agree would be the real test. Los Angeles and the film business had been connected to the history of the firm long before we opened the office there. It was seen by the partners in the early 1990s as an exciting outgrowth. Calgary was a necessary step in our evolution. Paris in the twenty-first century might have been similar in scope, but it was a first step in a completely new approach.

We embarked on the most thorough consultation in the history of the firm. For years the Executive Committee had been criticized for its lack of transparency; some of its members might have been brilliant at generating business but were not built to share information. While our management team was trained to filter information back to the partners in their groups, discussions within the Executive Committee tended to remain in the room. On this initiative Guy and I were leaving nothing to chance. We spent four months educating our partners on the markets where we saw value, on the team in Paris we were evaluating, and on the future of our international vision. All partners participated in the discussion about this next step in our evolution and some expressed concern, whether about risk management, tax issues, cost of failure, or reputation. Brian Burkett and Doug Gilbert succinctly articulated the core concern that others were not voicing but that lay hidden beneath the veneer of approval: "Norm, we're worried that the more we focus on international initiatives, the more we lose focus on our primary market, Canada."

The vote passed, but not before Guy had uttered the famous words that would haunt his final year as managing partner and beyond. "Paris will not cost us a cent!"

Meanwhile our Parisian partner Lucie made it clear that she was not at all interested in forming part of an expanded operation. She was a sole practitioner at heart with little interest in becoming a cog in an organization. There was no chemistry between her and Jean-François's group, so she left, shortly before the new group joined us in January 2011. Guy made bimonthly trips to the office in a newly renovated space not far from the Eiffel Tower, forming an association between our two independent businesses under the name Heenan Blaikie.

Our goal was to integrate over two years, but from the start the execution was flawed. The first blip in the road saw Jean-François's largest client balk at making the move. It took until the end of 2012 to convince the client to start sending African files. This blew a hole in our first-year revenue projection, which might have been filled through a joint-marketing effort that Jean-François and Jacques Bouchard were to undertake. I visited about six months after the opening. The problem, I discovered, was that Jacques had disappeared from the Paris landscape. He was focusing on initiatives in China and Africa, but seemed to have lost interest in our Paris operation. The combination of these factors demoralized the Paris staff, and I felt the full brunt of their Parisian frustration on my arrival. All too quickly the bloom had come off the rose.

The first-year subsidy to Paris was nominal, so while it was costing us money to support the venture, the loss was manageable. Mr. Chrétien and Kip had worked on an international mediation for which the Paris connections proved invaluable. Factoring in that, the first year was a modest success. If we could create any kind of positive momentum after the first year, we could escape the mire of recriminations. We had gone through this in Calgary. Building a new office took time and resources. However, Jacques continued to ignore Paris and work was slow in coming. Unlike our Calgary and LA start-ups, there was no one from the home office committed to the initiative. According to the team in Paris, the blame lay at our feet. Marketing was substandard and there was little support from the mother ship, which lay on the other side of an ocean. This proved to be as much a psychological as physical barrier. Frankly, most of our Canadian lawyers had no interest in our Paris office, and our French partners were beginning to feel insecure. The second-year operating loss, while not considerable, was an indication that things were not working according to plan.

Guy and I were not oblivious to this issue, and at the following partner retreat in January, on the anniversary of our Paris opening, we devoted a morning session to introducing our new partners, allowing them to share their objectives with all the partners, and encouraged mingling over the course of the weekend. We were certain that social interaction would help create the bonds needed to unite us, as it had with our previous successful expansions.

Jacques was also distracted by his new relationship with Ari Ben-Menashe, an Israeli living in Montreal who had fascinating international contacts. Ari had begun to make plans to connect Jacques with his contacts in Russia because he thought Jacques's relationships with certain African governments could prove useful. Russia wanted to provide funds and military equipment to these countries, as a way of counterbalancing China's sphere of influence. Ari was playing the middleman. The Executive Committee studied the question, and Guy and I asked our internal counsel to research international law and the type of transaction we would allow ourselves to be involved in as counsel, particularly if weapons were involved as part of an economic support package. We also canvassed Don Johnston, who had considerable expertise as former secretary-general of the OECD, for his views on the subject. As a consequence, we imposed various internal conditions on our participation in any transaction of this nature. The deal fell apart because our conditions could not be met, and we considered the entire matter to be academic; after all, it was difficult to imagine a ticking time bomb attached to a deal that never happened. Unfortunately, we were not imaginative enough! There would be a price to pay one day for the connection to Ben-Menashe.

— • —

Guy and I had started the internal discussion about what the future of law would be for the next generation of lawyers. How was our law firm going to remain relevant to clients, and how would we be able to market ourselves to the best and brightest of the next generation of legal talent? We were considering the pressures on diminishing profitability, the encroachment of law branches of the major accounting firms that were growing in Europe and Canada, and the development of outsourcing firms in India and elsewhere who were nipping at the low-value end of the practice. It was obvious that over a period of years these would all be a threat to portions of our practice.

We had always encouraged freethinking, risk-taking, and adopting novel approaches as our manner of competing. The accounting firms had run sideline consulting practices for years, over time building all types of businesses, including law firms, under their roofs, yet law firms seemed convinced that they should only be practising law. What did the accounting firms know that we had yet to figure out? We were learning that clients were prepared to pay for non-legal services even when they had strict budgets for their legal spend. And sometimes clients needed legal advice as part and parcel of other companion services, which we could deliver by hiring a few staff business consultants to supplement our services.

We began various experiments around the firm. In Adam Kardash's emerging privacy practice we hired consultants who could provide in-house training on management of confidential information in our clients' organizations. We could then not only teach them the law but also influence their daily practices and deepen their relationship with us. All my instincts suggested we needed to retrain our own lawyers to look at prospective clients more holistically and not merely from the perspective of solving legal problems.

HB Global, our consulting practice, was born out of this thought process. The name spoke to our future. We would be looking for opportunities for clients worldwide to assist with their business ventures. Our labour practice might use its services to expand to workplace training—their US colleagues were successfully implementing that approach. In our mining practice it would mean playing a more active role in matching mining opportunities in South America or China with investment appetite in Canada. Our lawyers were now moving around the globe. If we could marry opportunity in one country with equity in another, we could enhance both our bottom line and our reputation for being resourceful.

As our mining and energy groups became more focused on Colombia and Brazil, the Toronto Stock Exchange was focusing on making Canada a world financial centre for these financings. Steve Vaughan was the father figure for the mining group, and we added to the expertise by hiring a respected mining engineer, Wes Roberts. Our teams were commuting far and wide to look at resource projects that could be financed in Canada.

Guy hired Jacques Lamarre, former CEO of international construction company titan SNC-Lavalin. The news made headlines in the local papers in 2010 and was viewed by the media as a coup. This was all before SNC was to endure its own international corruption scandal. I recruited Igor Abramov, a veteran of the US Department of Commerce, who had incredible contacts in Kazakhstan, which were important for our mining practice and for a critical mediation that Mr. Chrétien and Kip Daechsel successfully negotiated. Peter Gall introduced me to Jessica McDonald, the former deputy premier of British Columbia, who at one point had run the entire civil service of the province. Peter had convinced Jessica to seriously consider joining us after she left government. Jessica was not a lawyer, so she could not practise law, but Peter was enamoured with the notion of the new consulting practice and was confident Jessica had the talent to help us build it.

At Peter's insistence I flew out to Vancouver to meet Jessica. I was immediately struck by her intelligence and the light in her eyes as she explained what she had accomplished in government. She also had a vision: she thought there was a unique possibility to affect change in the relationship between government, aboriginal communities, and business in BC, all of which were codependent in the ongoing development of the province's natural resources. While I had intended to keep the meeting short and head back home, I found myself instead arranging for her to meet other partners in Montreal. I felt that Jessica might be onto something of considerable impact, and the combination of her determination, energy, and contacts suggested she could be the right person to build the west-coast division of our consulting practice. Our business model for consultancy was still in its infancy, and I felt that if Jessica could be successful out of Vancouver, she could eventually run the entire process nationally and perhaps one day globally. At Heenan Blaikie we preferred to start with small steps on new initiatives, and once convinced we had the right people in place, we grew aggressively. In my mind this was the future of this practice.

I'm a big believer in the power of hiring the right people. Jessica had a proven track record in leadership, and she possessed something I'd seen in David Stratas, Ahab Abdel-Aziz, Peter Gall, Danny Kaufer, and others. It was an iron will to succeed regardless of what the facts might suggest. The plan for HB Global could take a number of years and would involve experimenting with various consultants with varying expertise, but I believed with Jessica at the helm we had a good opportunity to build something unique. I also hired Keith Stein, a lawyer who had been a right hand to Frank Stronach at Magna International. This was a gamble on my part. No firm would have hired Keith for his legal skills since he had little experience as a practitioner, but he understood how to make a commercial deal happen and he was very well connected in the business community. Keith demonstrated a unique rainmaker ability—rare among lawyers—that attracted all kinds of new files for our commercial group. He excelled at forming a team of high-functioning lawyers around him to perform the legal work for the numerous clients he brought in.

In Ontario Ahab had been running a large arbitration for a number of years that had consumed significant resources of our litigation group. He could see the writing on the wall and knew that this file would be completed by the.end of 2012. He was convinced the future was in international nuclear-plant financing, so we formed a team, using the counsel of Don Johnston and the services of Bruce Johnson, an associate with great promise as a business developer. This was Bruce's second career; he had started out as a film producer, where his claim to fame was the production in Canada of a *Dennis the Menace* sequel. The first movie, produced by John Hughes in 1998, grossed over $100 million. This one turned out to be a dud and shortly afterward Bruce made the shift to law. Bruce also had a close personal relationship with Bruce Hartley in Ottawa. Hartley had been Prime Minister Chrétien's chief handler for many years and continued in that role in the firm. Part of Bruce Johnson's unusual talents would see him acting as Mr. Chrétien's advance man on his trips across the Middle East. He had the chance to meet and form connections with many of the royal families from Doha in Qatar through to Riyadh in Saudi Arabia.

Ahab saw the raw potential in Bruce Johnson and latched onto him. Within a short time, the two were working on potential bid opportunities in Romania, Turkey, and China for nuclear regulatory advice tied to potential financings. We participated in joint ventures with some of the leading nuclear technical experts and were competing with some of the largest law firms in the world for these files. Only a small number of international law firms were involved in this lucrative work. We were dreaming big dreams about becoming a nuclear regulatory powerhouse (and this was all before the Fukushima nuclear disaster), but Ahab had the technical skill and knowledge to lead these files and Bruce had the knack of being able to access almost anyone in government in those countries. We were planting the seeds for the day that we would join the league of elite nuclear regulatory law firms. This was fascinating given that as little as three years earlier we did not have a shred of talent of this nature anywhere in the firm.

We were about to head into a new era at Heenan Blaikie, filled with leadership change. The world of legal services had shifted beneath our feet, and we were making adjustments to remain competitive on a global basis. However, many of the fine decisions that Guy and I had made in almost fourteen years of managing the firm were beginning to be overshadowed by the mistakes, which earlier in our leadership would have been forgiven or overlooked. The law of averages—that one out of four decisions was bound to be wrong—was catching up with us big time. A few failed lateral recruitments came first. Paris was second. Jacques Bouchard's distraction in Africa would prove to be the third. Against this backdrop, our global and consulting aspirations were becoming a source of tension among the partners, because we had failed to persuade them of the wisdom of our vision.

14

CHANGES IN LEADERSHIP

Guy announced his resignation to the Executive Committee in December 2010 and to the partners in January 2011, giving us a year's lead time. The process of replacing Guy as managing partner followed the theory of good corporate governance but had Roy's imprimatur. For the first time since we had assumed our roles, both Guy and I were excluded from an important process of the firm. To maintain the independence of that process, the incumbents could not be involved in choosing their successors. Roy had decided that his final acts as chair of the firm would involve leading the Executive Committee through the process of replacing both Guy and me and eventually him. Roy, however, was a visionary with little management skill. Had anyone canvassed Peter Blaikie about this, he might well have bellowed, "Roy, you're out of your mind if you think this is going to work with you in charge."

The Executive Committee began establishing the protocol for replacing Guy by first searching for Montreal candidates. The process suffered from three perceived problems: communication with the other partners was insufficient; the process took far too long; and many partners, particularly in Toronto, felt that for a national position there was not enough consultation. Whether this latter complaint was true became irrelevant because perception overwhelmed reality. The Executive Committee alienated itself from the rank-and-file partners in Toronto, some of whom cynically believed that with Roy running the process they would be getting Roy's choice of candidate.

The problem that ultimately unfolded would have been obvious to any competent corporate board of directors. We were an organization with annual billing that exceeded a quarter of a billion dollars and employed over 1,100 people. We had quadrupled in size since Guy and I took the reins. What business organization of that size and scope would hire a lawyer with no management training and little leadership experience to run their business? Only a law firm would contemplate this as normal behaviour. After all, no one understands lawyers better than their own kind. We also have a tendency to believe we know more about everything to do with our business, whether it relates to human resources, business development, collection of accounts, or any of a dozen other issues. Name the subject and most partners will assert that they can handle a problem better than their trained staff.

You would think, at the very least, that if we were resolved to have two lawyers replace Guy and me, that we would have our eye on the probable replacements well over a year in advance and send them out for leadership and management training. Harvard Business School executive leadership training is world-renowned: an expensive investment, but is that not what we instinctively should have been doing? McCarthys sent Marc-André Blanchard to study leadership and strategy before he took over as their CEO a number of years ago. After a very successful run as their leader, he recently retired to become Canada's ambassador to the United Nations. Yet not too many Canadian firms would make that sort of investment, which is shocking to consider. The thought certainly didn't occur to anyone at Heenan Blaikie. Perhaps we were spoiled, though I did take the

Directors Education Program offered at the University of Toronto's Rotman School of Management, which helped focus my own strategic thinking both as managing partner and as a director of Lions Gate Entertainment Corporation. At one point I suggested it to Guy's replacement early in his term, but it would have meant investing considerable time away from the firm.

— • —

The list of candidates in Montreal was impressive. The Executive Committee chose an eleventh-hour entrant in the race, Robert Bonhomme, whose selection was then ratified by the partners. Robert had joined the firm as a student wunderkind in the labour group in 1981, shortly after I started. Brought up in the richness of the firm's values, he was promoted to partnership a year ahead of his peer group. Robert specialized in the termination of executives and was recognized as one of the leading lawyers in that field in Quebec, publishing and speaking regularly on the subject. Over the years his practice blossomed, and he had a small team beneath him running a part of our employment practice. Tall, attractive, and charismatic, he was well liked. Robert would probably acknowledge that he was smarter than most people, and if given the chance to either speak or listen in a conversation, he would usually be the speaker. Listening was not his strong suit. He had developed theories about how the world worked and never shied away from sharing them. He was an alpha personality who made up his mind thoughtfully, but once he had made it up, he was rarely open to suasion. Though he had no management experience in the firm, he was a quick study, a diligent student, and a dynamic personality.

Like many Greek heroes, Robert's great strength would also prove to be his tragic flaw. Once he had established a goal, there was no moving him off the course. This trait had served him well throughout his entire career, but at a future moment, when heart would have to prevail over logic in order for the firm to survive, his rational mind would not get out of the way.

While he was still contemplating whether to throw his hat in the ring, Robert and I had dinner together. Though we had been partners for years, we really knew little about one another beyond the superficial, though we each respected one another's accomplishments. He wanted to get a sense of what my job entailed and, if he were selected, what it would be like to work with me for an entire year before my replacement was named. He would be walking away from a very successful practice into a new challenge, and he could not begin to comprehend what the implications of that might be for his future. I was satisfied that whatever decision Robert made would be well thought out. I left the dinner feeling that we could work together, and that if he were selected to lead, the firm would be in capable hands.

As it turned out, Roy had been warned in summer 2011 by a few labour department partners that they felt Robert was not a good choice for the job. They felt he could be divisive at times and had a hard time taking advice or listening to the views of others. By that time, however, Roy had made up his mind.

— • —

Robert and I were thrown together faster and more dramatically than either of us expected. In late October Jacques Bouchard had been approached by a freelance reporter to comment on an article he was writing about Ari Ben-Menashe. Ben-Menashe was an Iranian-born Israeli national living in Montreal who, for a brief period, had been a client of the firm. A business associate of Bouchard, he was a colourful character. A Google search on him revealed that he had served in Israeli intelligence for ten years, though a contact at the Mossad denied it; may have had some involvement in plots to assassinate Robert Mugabe; might have served some time in US prison; and had been debriefed by the Canadian government on security issues. He had international government contacts in Russia and Africa and was reported as the source of information concerning the Arthur Porter scandal in Montreal. He may have been involved in arms trading on behalf of various governments. There was no certainty about which portions of the story were true. After consulting with our firm's public relations expert, Guy approved the interview and sent one of our counsel along to sit in to make sure no confidential client information would be disclosed.

On November 1, a few days after the interview, Guy and Jacques happened to be in Paris for meetings. Jacques advised Guy that he needed to make some disclosures about the depth of his relationship with Ben-Menashe, which Guy guessed was a result of information that the reporter already had in hand. They met on November 2, and Guy was shaken by what he'd learned. We spoke when Guy returned six days later, and I concluded that we needed to advise our partners as soon as possible. Guy wanted a little more time to gather facts before convening the partners. I was convinced to wait until the following week. In hindsight that was a mistake.

On November 12, 2011, an article appeared in a Saturday morning edition of the *National Post* concerning the activities of Ari Ben-Menashe and Jacques Bouchard in the Central African Republic. The article shook the foundations of the partnership. Fortunately most of the business community missed it, but the fact that our partners woke up to it set in motion a viral reaction to what was perceived as bad press about the firm. The story related to Jacques's involvement with Ben-Menashe in an attempt to sell helicopters (which were stripped-down former assault helicopters) and other heavy equipment as part of a financial aid package from the Russian Federation to the dictatorial government of the Central African Republic. The transaction, which we were well aware of, was never consummated, largely as a result of the controls our Executive Committee had put in place while we contemplated our potential involvement as counsel.

From my perspective the reporter's goal was to try to embarrass the firm, using innuendo to create some kind of link between former prime minister Chrétien, a transaction involving weapons, and an African dictator. Reporting on scandals sells newspapers. Many of our partners were upset about the article, believing the publicity tainted our pristine reputation. While we had done nothing wrong, and our controls prevented the transaction from going ahead, the mere fact that a reputable newspaper suggested we were involved in a negotiation to sell arms was very upsetting.

Based on what Guy had learned from Jacques just before the article was published, in my mind there was no telling what else Jacques might not have disclosed about certain international activities. This whole affair was a rare source of tension between Guy and me. I felt betrayed and misled and wanted Bouchard out of the firm immediately. As far as I was concerned, this man was no longer my partner. Though he had explanations for his behaviour, I felt he had abused our trust and was now misleading us further in an attempt to cover his tracks. Guy, on the other hand, felt we should complete a preliminary investigation before taking action. It would add no more than two weeks to the process. From Guy's perspective, Jacques's explanations might be credible, and he wasn't prepared to accept that "Jacquot," as he had affectionately nicknamed him, had done no more than exercise poor, though well-intentioned, judgment—certainly not without more concrete evidence. The revelations precipitated an internal crisis over how to handle the investigation.

The better part of 2012 saw Robert managing the crisis, which was driving a wedge between the two largest offices. Montreal was prepared to leave the entire affair to the Executive Committee and Roy to manage, while Toronto, with a far more activist reaction, demanded a complete internal investigation. Toronto partners prevailed, but inter-office fights always leave winners and losers. In this case the big losers were Roy, Guy, and me. Toronto partners insisted I advocate on their behalf to install an investigation team that was independent of management. Arguing passionately for this were David Roebuck, Wendy Berman, Don Jack, and Ahab Abdel-Aziz. Suffice it to say that the Toronto litigators, who had been counselling their own clients for years about how to conduct internal investigations, believed we should be following best corporate practices. Roy and the Executive

Committee, where the Toronto members were in the minority, felt this was a matter to be reviewed by the managing partners with direct reporting to the Executive Committee, where the matter would be handled discreetly. Roy did not want this to make waves in the firm, where a full independent investigation would involve thousands of hours. Roy had always maintained that the firm's energies should be devoted to competition to bring in new work, rather than navel-gazing into internal affairs. He felt the firm's internal counsel could handle this on their own, quickly and efficiently.

The Executive Committee, and in particular Roy, had underestimated the degree to which the temperature on the issue had risen in Toronto. The Bouchard debacle underscored a growing rift between Montreal and Toronto partners on a number of different matters, not the least of which had to do with the transition of the chairmanship out of Roy's hands and the lack of clarity around that process. We held multiple meetings on the subject of the Bouchard affair in Toronto. During the second meeting I could feel the hostility in the room building, and I sensed the more militant partners were on the verge of issuing ultimatums. I knew there could be no good outcomes. I could support the Executive Committee and the decision it had made to minimize the investigation, which I was bound to carry out as managing partner. This would mean ignoring the strong demands of the group in Toronto, in which case I would have little choice but to resign. Or I could fight on behalf of the views of the Toronto partners.

In life we sometimes face crossroads where we know the next step we take will send us in a direction from which there can be no retreat, and will entail eventual personal sacrifice. This kind of decision is made at a moment in time that forever alters the future course of events. I knew what I was supposed to do: listen to the concerns of the Toronto partners, convince them that I would represent those views to the Executive Committee, then come back to them with a decision—likely the one they were advocating. But that process could take weeks. They were burning with anger and frustration and determined to have their way—not eventually but immediately.

Would they have quietly gone back to their offices if I'd asked them to be patient? I thought it more likely they might start making alternative career choices, which is the way partners mutiny. We risked a great fracture in Toronto that could lead to an exodus of partners. If I assumed the role of advocate of the Toronto partners in my final year as managing partner, I risked losing my moral authority within the Executive Committee. I would be accused by the Executive Committee of not following process, of having committed to a result that only it could decide. I would also be confronting Roy in a battle of wills, and the personal damage could be extreme. Not a great way to head towards retirement.

At that critical crossroads in the meeting, I read the room and opted to fight the Executive Committee on the matter. I promised the Toronto partners that we were going to have an internal independent investigation. I committed to it, though I had no authority to do so and had no idea if I could bend the will of the Executive Committee to this point of view. That commitment put my back to the wall.

Having managed this crisis, I could feel the tension receding and my authority returning, just as a proposal from the floor had us considering who would represent Toronto on the investigating team. This was a question best left for later, after I had convinced the Executive Committee, but there was no slowing the momentum of this meeting. David Roebuck suggested Wendy Berman, who had the litigation experience. The partners wanted one more name. I was immediately reminded of a ditty from my high school yearbook, which I never understood before that moment:

Death and doom
Stalk the room
Rent a tomb
You'll need it soon.

A long, pregnant pause ensued, but no other volunteer came forward. Finally one of the litigators suggested Henry Bertossi. There were murmurs of approval around the room. Everyone trusted Henry. "I don't think I'm really qualified for this," Henry said quietly. "But if no one else will do it, then I'll volunteer." He was clearly reluctant. This was his ultimate sacrifice, taking on a time-consuming, thankless job. There was only one partner who I felt certain to the core would not survive this process and that was Henry Bertossi. As he spoke those words, I knew he was signing his own death warrant with the firm.

I felt nausea rising from the pit of my stomach. Regardless of the outcome of this investigation, the revelations that would emerge about the Bouchard practice and the inevitable confrontational process with the Executive Committee would tear Henry to pieces. I knew it with every fibre of my being, but I could do nothing to forestall his fate—and perhaps my own.

A few days later we debated the matter at length at the Executive Committee table. The debate was stormy. I expressed the logic and, more important, the emotion behind the views of Toronto partners. The Executive Committee finally relented, but not before I had exhausted every last ounce of political capital I had left in the firm. I felt passionately that I had saved the firm from catastrophe but not without a cost. To the extent I harboured any hopes of succeeding Roy as chair of the firm, they were dashed, possibly forever. There was no recovering from the damage I sustained at the senior leadership level, where I was seen as putting Toronto's interests above those of the firm; or within the Toronto office, where it had taken me far too long to achieve the desired result. Years later Guy let me know that Roy was livid with me and the Toronto partners. Like Jean Potvin many years earlier, if Roy had had a gun he might have shot me through the head.

While we should have been spending 2012 planning for the future, building the roadmap of succession and a future of the firm for the next five years under completely new leadership, most of the year was spent managing the intense partner scrutiny resulting from the internal investigation process. In his final year as the chair, Roy's worst nightmares were being realized. Rather than fighting the competition, we were taking the year to shine the light on ourselves, so consumed were we in getting to the truth of what had happened in all of our international operations.

This also meant that Roy, who was now seventy-six, after years of slowly divorcing himself from the affairs of the firm had now solid-ified his grip, to the chagrin of many of the partners, particularly in Toronto. This was Roy Heenan's firm, so it would be handled Roy Heenan's way. Many wondered whether Roy was doing this to pro-tect the firm or his personal reputation. Perhaps in his mind, as the founder, the two were indistinguishable. Bouchard eventually and inevitably resigned from the firm, but not before the damage was done. While this damage might have been rooted in his untrustworthy behaviour, it manifested itself in the way we began to deal with one another. The subtle differences in world view between Quebec and the rest of the country were now magnified by anger and by mistrust in the approach to cleaning up the mess left behind.

The transfer of power from Guy to Robert took place in this stress-ful environment. The topic dominated all discussion. Though the tribute to Guy's fourteen years of leadership at the partner retreat in January 2012 was touching, the underlying tension underscored the entire weekend.

— • —

My final year was spent preparing for a transfer of the management mantle to my unknown successor. Toronto partners had not taken well to the process employed by the Executive Committee, led by Roy, to select Robert Bonhomme. They wanted my replacement to be named by a national vote of all partners. In some firms this would be seen as democratic process. According to many governance experts, however, careful selection of a new CEO should lead to a better result than a vote. However, the Toronto partners prevailed in having a vote for my replacement, though it took almost nine months for the process to be instituted and completed.

Winter turned to spring and then summer. While half a dozen candidates emerged, the vote had not yet taken place due to delays in instituting a campaign and a voting process. I realized that I had seen this problem developing for five years and had squandered the opportunity to groom a successor who would accept the role. Had our partners seen a successor being prepared to take over for me, the outcome might have been different. It's not as if I was ignorant of the problem. I had my eye on a number of quality young partners and involved them in management, grooming them for leadership, but they were reaching the pinnacles of their careers with little interest in running the business. While all the candidates in the election had been partners for many years and bled Heenan Blaikie blue, the colour of our logo, there was no sense that any of them were particularly qualified for the task at hand: co-leading a mature and diverse organization through turbulent times in the legal profession.

Over the course of the year Robert had revealed strong views on the steps needed to move the firm out of the era dominated by Norm, Guy, and Roy and to establish his own vision. While we worked well together, there was no question he was chomping at the bit to take the firm in a new direction. He wanted to end all the experimentation, eliminate weak partners and associates, get rid of the consulting division, rein in all international activities, shed Paris, and focus exclusively on the practice of Canadian law. I was an impediment on that route. Robert knew he needed to wait for me to get out of his way before he began dismantling the various initiatives and visions that Guy and I had put in place over the previous five years.

Would we have been better off moving away from the three-headed leadership monster and installing power in a single CEO? Should we have contemplated bringing an outside CEO in to run the business? We had many years to engage in that debate, though Roy had never considered it pertinent. Now it was too late. We were going to have a national election to select the second co-managing partner, though we were still incapable of making a decision as to how to replace the chair.

While there were numerous candidates, there was only one Toronto candidate who seriously wanted the managing partner job and was prepared to campaign nationally to get it. Kip Daechsel had been a partner for many years, was the nicest guy in the firm, and could communicate in perfect French. In the early years he could get no respect from many Toronto partners, particularly in the labour group, who believed he would never be a great success. He surprised them all. His practice expanded, largely as a result of work with Mr. Chrétien on international commercial mediations. He had become an important rainmaker as a commercial lawyer and had sat on the Compensation Committee for the past few years, so he had learned the firm and its partners. The best years of his practice were now behind him, so it was the perfect opportunity to take on a new challenge.

But Kip had his drawbacks. He had never spent a moment of his career in management and he had no natural ease or facility with numbers, so the firm's financial statements were a mystery he would have to decipher. As well, his practice style was slow and methodical. This was an asset for a mediation practice, but how would it translate to a new role where he would have to make a hundred decisions a day, even on those days when crises intervened? With the advance of digital technology, clients were not the only ones looking for immediate responsiveness. Our marketing department, our business development coordinators, our student and associate development all required attention on a weekly basis, even if it was only for a five-minute session. Could Kip learn to respond to the multiple demands on his time? We had discussed these challenges while he was considering the decision to run. In the end, there was considerable support for Kip's nomination.

— • —

Robert, in the course of the year, proved to be a quick study, a tireless worker, and a man who enjoyed engaging in minutia. We saw this manifested in his relationship with our managing director, Danielle

Chagnon. Although Guy and I would hold sessions during which she would update us on her admin team across the country, we gave her space. We wanted a COO who would run day-to-day management, leaving us to handle the legal business. Everything relating to IT, finance, marketing, space management, and human resources came under her direction, and included a five-year process through which she had replaced all our administrative team leaders. She ran a loyal and high-functioning team with military precision and had learned to run both domestic and international operations with equal aplomb.

While Guy and I settled into leaving Danielle's world to her to manage, Robert arrived questioning every assumption, reviewing every procedure, learning the business from the bottom up. I respected the time and effort he was putting into the job. Danielle had to accept that her life had changed under a new and very watchful eye. Many partners had felt for years that we should replace Danielle with a more business-oriented chief operating officer. We had debated the issue at the Executive Committee. I was comfortable with the set-up and had no patience in my last couple of years to train a new manager. I felt it made more sense to leave that decision to my replacements, who would choose someone in keeping with their vision of how the firm should be managed.

Guy wanted Robert and me to address the sagging confidence that our partners were experiencing from the loss of trust in our international operations arising out of "L'affaire Bouchard." We had learned lessons along the way and needed new processes to improve transparency and add operating controls so this could never happen again. Guy, now retired from his role as managing partner, volunteered to chair the committee, to be composed of partners who had varying views on the importance of international work.

Unfortunately for Guy, many partners blamed him personally for the failure of oversight that had led to the embarrassing revelations in the *National Post*. While this was neither fair nor accurate, perception again trumped reality. Many partners believed that the credibility of a committee led by Guy, despite its good work in emphasizing codes of international conduct, was completely compromised. For some partners the international committee became a symbol of failed leadership. Others simply wanted no part of anything outside North America. In many respects I believe this age-old approach of limiting our boundaries reeked of short-sightedness and xenophobia, because for many years international firms had been carrying on business in remote corners of Africa and South America, which included countries where the rule of law barely existed. Now China was beginning to open its doors to the world, and in order to remain relevant we needed to continue to explore opportunities abroad.

— • —

Launching into this inevitably short relationship with Robert, I felt a new strain in my life. For years I had come to trust Guy with every thought of mine, regardless of how esoteric, silly, stupid, funny, or childish. Our conversations over the years reduced our stress and allowed us to complain about lawyers, staff, and partners. We both believed laughter was an outlet for tension and allowed us to get back to serious decision-making. I could not immediately take for granted that Robert would react the same way. I could trust Guy, who was like my brother, with my life. I had no idea whether I could trust Robert with any of my thoughts. Underlying it all was the mutual knowledge we would be living with each other for only a year.

While Guy and I were both strong-minded we could reason with each other, and given enough time and patience one of us could convince the other of the merits of our argument. We used each other as sounding boards and often were able to see the error in our approach. Our personalities came from opposite ends of the spectrum, but we had learned how to adjust the volume controls. In fourteen years there was not a single moment when I thought Guy would ever do or say anything to knowingly undermine me. I didn't know Robert well; my natural inclination was to slowly build trust in the relationship, but we didn't have much time to work with. My network of confidants across the firm hinted that when Robert was frustrated with me he let it be known to others. I discovered that unlike Guy, when Robert had made up his mind on an issue, he was not going to be swayed. Ultimately, we lapsed into knowing that I could object, strenuously at times, and he would simply have to keep his checklist of unresolved items until the following January when I was gone.

In numerous situations Robert's views were not completely aligned with mine. He spoke to many partners about making changes in the way we operated. For example, he wanted to clean house of all the weak-link partners as quickly as possible. I had no argument with the principle, but I had strong views about how to proceed. The most difficult cases involved partners who no longer belonged at the firm due to flagging performance. We made a habit of allowing them to leave with dignity, and if that meant they stayed on an additional three to six months to allow for orderly transition, then the firm would pay those costs. These were situations that Guy and I made a habit of handling quietly by ourselves. The process might have been less cost-effective, but it was considerate of the partner's past contributions to our success. Robert had compiled his list, though, and was determined to speed through it. In some cases I made him wait.

I was not the only one feeling the strain. Years later Danielle Chagnon confided to me that Robert's approach was to deal directly with her administrative department heads, occasionally countermanding her instructions to them. She had hired and supervised every member of the administrative team. She considered Robert's approach as interfering in her role and undermining her authority. In her view this led to an inevitable demoralization of the group charged with running the day-to-day administration of the law firm.

According to Danielle, Robert's command of basic technology was lacking at the start. He had to learn to forward e-mails and many of his e-mail responses were dictated, typed by an assistant, and proofread before they went out. He double-booked meetings with Danielle's staff, leading them to conclude he was not focused on the issues. In Danielle's view he was spending too much time on the issues she had been hired to take care of and not enough on the directional issues that should have been his primary focus.

— • —

Much as I had been positioning myself to replace Roy as chair of the firm, the stresses between Montreal and Toronto had created backlash to Roy's leadership. Many partners wanted change and renewal. Elevating my status was not consistent with bringing in completely new management, which many partners wanted. Montreal partners such as Danny Kaufer and Gary Rosen were openly critical of Guy and me, and believed Robert represented a complete change in management philosophy, which they supported: a little tougher, and a little more bottom-line oriented. They wanted to clean house, undo the experiments, take the firm back to basics. I am sure they thought this would never happen if I could exercise any degree of authority.

Danny and Gary were not alone. Sonia Yung in Toronto, whose influence was growing, felt the same way, as did Jim Pasieka in Calgary. They all perceived the failed pharma addition, the expensive Paris office, the internal investigation that came out of the Bouchard affair, and the stresses under Roy's chairmanship as being attached to me.

I had dinner with Jim in Calgary that summer. It was a typically lovely evening filled with very good wine. Jim had a taste for the finer things. As we were relaxing, he became more serious. "Norm," he said, "the time is just not right for you to become the chair of the firm. I don't think the support is there."

"Really?" I was caught off guard. "I thought there was general support across the country for this. I'm pretty sure the smaller offices assume this is a natural transfer from Roy to me."

"I can tell you, Norm, that's not the feedback I'm getting. With all the tension in the firm right now, maybe it would be better to wait a year or so and let things cool down. I don't think it's a good idea for you to put your name forward."

It was a long flight back on the red-eye to Toronto that night. The disappointment sank in slowly and inevitably.

I have no idea how broad the anti-Norm sentiment really was, but there were enough key leaders not prepared to support me that it did not really matter what the rank-and-file partners felt. Did Robert want me to take on the role of chair? In our discussions he professed to being prepared to accept whatever partners wanted on the issue, though he reported back to me on conversations with other partners who advised him that I did not have sufficient support, particularly in Montreal. In my opinion, his friendly advice to me not to run for chairman had a personal bias. He had an agenda to execute and, in fairness, wanted the same freedom that Guy and I had exercised for so many years without interference. Having the former managing partner of the firm in the chair, there would be no escaping the probability that I would continue to call the shots on significant issues of direction. I had the ear of the Executive Committee and years of experience. For Robert there would be no escaping the possibility that all of his plans would require my approval.

Robert was headstrong; some would say too headstrong. He was comfortable pushing his ideas hard and steamrollering resistance. I respected him for that and if the roles had been reversed, I can't say I would have appreciated the incumbent looking over my shoulder. Though I must admit that was the relationship I inherited with Roy from the beginning of my term to the end.

Looking back, I can now see the irony in my own tunnel vision. As I watched Roy clutch at his authority in 2011 and 2012, oblivious to the tension it was creating in the firm, I had no trouble being critical of his insistence on staying on to the bitter end. Yet my attempts to remain in leadership beyond my December 2012 term were meeting the exact same resistance. The polite yet open rejection voiced to me by various key partners was a bitter pill to swallow. I couldn't see it at the time, but in my final year of management in 2012 I faced the same issues as a lame-duck US president at the end of an eight-year term. After fifteen years the partners were tired of me, particularly now that the end was in sight. As Robb Beeman so succinctly put it to me: "Norm, no one cares about any of the good decisions you made in the past. We're only focused on the mistakes."

I had experienced Roy's refusal to let go in his last two years, staying in the chair until he felt ready to leave, but long after many others, including me, believed he should have released us all. As it turned out, others were feeling the same way about me. Change is a healthy component of life, and it was time for me to adapt to a reduced role in the firm. Yet I was blind to this reality. I had persuaded myself that I was needed to replace Roy in the chair, and the more I considered it, the more obsessed I became in that quest. I broke every rule of the code of behaviour I'd lived by for almost twenty years in Toronto. Rather than allowing events to run their course, I actively sought the chair, ignoring the fact that the more I grasped, the farther out of reach it moved. By the end of spring 2012, while there may have been many pockets of support and even high approval for my years of leadership, the message from certain key partners was clear. It was time to back down and leave the firm in new hands. Robert and Kip would continue the journey, and the best I was going to do was observe the Promised Land from the wrong side of the Jordan River.

I sulked for a number of days as the rejection set in. Sharon was not the least bit surprised by the turn of events. She had seen this coming. It was time to accept that my career was going to have to move in a different direction, whether at the firm or elsewhere. The firm was going to move on without me, and I had to finally understand and accept that reality. I licked my emotional wounds and settled in for the final few months of my leadership career at Heenan Blaikie.

The appointment of my successor took much longer than the firm had originally planned, so Kip had very little lead time in 2012 to prepare for the January 1 changing of the guard. Robert had made good use of his one-year head start. He had dug into all aspects of the administration; he now had a command of the financial operations; and he had visited every partner across the country. While Guy and I had divided tasks and relied heavily on Danielle, Robert needed to be the master of everything everywhere. How would that work in a new relationship with Kip? Robert had prepared himself to run the entire firm. I was finally out of the way, but where would Kip fit into the equation, especially since he was a year behind on the learning curve? With some hard work, significant conversation, and a little luck, everything would work its way to a new equilibrium over the course of 2013. Based on that premise, Heenan Blaikie had always flourished.

The curtain finally fell on 2012. Given the bumps along the way, it all finished remarkably well. We had survived our internal investigation, and notwithstanding the squabbling between the offices, when our backs were up against the wall we had pulled together, dragged ourselves through a crisis, and come out the other side relatively whole.

— • —

The partner retreat in January honoured Roy's career as chair on Friday night and roasted me on Saturday. We had both come to the end of our respective terms in leadership. Heenan Blaikie was moving on. Despite what had taken place over the course of 2012, our camaraderie was reborn. One hundred and sixty partners crossing religious, ethnic, regional, and linguistic lines, young and old, celebrated together. We still genuinely liked one another. We enjoyed each other's company, and we benefited from the years of building links from Victoria to Quebec City that had allowed us to survive the kind of year we'd just experienced. Our imperfections once again became the butt of humour, and we were able to take an evening to laugh at ourselves in an impromptu roast.

Renewal carries with it new hopes and great challenges. Our 2013 partner retreat brought with it the aspirations of a brand-new leadership, prepared to steward the firm for the next five years. Guy had been out of management for a year and Roy and I were departing together, finally handing the reins over to Robert and Kip. Was I prepared for the handover? I couldn't see it at the time, but the firm and my place in it had become indistinguishable in my mind. We had grown up together as the firm had matured into a business that none of us could ever have anticipated. We were still a family with its love and dysfunction, its attractions and repulsions, its joys and sorrows.

I had yet to confront the reality that in short order my influence in the firm would come to an end. Perhaps this would have been an appropriate time to ride my horse off into the sunset and read about the exploits of the firm from my retirement. Even if I remained at the firm after withdrawing from management, could I really become a spectator while others steered it away from the course I had charted for so many years? A part of me had been amputated; perhaps it was the fist that had exercised its grip for so many years.

book III

FAILURE IN
LEADERSHIP
2013

15

THE **CRISIS** UNFOLDS

A professional services partnership does not run like a corporation, though in recent years some of the larger firms have become more 'corporate' in their approach.

A professional services partnership may have a person holding the title of CEO, or managing partner, but that person has nowhere near the authority of a corporate CEO. Not only are the partners the investors but also their work and client relationships are integral to the success of the business on a daily basis. In all but the biggest firms, most partners feel they have the right to participate in decision-making, so the managing partner must rely on the power and politics of persuasion. In our firm we were not simply resigned to that philosophy: we embraced it, all the way back to the days of Danny Levinson when I was a young lawyer. It was fair game to walk into my office or send me an e-mail to complain, though if you did, you might leave with the responsibility of fixing the problem you raised. Partners had the right and the expectation to second-guess, criticize, and affect decisions taken by the leadership they had elected.

Since the partners are owners of the business, they do not earn a salary. Instead they draw distributions regularly as advances from the partnership. Most firms will allow partners to draw a certain percent based on their previous-year or projected current-year earnings. Once the firm determines its profit for the year, the profit is allocated among the partners and any surplus over the draw is distributed. If the firm is financially healthy, the final distribution is made within a number of months of year end. Distributions made when expected make partners happy. If a firm does not have the cash to make a distribution, confidence is shaken.

A well-run corporation plans for the future. If it has a good year, it puts aside a portion of its retained earnings to fund growth or development. If it wants to expand, it raises debt or more equity from existing or new shareholders. By contrast, partners are taxed on their earnings whether or not the funds are reinvested in the business, so a professional services partnership distributes its earnings to the partners each year. Some partnerships withhold a small portion of the earnings, but not enough to amass significant capital to fund growth.

So what is it that holds this type of partnership together? Few firms offer pension plans upon retirement, so the notion that a lawyer would commit to the organization in order to collect a future pension does not exist. In most firms, when you become a partner you are obligated to become a stakeholder by investing capital in the business. In firms like ours, that amount could range from $100,000 for the most junior partner to as much as $800,000 or more for the most senior. Each firm has its own method and formula. Our capital contribution was adjusted annually up or down in proportion to a partner's increase or decline in earnings. Upon departure or death, the partner is entitled to recover the capital. In some firms all the capital is paid out quickly after departure; in others, like ours, it is paid out over time, possibly a year or two and often in instalments. Since departing partners can recover capital when they leave, the investment of capital is only a small part of the glue that keeps them from leaving.

Some partnerships protect themselves from partners leaving together in significant numbers for the same competitor by imposing penalties. Most partnerships have provisions that allow the partnership to delay repayment if there are liquidity issues. A departing partner might not like the rules, but he or she agreed to them on the way in the door. In the vast majority of cases, the risk that the capital will be lost or confiscated is very low, unless the business begins to fail. In most professional partnerships it is normal to see partners come and go. Sometimes key partners leave a firm to join a competitor, but you do not see law firms failing as a result. As long as a firm is growing, capital from newly admitted partners can form part of the base to pay out retiring or departing partners. Even small firms that have reached maturity will continue until a precipitating event, like the end of a lease, forces lawyers to consider their futures together. Lawyers are inherently averse to risk. Once they settle into an environment, even one they do not particularly like, they are inclined not to make a change. This final factor alone accounts for a considerable amount of stability—and unhappiness—in the legal profession.

For years I heeded the following adage: in a law firm the inventory walks out of the office every night between 6 p.m. and midnight. You can only hope it returns the next morning. That fact accounts for the amount of time I spent in lawyers' offices, making sure they understood what I thought were our key values and the important role that *they* played in supporting those values. Lawyers who feel appreciated and needed become much more resilient. When they stop feeling loved or valued, they start considering alternatives, just like a married couple.

Departing partners may express it in different terms: they don't like the direction of the business; they feel they may be better compensated elsewhere; a new client of another partner may create a business or legal conflict with their key client, obliging them to either leave the firm or lose the client. You may recall that this was how we recruited Henry Bertossi and his client Teva Pharmaceutical. He had an impossible conflict at his former firm, Blakes. Lateral partners who join firms in order to make more money are just as likely to leave a few years later for the same reason, like star baseball players. These departures, however, are considered to be normal business practice.

Great professional services firms have great leadership. A savvy managing partner understands how to lead, direct the board or executive to plan for the long term, manage the unexpected crises, remain consistent with the values of the organization, and make the difficult decisions no one else wants to make. The managing partner is not afraid to be wrong and understands that correcting mistakes is part of the job. A managing partner's most important quality is the ability to listen: listening rather than speaking and empathizing with a partner's problems rather than trying to fix them are critical attributes key to succeeding in the job. I benefited from professional coaching early on to improve this skill, which did not come to me naturally. But now my term was coming to an end, and the time for replacements was upon us.

— • —

We exited 2012 with the old guard stepping down and believing we had left something built to last: an environment where people came first, before profits, egos, or status. When we said that people mattered, this was not some facile recruiting come-on, but rather an everyday reality. Our people were excited to come to work in the morning. Above all, as Don Johnston and Peter Blaikie used to say, if ever there was a knife to be wielded, it would go into the chest, as had always been the case, and never the back—since we had each other's backs.

Our long marriage as partners, as in most other firms, had its ebbs and flows. We danced through periods where we were deeply in love, infatuated with our success, and through times when we could barely look at one another, so strong were the contemptuous feelings that briefly tainted our relationships. But like most organizations we toughed out the difficult days, always remembering our common values and our vows to weather the storms together, and we awaited the next period when the love would once again prevail.

The institution could survive the foibles of leadership because deep down we respected one another, and personal greed always took a back seat to the spirit of what we were creating together.

The keys that I handed over to Kip Daechsel unlocked some treasure chests, but there was no shortage of trap doors. Ahab's litigation file, which had delivered significant billing performance and fed the firm for five years, had just come to an end. The many lawyers who had devoted their lives to the case had to be reintegrated into the general practice, a process that was likely to take some time. We had endured a similar experience with our litigation group in Montreal a few years earlier. One of our young litigation partners, David Joanisse, took over the leadership of the group to manage the process of reintegration and, in some cases, departure from the firm, while other areas of the firm picked up the slack financially. David Roebuck had been a shining light for our practice; he had delivered important clients and files while training a new generation of commercial and securities litigators. But David had cancer and it was now entering its final stages. Some of the partners in the group would leave the firm, having realized that an important source of referral work was no longer going to be available.

Furthermore, the process of dealing with the Jacques Bouchard matter had left fractures between our two major offices. Time and wise leadership were needed to salve the wounds.

At the very end of 2012 Henry Dinsdale and Jeffrey Goodman announced they were leaving the Toronto office for a labour boutique. Though Brian Burkett and Doug Gilbert had built a solid core that could withstand the departure of two senior-level partners, it was still a blow. Were they leaving out of concern that the direction of the firm was becoming too diversified? They told me they had become disenchanted because the firm seemed to be headed in a direction that would de-emphasize the importance of their group. Or was it simply a matter of a better financial offer?

The Paris office was heading closer to profitability, but it was still not meeting expectations. Europe's slow recovery after 2008 and the gradual slowdown of the Chinese economy, which had been a huge consumer of resources and an engine driving profitability for many businesses globally, were impacting our economic performance, which continued to be a sore spot for Jean-François's group in Paris and for our partners in Canada.

Strong and united new leadership was the remedy for all that ailed us, as it is for every professional services organization.

FEBRUARY 2013

The phone was no longer ringing and my e-mail volume had slowed to a trickle. My calendar was empty, and the meetings and unscheduled visits for advice and direction had ended. In the span of thirty days I became yesterday's man. I had no access to daily financial information—I'd been cut off. A month earlier I had my hand on the pulse of this living, breathing business, my every sense engaged at all hours of the day and night: on call for emergencies from Vancouver to Paris, making hundreds of decisions a day. Now I had become a rank-and-file partner. My job was undefined and I had to rebuild a law practice. Is this what I wanted? Should I have remained or gracefully exited the firm for new life challenges? I polled clients, all of whom recommended that I take a year to observe and reflect, not make any rash decisions, and retreat to the role of *consigliere* for clients and within the firm as and when Kip sought me out. In twelve months I would decide how to reorient myself. In the meantime I resolved to follow the formula that worked effectively for most of my career: "Don't chase the first opportunity. Let the right one approach you." I needed to rediscover who I was underneath the mask of past achievements and without the identifying cape of managing partner.

February and March 2013 were particularly slow months for the firm, so much so that the entire first quarter had been the worst in our history. From my vantage the entire Canadian legal economy fell off a cliff on New Year's Day. After a robust fourth quarter in 2012 M&A came to a halt at the end of December. Commodities prices slid and Chinese consumption was in serious decline. The banks were no longer lending other than to renew lines of credit and borrowing facilities of existing clients. Little borrowing was available for corporate expansion. In this type of economy businesses fail, so there would normally be plenty of insolvency work, but the banks were seeking to avoid client defaults and not executing on non-performing loans. The workload of commercial lawyers ground to a halt, not just at Heenan Blaikie but around the continent.

The cycle was not going to go on forever, but I thanked my lucky stars that my term as managing partner had ended in December. This market, which would continue through April, was every managing partner's worst nightmare. How do you keep lawyers calm in a tough economy? Busy lawyers may worry about workload and stress, but they have no time to complain except about how busy they are. They put aside their natural insecurities. Lawyers with time on their hands are management's worst nightmare. Like dogs who run in circles, pee on the carpet, and chew on the furniture when they haven't been walked in the morning, lawyers with nothing to do discharge surplus energy by engaging in destructive activities within the firm. They have the time to second-guess every decision, gossip in the hallways, and exchange views on who is responsible for the problems of the firm.

This baptism by fire that Kip and Robert faced together required them to keep the partners calm and pointed in the right direction until the cycle finally turned for the better. The firm had never endured four continuous slow months, but we were not alone. Most of our competitors faced the same challenges. The situation called for a steady approach, serenity to wait out the tumult, a well-executed internal communication campaign, and two managing partners who were very visible. Partners needed to see the leaders presenting an optimistic yet realistic face. We had endured many crises in the past with Guy and me projecting that confidence in the future. We just needed to climb out of this trough together.

— • —

The first quarter of every year at Heenan Blaikie is dominated by compensation, and 2013 was no different. In the previous couple of years the Compensation Committee had become far more activist oriented and had added the assessment of all counsel arrangements to their traditional responsibility of compensating partners. This increased their workload. On a more practical level it also had partners inquiring into every economic relationship in the firm, including our arrangements with everyone from Jean Chrétien to part-time counsel and young contract lawyers. While most partners didn't care, believing they had delegated that responsibility to management, the activists saw this as a victory and contended they were uncovering the "culture of secrecy" that surrounded all the "special arrangements" in the firm. Although in my view this was complete nonsense, repeated often enough, as with all other propaganda, it became true. In Montreal, in particular, partners were repeating these rumours as if we were finally emerging from a Soviet-style era of secrecy, which the Compensation Committee would be replacing with our new style of glasnost.

The committee insisted on meeting with virtually every partner and counsel, adding countless hours to this non-revenue-producing activity. This led to both managing partners being consumed for well over two months in an enormous process.

— • —

Something more basic was happening in the compensation chamber. I had begun to note in my final year as a member of the committee in 2012 that there was a change of atmosphere in the room. The committee was no longer a welcoming forum for many partners. As noted earlier, compensation strikes at the heart of the insecurities of each and every partner, and for many the process is an intimidating experience. All partners wish to present their cases in the most favourable light, and some occasionally stretch the bounds of credibility.

One of the members of the committee from Montreal, Gary Rosen, was a tough litigator and a dedicated partner. Gary had been a candidate for managing partner in Montreal and had very fixed views on what was wrong with the firm and how he was going to change them. Guy put Gary's name forward when a Quebec vacancy opened on the committee a few years earlier. With Guy's endorsement, Gary ran unopposed; it is unlikely that he had enough support to win an election. Gary could be a polarizing force, although the positions he staked out always put his interpretation of the firm's interests first. While his views were often in the minority and thus usually taken with a grain of salt, his presence on what was arguably the firm's most important committee sent a message to partners. He came to each compensation interview well prepared, challenging assumptions, and aggressively counterattacking. That aggressive approach was noted by many unhappy partners, who bore the brunt of his talent for incisive cross-examination.

From what I gathered, 2013 was even worse. Many partners left their meeting with the committee feeling they had faced the Spanish Inquisition. Robert and Kip were exercising little moderating influence on the proceedings, and many partners were so upset that they vowed never to return to the room. Outrage was building among the rank-and-file partners. The process had become unpleasant, with a hard edge that, without being so intended, was perceived as meanness.

I did not recognise it at the time, but if the Bouchard internal investigation had strained the bonds of our partnership through 2012, the compensation process was beginning to tear at its fabric. This new anger and mistrust was engendering a perceptible change in values. Profits were beginning to trump people. This is not to say that the concept was wrong-headed: "Rid the firm quickly of the poor performers; revel in our excellence; clean house; get rid of the mistakes; and do it all quickly." It all sounded good in theory. Robert's group of followers had been advocating for this for years. As we later discovered, it did not work out so well in practice.

Meanwhile, the market for legal talent had grown more competitive in a very tough economy, and headhunters actively solicited lawyers with big practices, offering them large sums to move and solve the problems of other firms. Cherry-picking season was underway, and every high-performing partner was fair game. The committee made the strategic decision to protect the top-end-performing partners, offering them the maximum possible permitted in our system, so not everyone was unhappy with the results! With partners who were performing below expectations, however, the committee drew a consistent hard line. It made deep cuts, sending a message that those partners, perhaps seven or eight in number, were on thin ice. The committee was blunt; it was time for those partners to leave, or slip through the ice and drown.

—— • ——

This was not in keeping with our tradition. Certainly, compensation was about money and reward, but if someone was no longer of value to the organization, I always thought it best to visit them in person, laying out the reality and helping them with their career plans. Ideally, compensation is the art of managing rewards and egos; showing respect, regardless of outcome; and creating a process that not only is fair but also appears to be fair. This principle of fairness is drummed into lawyers beginning in first-year law school. By contrast, envelopes at the end of March delivering the message that the recipients' incomes had been reduced could be seen as cowardly and disrespectful, or at the very least insensitive, and hurtful to the partners affected, who in turn would hurt the firm. Other partners, who inevitably learned how their colleagues had been mistreated, would remember it, perhaps wondering when their turn might come. The damage to morale might not be visibly apparent but it was very real.

Between the high earners and the underperformers sat a third group, made up of mid-level partners, who were unlikely ever to climb to the top of the compensation ladder but on whom the firm counted for day-to-day production. They all had practices with a steady client following that covered the overhead and left a modest profit for the firm. They could be counted upon to deliver consistent performance.

Some had wonderful reputations in their practice areas and brought distinction to the firm. All they wanted was a demonstration of a little respect and love. They knew their value in the market, were regularly solicited to leave, but would always feel the gravitational pull holding us together—at least as long as they felt needed. Their income levels rose and dipped, like corks floating on the waves of the firm's economic performance.

While the committee stretched to reward the high performers, they taxed some of the mid-level partners. Each partner had a sense of the high end and low end of the compensation they could expect. Some were downgraded to just below the low end of their expectations, in some cases by as little as $10,000. However, coupled with the strong positive message sent to the stars, this move sent a powerful negative message, whether or not intended. Some partners felt disrespected. Their diminished compensation suggested that the committee saw them as having diminished value to the firm, and that the new managing partners endorsed this view. This response might have been irrational, or maybe they were overreacting. But most lawyers have fragile egos, and even small discrepancies between what they expected and what they got were shattering to some.

What was lost in the compensation process was the role that Guy and I had played in that room. It was a role we inherited from Jean Potvin and which he had inherited from Peter Blaikie, going back to the origins of the firm. The managing partner's role was to modulate influences, to understand that maintaining the harmony in a law firm wasn't always about being right. It was about understanding our partners, what made them tick, what motivated them, and what could demoralize them. Kip and Robert had not done well in their first test of leadership. In Robert's case many partners genuinely believed the committee was carrying out his intended plan: Drive out the non-performers quickly. Bet that the rank and file would accept a little less. Protect the high performers at all costs. In Kip's case, it was taking time to understand the difference between sitting on the committee and leading it. It represented the first in a growing number of situations where the politics of the situation were challenging him. Some will say he is the nicest and classiest man they have ever met. I will be among them. But those qualities are not relevant to this job.

SPRING 2013

Robert began to execute his plan to reduce the size of the firm, attempting to jettison lawyers who, simply put, were not profitable, and practice areas that were slow to develop. He needed to make it more efficient and higher performing. For many years we had a few practices where we earned gigantic premiums (such as my film-finance practice and Kip's mediation practice with Mr. Chrétien) that allowed us to achieve overall good results without having to confront these issues. In Robert's view this was a failing of Guy, Roy, and Norm. Perhaps he was right. Those days, however, were over and the axe came out.

It started with the consulting practice. Very quickly HB Global was reduced to a shell. Jessica McDonald, our Vancouver-based consultant who was growing our west coast business, met with Robert shortly after my resignation as managing partner. Robert made it clear that he had little interest in continuing an experiment that was not yet profitable. Jessica understood that the vision to build, which would take a few more years, was not on his agenda. She made other plans for her career and later became the CEO of BC Hydro. Robert viewed most of the consulting business as a black hole, and the patience to see what it might become no longer existed. Through the efforts of Martin Cauchon, a former federal Cabinet minister, we had been involved in ongoing discussions to open a small office—part law, part consulting—in Beijing. Robert scuttled that plan as well, and Cauchon eventually got the message and left the firm. Many in Toronto supported that result. They were unconvinced that any steps in China were worthwhile at that point and also questioned whether the team we had assembled to execute the plan was strong enough to succeed. Guy, Roy, and I originally believed we were on the right track, but few were sad to see the dismantling of the China initiative.

The perfect storm began to brew over the skies of Heenan Blaikie. The non-performing partners got the message: time to polish up their resumés and look for a new platform. Feeling aggrieved, they had nothing nice to say about the firm in their searches for new firms. Previously, they would have left under arrangements that included assistance from the firm, and we would have benefited from their goodwill. At the same time the offended mid-level partners began responding to the calls of headhunters. When partners of quality like Gavin MacKenzie, Jeff Citron, and Noam Goodman left the Toronto office together for Davis and Co. (which subsequently merged with DLA Piper), the rumour mills in Toronto began to hum.

David Roebuck, the soul of our litigation group, finally succumbed to the cancer that had ravaged him for the previous eighteen months. His loss hit hard. Few are the litigators of the modern age like David, who are also respected as gentlemen. One of the moral leaders of the firm had passed on. Between September 2012 and April 2013, four other key partners of the group departed, partly as a result of David's illness and partly over compensation issues. There had also been a slow but steady stream of departures from our labour group over the past year. Others who were unhappy with their compensation reviews were actively looking. Nothing we did could counter the message that the market took from these developments: something terribly wrong was going on at Heenan Blaikie.

When rumours of problems are circulating within the world of law firms, few partners of other firms show up with tea and sympathy. Instead the headhunters rush to the phones calling partners in an effort to extract any information or gossip that may help them pry others out the door. One headhunter in particular was calling partners whom she had recently placed in the firm to see if she could move them elsewhere. I had seen this disaster play out before when the vultures were swooping in on Goodman & Carr in 2007.

Robert keyed in on the fact that something unprecedented was going on in the firm. He felt strongly that drastic action had to be taken. His focus was on Toronto, where a large number of lawyers were working well below capacity as a result of several concurrent factors: the bottom had fallen out of the commercial world, we suffered a slower performance in the pharmaceutical practice, and Ahab's litigation group was in transition.

Robert smelled catastrophe and took immediate action in Montreal, imposing cuts on administrative costs and staffing, which sent local morale into a tailspin. In his view, cancer was growing in the firm and needed to be cut out quickly to save the patient. April's results were not much better than the first quarter's, and we had no idea when the curve would finally turn upward. Robert was certain, however, that we were rushing headlong into oblivion. The time to make bold, slashing moves was upon us. His tone was dire, but consistent. It was a tone that neither Guy nor Roy ever would have used.

Meanwhile Kip was four months into a new job. Given that he had only been appointed in the final quarter of 2012, he was pursuing his crash course in firm systems and operations. He had surrounded himself with a group of advisors in Toronto, who visited him regularly to interpret for him the goings-on in the hallways. He spent countless hours with Danielle Chagnon, poring over the financial situation and learning how to explain the financial statements to our partners. In a normal year this would have been time well spent, and few would have noticed. In the context of 2013 some partners began to wonder whether he was keeping apace of the problems the firm was facing.

In fact, Kip understood the gravity of the situation, but his personality was geared to taking a measured approach. Slow on the uptake, he needed to process and understand before taking action. That was his nature. He had also grown up in a system where he perceived that decisions were made slowly and thoughtfully. He was not convinced that immediate, radical surgery was in order. He was certain that life would eventually get back to normal in Toronto as long as no one panicked. So while the feeling in Robert's corner in Montreal was that Toronto needed to make some very tough decisions *now*, Kip balked. While the other Toronto members of the Executive Committee favoured a more measured approach, personal support for Kip was not unanimous. Kip was still not too worried, although internal rumours began to spread that he and Robert were at odds over the direction the firm should take.

Robert was sensing panic, and his group of advisors in Montreal pointed to the litigation and commercial groups in Toronto as the source of the problem. Jim Pasieka from Calgary had joined the battle at the Executive Committee and, perceiving a lack of action by leaders in Toronto, was becoming progressively more frustrated. Robert felt that if he couldn't convince Kip to take control of a developing crisis, he would carry the load on his own broad shoulders. Robert took his plea directly to the Toronto partners to convince them himself. The partners began to understand that the two managing partners were split on the direction of a firm in crisis. Kip did not agree with Robert's slash-and-burn approach, but he seemed unable to stand up to his Montreal partner. What's more, in some Toronto partners' view, Kip was weak and dithering, out of touch with hard reality. Actually the opposite was true. Kip had a very strong stubborn streak and a firm backbone. He might be slow to decide, but he would not bend easily on matters of principle. Robert was cut from the same cloth and could be equally unyielding. He had made up his mind about what had to be done and Kip was now standing in his way, so Robert would take his fight to the street and undermine Kip's position until Kip capitulated. Kip was not a street fighter.

As one Toronto partner later put it: "Robert sat down with me and explained that Toronto was now a problem; to save the business we had to swiftly make some severe cost and lawyer reductions. I explained to him the problems with that approach: that morale in the office would be flushed down the drain; that eliminating law-yers would also mean eliminating revenues. We were living in a fragile ecosystem and there would be untold negative consequences from moving so harshly and so swiftly. Robert listened carefully and absorbed everything I had to say. I appreciated that at the time. Then he left my office and completely ignored my advice. He had obviously made up his mind before he walked into my office."

It was not long before Toronto partners began to resent Robert's visits to the office. Regardless of how partners felt about Kip, they were unhappy with Robert's meddling in Toronto affairs. In short order Robert had become an unwelcome visitor on the Toronto premises.

Kip's work habits would slowly colour partners' perceptions of him. If Robert was a quick study, Kip was at the other end of the spectrum. The recent success in his career stemmed from his slow and methodical approach. His determination allowed him to master four languages and had yielded impressive results in his practice. He had been focused on promoting the firm's interests in Central and South America and had also established contacts in France, Spain, and Italy. He was a dogged and patient mediator. However, when these skills were applied to the current situation, which some were portraying as an existential crisis, they did not translate well at all. Kip could be an impressive statesman, representing the firm in all his elegance, but he could not manage the daily e-mail flow and he would disappear into meetings for hours on end while questions that demanded immediate attention would sit for a week. He had not come to terms with the need for a triage system that would allow him to process issues in a timely fashion, and the list of questions—small, medium, and large—piled up unanswered.

The sheer volume of meetings and trips to Montreal and around the country that Kip undertook prevented him from walking the halls in Toronto, a process I had found invaluable throughout my career. He was invisible to staff, lawyers, and partners, other than those involved in his routines. Kip did not seem to be around. At a time when partners were announcing departures, the office was missing a calming influence, someone who could put the news into context. More than anything else, people were just looking for a role model of confidence in the firm, that it was in good hands and that everything was under control. Partners like Mark Jadd and David Steinberg were providing ongoing feedback as to who needed a reassuring visit, expecting that Kip would act on those cues immediately. By the time Kip had gotten through his own daily agenda, there was no time left to do the little things that can add up to big gestures. A visit to a partner at a critical moment might be the difference between her walking out the door or committing her loyalty to the firm. It had sometimes driven my own advisors crazy that the words were barely out of their mouths when I would be on my way to make the visit. Talking to people individually had been a critical component of my management style, and it had gone sorely lacking for five months.

Meanwhile, as I had promised, I was staying out of the way. I had vowed to myself and to Kip to be available for consultation whenever he needed me, if asked. But partners wanted and needed a breather from me, and any attempt to reinsert myself would have further diminished Kip in the eyes of partners. I would also have been perceived as the former leader who refused to let go. I took to business development activities to rebuild my network of connections and assumed these dark clouds would eventually pass as Kip found his sea legs and matured into the role.

— • —

Jim Pasieka was now overtly pressuring Robert and Kip at the Executive Committee to take aggressive measures to deal with the problems in Toronto. If that meant further cuts to the size of the office, then in his opinion we should be getting on with them immediately. While Jim was still among the leading rainmakers of the firm, he had not been easy to manage in the previous eighteen months. At the end of 2011 he had been actively wooed by one of the major firms to become the lead partner in their new Calgary operation. We had leased brand-new, expensive space in the market, and expected Jim and the other partners to dedicate themselves to the success of the enterprise. Yet when the other firm came knocking, Jim took the meetings and peered over the fence at the green pasture they were offering him. I knew he wouldn't leave; I had sensed he needed Guy and me to show him some affection (as well as a path to overall leadership in the firm), which we did. It was no surprise to me that he let them know at the eleventh hour that his commitment to his existing partners was a bond he was not prepared to break. The gravitational pull of Heenan Blaikie was stronger than any force beckoning him to leave.

Six months later, however, Jim's team was purportedly considering abandoning the ship for other firms offering more money. Knowing only a few months were left in my term as managing partner, the Executive Committee believed this was a test for Robert to handle.

I knew that not a lawyer in the bunch would leave the firm without Jim. He was the source of the work, so the rumblings about the group departure appeared to me to be really about Jim reconsidering whether to stay. We were faced with deciding which of two bad alternatives would cause the least damage. Either we agreed to the increased payment demands and set a horrible precedent for the rest of the partners, or we drew a line in the sand, letting them know the partnership principles preventing mid-year adjustments would not be bent for anyone, and took the risk they would depart.

— • —

Robert ably averted the crisis, but the deal he negotiated saw us make unprecedented commitments to Calgary partners to keep them from jumping ship. The deal left a sour taste in the mouths of partners across the country. Feeling we were between a rock and a hard place, I had supported the deal, so I had to share responsibility with the Executive Committee for putting pragmatism above principle. We simply couldn't afford to jeopardize the entire office through such a significant loss of talent. There is always a risk, as my friends Brian Burkett and Henry Bertossi would say, that if we give in to pragmatism, we may discover that no governing principle remains to guide us, and we are left without direction. Who would be the next lawyers to put a gun to our head?

Eight months after Jim and company had been convinced to stay, Jim fired his first shot over the management bow, levelled at Kip: either make swift and decisive changes within the firm, particularly in Toronto, or watch Jim's back as he made his departure. Was this an idle threat, a way to vent his frustration with the firm's lack of direction, or was he serious?

The first four months of the year had me watching the firm from the sidelines. It was slowly driving me crazy and Sharon was bearing the brunt of my frustration. She reminded me that my term was over and with it my responsibility for the present and future. Like the parent whose children had grown up and needed space to take charge of their own lives, I had to step back and let the next generation take charge of its own destiny.

Cash flow for the summer was going to be poor based on weak first-trimester billings. We were due to make a significant partner distribution at the end of June, but it was no longer feasible; at some point the Executive Committee would have to notify the partners that the distribution would be delayed. I had lived that situation twice in fifteen years and managing expectations had been challenging, even though the delays were never more than three months. The delay in distribution was one more difficulty atop an increasingly precarious pile that Kip and Robert would have to keep in balance.

The Executive Committee met more frequently, digging into the day-to-day management of the firm to the point that the National Management Committee had become superfluous. We now had two groups looking at management issues and no one considering direction. Robert pushed hard for more departures to cut costs and asked the various groups in the firm to come back with their lists of those who should be shown the door. This might be standard procedure in a corporation where the CEO orders job cuts and the managers comply without asking questions. It didn't work in our law firm, where most department heads felt they lacked any such authority and chose not to comply. For years cutting staff had been a task the managing partners carried out with consultation, but never by delegation. To make matters worse, word got out that the Executive Committee was compiling 'hit lists' of personnel to be voted off the island in an HB version of *Survivor*.

None of the Toronto Executive Committee members had a taste for this game and Kip could not abide by this strategy. Some Toronto partners, particularly in the litigation group, which had been the heart and soul of the firm's financial support for five years, reflected Kip's view that those who were no longer performing needed time to re-establish themselves and had earned that right. But Kip was perceived as the obstruction on the path that Robert and Jim were certain must be followed.

The real question was how to address the growing unrest in Calgary and Montreal, where Toronto was felt to be 'The Problem' and at the root of every threat to the firm. The rift between Robert and Kip was now public. They openly disagreed in meetings. The Executive Committee was unable to manage their differences in opinion. There were now two leaders and no leadership.

— • —

In hindsight, in the course of leadership transition we had failed to address the basic issue of whether a system of co-managing partners could continue to function in the event of deadlock. Guy and I had made it look so easy over the years that everyone assumed this was not an issue that needed to be addressed, and Roy Heenan refused to do so while he had the chance. Now we were facing the dire consequences of a non-functioning leadership system. Would a single CEO have been the solution? Yes, I suppose, if we had chosen the right person. Other firms were suffering similar economic problems and managing to sail through the storm. In our case, two-headed leadership had become a recipe for disaster.

For years the Executive Committee had been the sounding board for new ideas and direction. While Guy and I would set the agenda for new initiatives and the direction of the firm, we would review these ideas with Roy and present them to the Executive Committee. Like a good board of directors, it would assess management's ideas, criticize them, improve them, and sometimes reject them as we charted our plans for the future.

The role of a successful board of directors is to assist management in developing strategy while staying out of operations. Their primary responsibility is to choose the right CEO to lead them, and then leave it to the CEO to run management. In many companies, when the board begins to take over the role of management, the entire organization suffers. The Heenan Blaikie CEO structure, which for years had functioned very well, was floundering through the management transition. The Executive Committee had no previous experience managing and, frankly, was not composed of the right talent to manage. Once the two firm leaders were in deadlock, the organization had no effective means to pull itself out of its tailspin. The economics of the firm were either going to improve quickly so the crisis would abate, or we were headed for drift.

The business cycle began to turn in May, and we finally believed we were heading back on track. Still, how you read the tea leaves depends on whether you are a pessimist or an optimist. Had we come around a corner on the way to a recovery so that within four or five months this nightmare would be all but forgotten? Strong voices in the firm led by Jim Pasieka, Robert Bonhomme, Danny Kaufer, and Gary Rosen believed that kind of speculation to be irrelevant: it was imperative to take action immediately. Meanwhile morale in Montreal had descended to an all-time low as a result of some sweeping terminations in that office, while tensions between the two offices had risen to an all-time high. Some Montreal partners were openly hostile to Kip, who continued to radiate positivity.

Riding on a crest of optimism and popularity, Kip had been tough enough to run an astute campaign to get elected managing partner. Once in the seat, his agenda was overwhelmed by events. While he may have been solid in conversation, he seemed to lack talent for reading a room, and showed little natural understanding of how to turn a hostile room to advantage.

— • —

The financial situation continued to improve but the frustration was increasing, as much for me as for other partners. Were we on the precipice? How could the situation have turned so badly so quickly? To Robert it was now clear that we were in crisis. Kip felt strongly otherwise and was convinced Robert was leading us to a catastrophe. Robert was no longer welcome by many partners in Toronto. I was not hearing much from Kip throughout any of this, but Robert called to see if I could intervene.

Robert was now beginning to advocate for a separation of the offices economically. In his view, if Toronto wanted to adopt its own approach to the current situation, perhaps the answer was to move away from a single profit pool in which all partners shared and replace it with regional accounting, with each region sharing only that region's profit. This idea was antithetical to every principle the firm was built upon and was being proffered at a moment when Toronto would be having a miserable year. Despite that fact, a number of Toronto partners were convinced that if we swallowed the bitter pill in 2013, when things finally turned around, the subsidization of the Quebec region that had been financed out of Toronto for much of the past twenty-three years would finally be over. I knew this was all short-sighted reasoning. Once the firm became balkanized we would begin to ask ourselves what was the point of any affiliation at all between the different regions. A form of 'sovereignty association' with Quebec might be the first step towards complete separation.

As the situation worsened, the Executive Committee became more engrossed with management to the point where our National Management Committee had become redundant. For years that committee had been filled with our best departmental coordinators. Now the Executive Committee had taken over and abolished the management committee, and while the Executive Committee included some great business leaders, they were generally poor managers. At one point I asked myself, "If the Executive Committee is spending its time managing, who is leading?"

Here we were, midway through a very difficult year, with leadership openly discussing whether the single partnership foundation on which the entire firm had been built should be reconsidered. The management structure of the firm had now been recast. Swiftly and without partner consultation, the firm's constitution was changing. Who, beyond Robert, was supporting these changes? It was not entirely clear. But as I would find out, other partners were engaged in discussion about what to change next.

The situation we faced in winter 2013 was horrible, to be sure, yet it was the same for all but a few law firms. We were not going through anything different than our contemporaries, particularly in the Toronto market. The smart firms were gearing up to raid the best partners from their competitors in order to boost their own results. Normally Heenan Blaikie partners did not respond to such calls, but this spring they began to do so. Some of them might have been frightened by the Bouchard affair, but in my view a lot of that dust had settled. What had not settled were the recriminations from disgruntled partners from the round of compensation reviews. If our firm mission in the past had been to leave everyone a little unhappy and no one unloved, the game plan had changed. Now we had high-performing partners relatively happy with their earnings, while a number of mid-level partners felt disrespected.

Robert was acting as if we were on the *Titanic* and he was trying to save us, and he let everyone know it. Robert rejected Roy's philosophy of tempering bad news and looking for silver linings. As a result, partners were overly nervous. Kip projected calm, but with Robert projecting the risk of a looming crisis, one of them had to be wrong. Which one? The only thing that partners knew was that others were beginning to leave. Under our partnership policy, if they left they would get their capital out in instalments over the course of a year or two. Of course that presupposed that the firm had the financial wherewithal to make the payments. The system was built to accommodate a small, though regular, departure of partners. It was not designed to accommodate an exodus. If the rumours on the street were true, however, the firm was headed for a crash and maybe the wise thing to do, if you had the option, was leave while you could still get some of your money out in instalment payments. The only risk you were taking was that if this turned into a run on the bank, you and everyone else would lose everything.

— • —

Something fundamental about the firm culture was changing, which we had yet to perceive. I am reminded of a meeting that took place in Toronto shortly after I became managing partner. Roy Heenan, Guy Tremblay, and I, along with a few key partners in Montreal and Toronto, organized a dinner with the leaders of Coopers & Lybrand. At that time they were our largest client and our auditors. This was a social evening designed to look for opportunities to deepen our relationship. After dinner we went around the table introducing ourselves and our business objectives with a view to finding some common ground. Roy began, explaining how "Heenan Blaikie is about the practice of law at the highest level in a collegial atmosphere among people who genuinely like working with one another. We take care of clients and one another and let the bottom line take care of itself." A few minutes later it was the turn of the chair of Coopers, who said, "We run a business with a view of maximizing our bottom line." He had nothing more to add.

The contrast was stark, but it said everything one needed to know about our two firms and how different they were. We were, perhaps, an unusual organization, one that sold itself to staff and lawyers as a firm where how we interacted with one another in the workplace came before everything else. This was the force of our attraction; this is what allowed us to survive crises, pulling together instead of pulling apart. We lived it and we breathed it for thirty-eight years. We always placed people above profit. In so doing we still managed to run a business that for four decades earned what we considered to be an entirely respectable level of income for our partners, our associates, and our staff. In a very short time period the paradigm for the firm was changing. Robert believed we needed to start putting profitability at the front of the line in order to save the firm. No one was psychologically prepared for this kind of shock treatment. We were drifting from our basic firm philosophy. Like chemotherapy, the proposed cure was killing parts of the patient.

I have always believed that the true test of partnership, as of marriage, is how you weather the rough times. It's easy to gloss over problems when things are going well. For better and for worse we struggled together over the years, celebrating our victories, licking our wounds over defeats, and never questioning our marriage vows.

In the tough times of 2013, though, the market stresses and our compensation process weakened the cultural glue that held the marriage of lawyers together. People no longer came first. We had moved the profitability cart in front of the horse. We were adrift, angry and upset. No one in leadership was talking to the troops, building up the morale.

I was still on the outside of the fishbowl looking in, but things were about to change dramatically.

16

THE SPARKS **REKINDLED**

For years my partners heard me repeat the same mantra regularly. The test of partnership is not how you celebrate the victories, or how economically successful you may be in the good times. Rather, the true test of partnership is how the partners weather the difficult periods. Do they pull together or do they pull apart?

This was the summer of our discontent. The rumours were circulating like poisonous gas on the street. Clients were asking us discreetly, "What's going on at Heenan Blaikie? Is it true you're going bankrupt? Should I be concerned?" While all our clients remained loyal, we could not have scripted a scenario with a bleaker appearance. Ironically, billing and work volumes were now steadily rebounding, and while we were going to miss our June partner distribution, the economic signs suggested that at this rate of recovery, the delay might be as little as four months. Unbeknownst to me and many others, Jim Pasieka had made good on his threat and was preparing to leave for McCarthys, along with most of his team. Jim's disillusionment with management, from his perch atop the Executive Committee, left Robert and Marcel

Aubut with a mission to talk him back in off the ledge. They failed
and he resigned, to the shock of many partners, me included. Five
partners in all were leaving—the same group for whom we had made
significant economic concessions a year earlier. They were prepared
to take the risk that they might not recover their capital. There was no
way we could afford to take this economic hit and at the same time
agree to a payout.

Mark Jadd phoned with the news at the end of the month. As I
felt my fury rising, I knew at that moment my self-imposed exile was
over. It didn't matter to me whether I was wanted or whether feelings
would be hurt. My life work was going up in smoke. I'd stood back
helplessly for six months. It was now time to take action.

I immediately contacted Robb Beeman, newly appointed head of
the Calgary office, who confirmed the story. The remaining partners
were numb and feeling betrayed, but had no interest in giving up or
giving in. They would scratch and claw to rebuild. Ed Wooldridge,
our young banking partner, was prepared to help Robb pick up the
pieces and shoulder the load. They were sure there was a silver lining
in Jim's departure: the door to recruiting was now open. Over the
past three years the office had contracted, and recruiting efforts had
been challenging. I offered my assistance to Robb in any leadership capacity that he saw fit. We'd been partners since the day I had
opened the Calgary office and we were close enough that he felt he
could be blunt.

"Norm, you may have done great things as managing partner over
many years," he told me. "I wouldn't be here today if not for you.
Understand though that there are a group of partners who've had
enough of you. All they remember are your recent mistakes. Now they
may not have been your decisions, they may have been Guy's, but
right now they're yours. They don't want you back." Perhaps Robb
was including himself in that group. Although I'd heard all this before,
when I was aspiring to be chair, it was still a stinging slap across the
face and a harsh reminder that I was still yesterday's man. But was it
enough to prevent my return from obscurity?

The Calgary bombshell was a blow that sent shock waves across the country. The Executive Committee sessions were sucking up enormous amounts of time. There was no end in sight to the misery. Panic and depression set in. I spoke to Sharon and I decided to take action. I couldn't formally intervene in this crisis, but I was not dead yet and I needed to take an active but non-threatening step.

— • —

A meeting off-site with a few key opinion leaders was the logical starting point, just to talk and share ideas. I had no agenda, no plan, and no scheme. Being so far out of the loop now, I also didn't have much information. All I had in my back pocket was instinct and experience, which were telling me we desperately needed to talk among ourselves. I began on safe ground by visiting Jon Stainsby, the head of our pharma group, as well as Allen Garson, Mark Jadd, and David Steinberg. They shared the same perspective: they were frustrated and angry and had no idea what to do next. There was nothing to lose in sitting down to talk. Mark agreed to recruit Kevin Rooney and Sonia Yung, while Jon agreed to speak to the litigators and Steinberg to the entertainment lawyers and a few other key partners. I asked the groups to select a representative handful of partners to discuss the problems. No management would be in the room, which would allow for open discussion. Within a couple of days we had a core group of twenty partners to attend an evening meeting in my dining room at home. The twenty were representing forty, which included younger and older partners, all of whom had considerable history with the firm. The 'delegates' would report back to their larger groups.

Adam Kardash felt his position on the Executive Committee conflicted with his attendance (not that there was any intention to discuss insurrection). The idea was not to create a Star Chamber to combat management; rather, we had to find a way to pull ourselves out of the tailspin that threatened to crash the firm into thousands of pieces.

The partners filed in at 7:30 p.m. on a warm summer evening. Sonia arrived a little early, announcing she was starving; Sharon fed Sonia dinner, telling her the food was leftovers when in fact it was Sharon's dinner. This was perhaps the ultimate irony. Our house had been the venue for our annual partner-and-spouse dinner each holiday season for as long as anyone could remember. They began as smaller, intimate affairs in the first week of December. Sharon would spend hours working out a menu for about fifty people. In December 2011, for the last party we hosted before I stepped down as co-managing partner, she insisted on holding it over two back-to-back evenings with seventy-five people attending each night. The ambiance was warm; the opportunity for partners, counsel, and their spouses to reconnect each year in the setting of our home had taken on a life of its own. For most, it was the highlight evening of the year: a chance for each of us to remember how special these relationships were. We might have grown from an office of four to over two hundred, but the ties that continued to bind us together were social and powerful. Sharon insisted on reminding us of this each year.

Convening in the dining room may have brought to mind better times; however, this night was all business, and once the discussion began the floodgates opened. Never had I listened to such dismay, anger, hurt, and frustration. We went around the table, people taking turns.

"The problem's in Montreal."

"The Executive Committee is lost."

"This was a legacy of previous management."

"Paris is a black hole of expenses!"

"No one is leading."

On and on it went for two and a half hours as they fed off one another's despair. They were all well beyond anger. Mark Jadd admitted that he now preferred working from home—a pall had descended on the office that depressed him as he drove into the parking lot. I could see the nods of agreement around the room.

They agreed on only one point: this was no longer the firm they had joined. We had been a firm that put a genuine premium on environment and values, and that actively tried to be different. We were now as miserable as any other law firm. Everyone was prepared to make a sacrifice to work at a firm with strong values that supported their individual dreams. No one was prepared to make any further investment in a firm they no longer recognized or felt part of. The alienation was complete. The firm culture had been stolen. It was gone, nowhere to be found. And each person at the table admitted they had an eye on the exit if not one foot out the door. The Calgary departures were the last straw: a sign of a firm that was lost, adrift, without direction; a ship dead in the water. Perhaps it was time to abandon it before it sank.

At 10 p.m. and in great distress myself, having listened without comment, I faced the room and asked a simple question: "What are we going to do about this?"

David Steinberg looked around the table. "I've worked with all of you for at least ten years," he said, "some as many as twenty. My legal career was reborn here, and there's not a person in this room that I don't love working with. I am not prepared to give this up without a fight."

He spoke for five minutes and reminded everyone of what we all found important. He reinforced what we all knew without having to be told. We had come to love working with one another. We owed it to one another to stick together and battle our way out of this corner. If for any reason it was too late to save Heenan Blaikie, or if the actions of others took that possibility out of our hands, then his strong preference was to keep this group together. We were, after all, the core foundation of the Toronto office.

David sat down and one by one the other partners were moved to respond. It was as if magic dust had been sprinkled in the air. They took their turns reaffirming their connection to one another. What we had built together was a bond that no one from Montreal or anywhere else could break. After forty-five minutes we concluded that as a group we would do everything in our power to stay together. No one would consider a job offer before the end of the next compensation review, which would take us to the end of March 2014, and for now we would put our heads down and fight to get through the second half of the year. We'd then propose changes to the Compensation Committee, which was still being vilified as a root cause of the social disorder.

We thought it would be a good idea to ask Robert not to visit Toronto, at least for the next quarter. Toronto had to regain control of itself. We needed to reintegrate Kip into that process and show the firm what Toronto intended to do to get back on course. We would stand together or fail together, but there would be no risk of further departures.

Everyone in attendance agreed to report back to the group constituents to broaden out the discussion. We had begun to trust one another again. I had not seen this level of positive energy in a room since our partner retreat in January. We left that night with a feeling of power and a sense of control over our destiny that until then had all but been abandoned. We were no longer going to stand by and watch while the firm was being wrested from our grip, though we did have considerable work ahead of us.

— • —

As word slowly seeped out over the following days about an important meeting that had taken place in Toronto, my next stop was to speak to Marcel Aubut, still recognized as a key Montreal leader. I explained to him that there was a new sense of purpose and responsibility in Toronto and that it emanated from open discussion and focus on the values upon which we had built this organization. If he wanted to accomplish a similar morale boost in the province of Quebec, he might want to take a page out of our playbook.

Marcel let me know that Robert had tried to tender his resignation and it had been quietly rejected. Robert saw no future in trying to work with Kip. It was an endless source of frustration. He was also beginning to doubt the future of the firm as a national endeavour. Perhaps the best way to handle Toronto, as far as he and a few of his supporters were concerned, was to cut it off. He could see only two possible routes to solve the problem: resign and step out of the way, or take on the entire mantle of leadership—because a system with two leaders was no longer workable if the two leaders could not agree on fundamental issues.

Marcel knew he could not allow Robert to resign. It would have been a show of complete non-confidence by Robert at a moment of growing crisis. Inspired by what I had organized in Toronto, Marcel now believed we needed to assemble the business leaders of the firm from across the country, outside of any management structure, to talk to one another, confront the issues, and resolve our differences. I admit I thought the idea of gathering forty or fifty partners together was practically unworkable, but Marcel was not to be deterred.

Within two weeks we had organized a sizable group of Montreal partners to visit Toronto for an afternoon, along with a few key partners from the West. I arrived at the afternoon meeting with great trepidation, as Marcel and I were to co-chair the event. Opening statements were respectful, but within minutes the tone changed. Many Montreal partners became hostile over Toronto's perceived fiscal irresponsibility. It seems that before they'd left Montreal, they had received financial information that was inaccurate and misleading. The assumption was that Toronto was bloated and not dealing with an overabundance of staff. In fact, the office had shrunk by 25 percent over the previous twelve months. Unfortunately, since some of those departures had been steady revenue producers, this had some negative impact on results. The perception that Toronto was not cutting fast enough was not only inaccurate but also the reverse of what was true. There was a growing risk that the continuous shrinkage in Toronto was causing us to shed too much too fast.

More than two angry hours passed before tempers began to subside. I watched as Kip confronted the hostile room. Although he approached the issues calmly, the points he insisted on driving home were not the ones partners were focusing on. So while the group was making progress, Kip was losing the group, along with his moral authority.

Though we could not get through all the issues, people were finally beginning to listen. We had made some headway in bringing down the walls of misunderstanding and recrimination. We agreed to speak more to one another outside of any formal committee structure and we planned for a second meeting at the end of the summer to continue the discussion. We also hoped to see economic improvement over the course of the next couple of months.

Robert's contingent, which included Danny Kaufer, still believed we should be continuing as individual operating units under the name of Heenan Blaikie. A growing number of Toronto partners, seeing the turn in the business cycle, were beginning to believe that our performance would continue to improve, and economically we might all be far better off without Quebec or BC. All this whispering of separation invited the question of how we would deal with our Paris office and the considerable counsel cost in Montreal and Ottawa that benefited the entire firm. Dividing us up would be akin to Canada agreeing to the sovereignty of Quebec. The division of assets and liabilities might sound simple, but in reality it would take years to unravel all the common threads woven over two decades together. As far as I was concerned, going down that road was not an option, and Marcel felt the same way. We had to march forward together or perish.

One of the few sources of inspiration over that summer and beyond was Calgary. By every objective standard the departure of the energy practice should have sounded the death knell for the entire office. Undeterred, Robb Beeman and Ed Wooldridge refused to acknowledge defeat, instead viewing Jim's departure as a chance to recruit and remodel the office, albeit without an energy practice. The space was expensive and needed to be filled quickly. Ed, a former football star, and a protégé of mine over the years, had longed to lead. Together he and Robb spent the summer rallying the troops. Robb strengthened the litigation component while Ed recruited a new real estate team. HB Calgary would henceforth be an office that incentivized opportunity and practice building. Given that the energy market would begin to collapse in the near but unseen future, the repositioning of the office was, in hindsight, timely. If we could rely on the same fire, intensity, and commitment from other sectors of the firm, we might steer ourselves out of trouble.

— • —

Ottawa had been galvanized in a similar fashion in 2012 after the departure of Ron Caza, himself a contingency-oriented lawyer, who had helped us build that office. Ron was the recognized leader of the office, and his support of minority language rights in Ontario was very appealing to our senior counsel, Jean Chrétien, and former Supreme Court Justice Michel Bastarache. However, the more senior Ron became, the more he felt compelled to take on underdog cases, many of them complex and all of them expensive for us to carry. As Guy and I became aware of Ron's penchant, we imposed all kinds of limitations on his ability to take in new cases. The amount of time and effort spent on non-paying files was sinking the office in red ink, and Ron realized that if he wanted to continue he would have to do so under his own roof.

At the beginning of 2012 I went to Ottawa to join Ron for lunch and waited for him to unload his frustration with the handcuffs we had placed on him. By dessert he was finally able to get off his chest that he needed to leave and open his own boutique to follow his dream. The separation was necessary but also painful because he left with a number of our litigators. However, Ron's departure allowed Pierre Champagne and Dan Palayew to step out of the shadows into leadership positions. Other young partners like Benoit Duschesne also rose to the occasion, taking over the important City of Ottawa account, and Claire Vachon, the leading light in our labour group, was relieved as the tension level in the office dissipated. Mr. Chrétien and Justice Bastarache also made adjustments to the new young leadership in the office.

There was much reason to believe that rather than Calgary representing a calamity, the future could—with a little heroic action from our partners and a little time—be brighter. We just had to find the will to continue and search for the light at the end of this tunnel.

Our satellite offices in Quebec City, Sherbrooke, and Trois-Rivières, which prided themselves on strong local management, continued to function effectively, while Vancouver was turning a modest profit under the watchful eye of Craig Munroe, a young partner who had taken over the management there.

Our problems were centred in our two major offices. By the end of July, however, it appeared that the worst of what the business cycle had to dish out was over, and lawyers had gone back to work. This was still going to be a 'big miss' year: all signs pointed to a drop in profitability in the neighbourhood of 20 percent. It couldn't have been otherwise given the sheer reality of fewer lawyers due to departures. We would all have to accept that we would earn less, though the reduction meant that most of us would be owed little after year end. Ordinarily during the course of the year the partnership advanced to each partner approximately 75 percent of the previous year's earnings. After completing the compensation process in the spring, we made adjustments and then paid out the final distributions. There would be little left to distribute after the 2013 year end, if the estimation proved to be correct.

The partners continued to meet regularly in Toronto over the next few months. Many of us were becoming convinced that we were now pointed together in the right direction, and we were engaged in more open dialogue. Disturbing rumours that Robert wanted to resign were still making the rounds, although Toronto morale had steadily improved since he stopped making trips to Toronto.

Were we deluding ourselves that the firm could be saved at this point? Were we past the point of no return? If we could have gotten past the leadership deadlock, if our leaders had dedicated their time and resources towards showing our partners that the cloud was lifting, that business was improving, that pulling together would lead us back to profitability, we may have had a chance. If they had only taken the time to listen to partners and to offer hope. Lawyers are no different than other animals. They thirst for leadership, and if they cannot find it at home they will search for it elsewhere. In his heart of hearts Robert simply did not believe the firm was viable. He also knew he could not work with Kip. With each passing month his view was solidified further. We no longer had role models to follow; consequently many left to follow other leaders elsewhere who offered hope and opportunity.

Sadly, as I had predicted to myself the evening of the fateful Toronto partners meeting that created the Jacques Bouchard investigation committee, Henry Bertossi was mentally fatigued from his eight months on the investigation and the accompanying battles with Roy Heenan. Henry grew increasingly alienated from the goings-on around him. It was no surprise when he finally announced his departure, for Miller Thompson, but it could not have come at a worse time. There was no quelling the daily rumours in the market of our inevitable decline. Partners, associates, and staff were bombarded by an endless stream of stories of our imminent demise. This sideshow was a distraction, and many outside the firm were wondering if this would become a self-fulfilling prophecy.

— • —

At the end of the summer Marcel and I took one final step towards attempting a rescue. The plan came together gradually and we did not share it with others, believing that if we planted the right seeds and allowed the partners to come up with the solution on their own and with our guidance, the solution and the firm had a chance. We understood very well that any plan perceived as being imposed by us was destined for rejection.

Key partners met once more at the end of August with Marcel in the lead, because once Roy had resigned as chair in January, he had essentially retired from any leadership role in the firm. Like me, he had spent the first six months of 2013 watching from the sidelines with growing frustration, though he was not returning (nor was he invited) to participate in a rescue mission. This had to be agonizing for him to observe.

Marcel and I had weekly discussions over the summer. We were developing a notion of how to bridge the morale gap between the two major offices and how to work around the ruptured relationship between Kip and Robert. We planned to create a working group composed of the four of us, with Marcel and me aiming to improve relations between Robert and Kip. We believed all of our partners would see this as a step towards improving morale. We understood that the partners did not want Marcel and me running the business for the long term, but Marcel and I felt this working group could carry the firm until we found a new CEO from industry to take over the ship. Regardless of how Kip and Robert might feel about this, we would be in position to either work with them or accept their resignations if they were not amenable.

Marcel and I had both reached the point where we no longer cared whether there might be some opposition to this plan. We just needed to garner enough support to approve it and allow us to move on. We saw what the future held if we did not proceed, and it was bleak. The key was to stabilize leadership, patch the holes in the ship, and keep the partners talking about the future.

The second meeting in our Toronto boardroom went considerably better than the first. We began to move towards a rapprochement, though no matter what Kip had to say, the tension in the room appeared to mount each time he spoke. Marcel managed the meeting with an adept hand, leading us slowly, inexorably, to the conclusion we sought: a resolution from the floor that Marcel and I be appointed—without title, role, or compensation—to assist Kip and Robert for the balance of the year. Essentially we were to become a four-person management team, reporting to the Executive Committee.

Alas, when Ahab Abel-Aziz stood up, I could feel the ghost of poet Robbie Burns lurking in the corner of the room, smirking directly at Marcel and me and whispering, "The best-laid schemes o' mice an' men / Gang aft agley." Ahab had always been a strong supporter of mine, did not care for Robert at all, and thought the treatment of Kip had been unconscionable. But Ahab had a habit, unfortunately, of trying to help me at the most inopportune moments. Marcel was about to table the resolution when Ahab pointed out that while a support group for the managing partners was a wonderful idea, under our governance policy only the Executive Committee had the authority to appoint it from among its members.

It is amazing how at critical crossroads we can see, in a flash, a vision of some impending catastrophe unfolding in slow motion as we remain helpless to avoid it. In that moment I thought, *Ahab, don't you understand that the Executive Committee is at the root of this problem? Kip and Robert have been stalemated for months and the Executive Committee hasn't come up with a solution to deal with it over the past seven months other than abolish the National Management Committee, which in my opinion is no solution at all. No one in leadership has been leading. Can you not appreciate that this requires outside assistance? Are Marcel and I the only ones who see this?*

But lawyers will always be lawyers, and the tidal wave of support for his suggestion, which was in keeping with good firm governance, spread through the room like wildfire. Ahab had reminded the lawyers in the room that we had elected Executive Committee partners to deal with this crisis, so let them do their jobs. Marcel's proposal that he and I step in never made it to the floor.

In three short minutes the fragile solution that Marcel and I had carefully crafted, the product of an entire summer's work, was knocked from our hands and shattered into a thousand shards. Ahab had unwittingly succeeded in returning me to my office to wait for the phone to ring. Marcel and I were being relegated to the outer fringes of leadership. Maybe we were kidding ourselves. Perhaps Marcel and I could not have bridged the differences between Kip and Robert. We never had the chance to find out. Kip and Robert were dysfunctional, and the Executive Committee had neither leadership nor direction. Instead of building on some of the goodwill we had created over the summer, they appointed a subcommittee whose sole responsibility was to figure out who else to fire.

— • —

Since the end of 2012, when Roy had resigned as chair, no permanent replacement had been named, and the Executive Committee had
rotating meeting chairs. Many partners thought it was not necessary
to appoint a new permanent chairman. Roy had always believed his
role as chair was to insure that the values of the firm were maintained
despite our growth. He played a unique role in the recruitment of
prime ministers and Supreme Court justices. He participated with Guy
and me in the long-range vision of building a law firm. He kept his
nose out of management. The role was uniquely suited to Roy. There
were reasons the partners had not replaced him. First, there was no
one else like Roy in the firm, and second, the Executive Committee
had not yet figured out what they wanted from his replacement.

The compromise, to appoint a rotating chair, was a short-term fix
to what was becoming a long-term problem. The partners needed a
breather from Roy in the chair and were not agreeing on a suitable
replacement. My old confrere from Montreal, Neil Wiener, had ably
run a number of meetings. However, the Executive Committee was
spinning its wheels, spending considerable amounts of time trying to
address what had become an insoluble problem. The meetings of the
Executive Committee continued, each one seemingly endless and with
little purpose or real direction. Agendas for their meetings ran three
pages long, and meetings would see them revisiting issues without
finding solutions. They were putting in long hours, but with no clear
direction, they were achieving very little. Eventually there was a consensus, led by Kip, to organize a fall weekend Executive Committee
retreat to deal with strategic objectives. Was it realistic to believe this
was going to be a constructive exercise? We would all soon find out.

17

BONHOMME'S GAMBIT

NOVEMBER 2013

From the moment Kip stepped into his leadership position, he and Robert as the new managing partners knew they would have to chart the direction for the firm. They fought and struggled their way through the year without addressing strategy until the fateful weekend of November 9. The Executive Committee was finally scheduled to meet with three independent legal consultants for two days in Montreal to begin the process of strategic review. Danielle Chagnon and her administrative staff had devoted countless hours to prepare financial analyses that broke down the performance of the various practice divisions and regions from Paris to Vancouver. Almost everyone was in attendance: Sonia Yung, George K, and Adam Kardash arrived from Toronto, and Marcel Aubut, Marie-Josée Hogue, Neil Wiener, and Danny Kaufer from Quebec. A number of other firm leaders from around the country were invited to attend. Peter Gall sent John Legge to represent the Vancouver office, and Ed Wooldridge flew in from

Calgary. The strategic planning session was Kip's initiative and he arrived with great expectations.

Kip lacked a good sense of Robert's political savvy, or where Robert was coming from or headed to on particular issues. This day would be no different: before the Saturday morning session gained any momentum, it was sidetracked by surprising news. Robert had arrived at the meeting with his resignation in hand, this time formally tendered. He let the Executive Committee know that he was no longer prepared to continue with Kip. They would have to choose. As far as he was concerned they could even choose a third party. It was a shock that cut to Kip's core. He was completely bewildered by the events, though others in the firm might have seen this coming from ten kilometres off. The two were still not working as a team, and Robert, in his frustration, believed the only alternative was to trigger a constitutional crisis.

The Executive Committee, after receiving Robert's resignation, knew it had to move swiftly. After asking Robert to leave the room, they let the consultants know the morning session would be delayed. Then they asked Kip to leave as well so they could hold an in camera session. If Kip was surprised by Robert's resignation, he was flabbergasted at being asked to excuse himself. After all, he was not the one who had just resigned. He might reasonably have expected at that moment to become the sole managing partner.

By then, Robert was at the nadir of his popularity in Toronto, but he was not the only one who was unwanted. I am not sure Kip realized he had little support in the West, and even less in Quebec. To break the deadlock between Kip and Robert, Danny Kaufer had been openly advocating for a single managing partner for awhile. Who would it be—Robert, Kip, or someone else? Had Kip done any positioning for this moment? Likely not; he wasn't hardwired to live in a world where people couldn't be trusted, where partners would stab him in the back. That had never been the Heenan Blaikie way. But the time for open confrontation had passed, and this knife was not going in the chest. It never occurred to him that he needed to understand his fellow Executive Committee members, to learn what made them tick, to prepare for an unthinkable moment of truth such as this. These skills did not come naturally to Kip. Robert's move would be the biggest blindsiding of Kip's life. Where was the support of the Toronto committee members? As he left the meeting room, Kip might well have been thinking, *Et tu, Brute*?

The Executive Committee deliberated for hours before asking the two to return to the room. The dual managing partner structure, they said, had proved to be unworkable. For the sake of the firm, Robert would be reappointed on an interim basis as the sole national managing partner to finish out the year until a new structure could be organized. Kip was out, though he could return to Toronto as managing partner of that office. The Executive Committee, unless it decided to reaffirm Robert, would begin a search for a professional manager to take over as CEO in 2014.

Robert knew he was taking a risk, but it was one he had to take regardless of the outcome. He could no longer function in this arrangement. While the more cynical might say he had orchestrated the entire event to emerge as the victor, I don't believe that was the case. He was desperate for a solution and was truly prepared to walk away for the benefit of the firm if the Executive Committee had come up with a different solution. This interim arrangement could not have been what he'd hoped for, but I give him credit for having the balls to take action. Regardless of his motives, Robert seemed certain he was putting the firm's interest first in taking this step.

Kip, on the other hand, was emotionally distraught. He felt unsupported and abandoned by the Executive Committee. This was a very harsh pill to swallow and it had to hurt him enormously. Yet he refused to wallow in self-pity, and after a few days he pulled himself together. He took on the role of Toronto managing partner and soldiered on, putting the welfare of the Toronto office above any other preoccupation, wondering all the while how matters had taken such a dark turn.

— • —

While the weekend had been intended as a turning point for our leadership—a long-awaited first step in organizing for the future—the Saturday morning political crisis upended the planned agenda before it got started. The new focus would have to begin with a search for a new leader. Quite coincidentally I had been put in touch a few months earlier with Paul Wilson, a British businessman and CEO of a UK law firm, appropriately called Shakespeares. Paul was a CPA, not a lawyer, but he had a strong background in business, finance, and consulting. He had stepped into a law firm that was struggling in 2008 as a result of the financial crisis and had engineered its recovery, while also building up all aspects of this UK enterprise. His strengths combined an ability to listen and reflect back to partners what they said they wanted, a consistency of approach, the skills required to develop and execute a business plan, and a knack for holding partners to their commitments. In short, Paul's long suit had every card in the deck we now so desperately needed. He had fallen in love with a Canadian woman (whom he'd met at a Harvard business leadership course) and was planning to relocate to Toronto.

I first met with Paul in June out of curiosity to see if I could help him find a job. Over time I began to see how he might be the solution to our problems. He met with the various Toronto members of our Executive Committee, all of them quite skeptical about bringing in an outsider. Eventually, they too became persuaded that Paul might well be the CEO candidate that our fall crisis called for. Once Robert's interim appointment had opened the door to look for other candidates, I asked Marcel to arrange for Paul to meet key partners around the firm. Over the next couple of months, the notion had shifted from Paul as a wild long shot to Paul as a likely successor to Robert.

Paul's arrival on the scene coincided with a deep sense of hopelessness that quickly descended on Toronto after Robert's coup. While no one believed the Kip/Robert duo was functional, people found Kip's humiliation in this fashion unacceptable. There was a quick rally of support from most Toronto partners, who could not begin to imagine how difficult this must be for Kip. Although they believed that Robert expected his interim appointment to become permanent, most of those partners agreed that anything other than a short-term appointment was now untenable.

— • —

It wasn't long before Robert was having serious doubts about the firm. Over 10 percent of our lawyers had departed in under a year along with a host of support staff; revenues were now projected to be down 12 or 13 percent and profits at least 18 percent. He projected that 2014 would likely not be any better. For five months his belief had been growing that the national enterprise was no longer viable. From his perspective, an intelligent leader would prove that hypothesis, and if the business could not be saved, better to accept that reality swiftly and deal with it.

For any partner who wanted or needed to believe in the future of the firm, the worst possible nightmare was playing itself out. We had installed as our interim leader a man who was coming to believe that there was little hope for the enterprise as a going concern. Without any discussion at the Executive Committee level, he hired accountants to conduct a review of the financial situation and report back on the viability of the firm. To my surprise he called to let me know what he was thinking.

He wanted it to be prepared by early January to face reality. The enterprise might not be viable, and if so, he concluded that the best time to disband it would be in the first quarter of 2014, when the cash position of the firm would be at its strongest.

Instead of putting his considerable talents and energy into steering us away from the rocky shore, he was prepared to mobilize the life rafts. Would he change course? I doubted it. It seemed I was the only person who understood this. If it was to survive, the organization desperately needed a dreamer, a committed optimist, a group of optimists, to lead us forward. People like Neil Wiener, Marcel Aubut, Eric Maldoff, Mario Welsh in Quebec, David Steinberg, Robb Beeman, and so many others across the country who had built the firm, needed to step up and commit themselves. While we needed a leader to convince all of our partners to believe in the future, to preserve their capital, and to hold on because better times would inevitably return, Robert relied on the numbers, which were telling him it was best not to continue.

We were not yet at the point of no return as an organization, but it would only take three or four more key partners to get nervous and desert the firm, leaving us with no reasonable alternative but to collapse. I had a strong sense this would not happen in Toronto, but there was no telling what might happen in Montreal.

— • —

On November 15 I had entered the hospital for a right-knee replacement. I was scheduled to be completely out of commission for six weeks. The plan was to lie low until after the holidays and get back to serious work at the beginning of January. I had been home for a week. I couldn't sit at home any longer. On November 25 I returned to the office, limping badly but prepared to formulate a plan and convince my allies to support it. I believed the firm could still be saved, but it would take single-minded determination and our key partners' willingness to stand up to be counted.

Mark Jadd and Allen Garson, however, were telling me there was still no sense that enough partners would support my return to any position of authority, with or without Kip. Robert had not shared his thinking with very many people—at one point I wondered if I was the only one who knew—so there was still no crisis that would precipitate immediate action. I would have to continue waiting and attend to my own recovery while the firm did the same.

DECEMBER 2013

Most partners in law firms have mastered the art of dealing with the work pressures caused by unrealistic deadlines, impatient clients, or fools as adversaries on the other side of a transaction or litigation file. We can be completely objective about our clients' crises and we have no issue returning to our normal lives after a day at work and sleeping at night, knowing we can be objective again in the morning. When the crisis is of our own making, however, all objectivity flies out the window and different rules apply.

December was a time for cold logic, a decisive approach, and a firm guiding hand to pull us from the precipice. Had my partners been objective outside advisors, they might have known what to do next.

I learned from personal experience that when crisis besets an organization, the normal rules of conduct vanish. That is because there is no normal. Most partners I spoke to after the crisis experienced the feelings I am about to describe. Although some were better equipped emotionally than others to deal with the situation, the stress was enormous and unremitting. They would wake up with it in the morning, and getting through the day became a challenge. Soon their ability to make even simple decisions diminished. As people entered the office building, depression set in. They tried to lose themselves in their work, but the cloud that had descended on the office greeted them every morning.

I still remember the first crisis I faced in 1998—dealing with Oscar, the rogue partner. Waking up in the morning and putting on my game face was a chore. Each day I worried about what new calamity I would be facing. Who would be the next to announce they were leaving? The boat was listing and I had to deal with it. The distinguishing factor was that I had Guy's moral support throughout, and that helped get me through the long days and nights. We projected calm and a sense that we were in control. No one panicked. It helped that we had done an outstanding job of keeping a lid on the information. Outside the firm there was no inkling that we were having a problem. The partners trusted Guy and me and the team of experts we had put in place to handle the situation. We waited out the storm and life slowly got back to normal.

This time was different. Kip had been fired as managing partner, Robert held the reins, and the senior management was sidelined.

Roy had retired, Guy was ignored, Jim Pasieka was gone, and I was still marginalized. Robert, the interim leader, had lost his faith in the enterprise. The tension between Montreal and Toronto persisted. Economically we were about to have one of our better Decembers, but that good news would only emerge in early January. We were in the process of bidding on major commercial files for the new year: files that might change the outlook of the entire firm. We would normally be revelling in the excitement of the chase. Now we were trying to hide our uncertainty as to whether the enterprise would still exist in six months. From a Toronto perspective, factors beyond our control were in play. A few key departures in Montreal might be enough to take us over the edge. At what point would we have too much overhead and not enough partners to shoulder the load? We all knew we were very close to that line. On top of that, the stress was affecting partners in ways they were just beginning to comprehend.

Some partners admitted later that they could no longer make decisions of any nature. A few had been through the shock of breakups in other firms and were showing classic symptoms of post-traumatic stress. One partner's family was very concerned; when he talked about Heenan Blaikie, he would call it the name of the firm he had left twenty years prior. Day-to-day existence had been reduced to surviving enormous levels of anxiety. It wasn't just about losing money if the firm went down. It was about confronting the pain we were now all feeling and the sense of helplessness and drift that was dominating our lives.

By now all of our key partners were being actively solicited to leave. This would have been unthinkable as little as a year earlier, and many of those partners would not have even considered taking the calls, which were increasing in frequency. How could the atmosphere have changed so quickly? The only thing I felt confident about was that the Toronto partners who had pledged to one another at my house in July to stay would not break those vows. I am sure they were still weighing options, but all were sticking it out. At least for now.

Word began to leak out in late December that Robert was working on a dissolution analysis. Every ounce of leadership in every corner of the firm needed to be dedicated to saving the organization. We needed key people to build morale and outline to everyone what their role could be in our war of survival and re-emergence. No one was filling that role.

Ironically, our bank lines were well within their limits, our distributions were all up to date (including the June distribution that had been delayed), business volume had picked up, and with any luck 2014 would be a much better year. Projecting out 2013 numbers could suggest that profits were unacceptably low, but in a slimmed-down partnership we might be able to improve profitability in significant ways, if not for 2014 then certainly by 2015, as long as we all stayed together.

Around December 15 the anvil dropped. Mark Jadd walked into my office to let me know that Eric Levy, our young securities leader in Montreal, and Manon Thivierge, the head of our tax department, had announced they were leaving to join Oslers; simultaneously Marie-Josée Hogue, our top litigator in Montreal, had made the decision to move to McCarthys. Without thinking, my response to Mark was "It's over." These were no ordinary Montreal partners. They represented the past, present, and future of the firm. Eric was reputedly one of the top mid-cap securities lawyers in the city, very well known and sought after by every major firm. Manon had trained under me as a student and was one of the leaders of the Montreal tax community and former chair of the Canadian Tax Foundation. Marie-Josée was also a Heenan Blaikie 'lifer' who had seen the firm through all its trials and tribulations for as long as anyone could remember. Manon and Marie-Josée had served on the Executive Committee, and their departures were an unmistakeable signal that we were in serious jeopardy.

Was it a case of greed, or was it battle fatigue that led them to leave? And did it really matter? Eric would later explain his reasoning as follows: "A few partners came to me about rumours they were hearing that I was thinking of leaving. They told me the firm wouldn't survive if I left. I always trusted management and thought the firm was resilient until that moment. I'm figuring, if the firm is so weak that it can't survive me leaving, the situation must be much more desperate than I thought. That's when I got really scared."

The Toronto reaction to the news was far more extreme than in Montreal. Montreal partners felt angry and betrayed. Toronto partners believed the sky was falling in Montreal. Tim Lawson's announced departure for McCarthys from our labour group in Toronto happened at about the same time, and from a psychological perspective was as damaging as the departures in Montreal.

Had the firm now hit the tipping point? My head said yes, but my heart would not accept it. The head began to work on contingency plans for the Toronto office in the event of a firm collapse while my heart drove me to action to try to save the firm.

18

THE HAIL MARY

The recent events drove me into high gear. I no longer had questions about what to do. If the ship was about to sink, I was not going to be a spectator, and I was certainly not going to head for the lifeboats. I sprang into action and Marcel followed suit.

Over the next week leading up to the Christmas break I met with and phoned a growing number of partners. I had managed crises in the past, and I had in-depth knowledge of every corner of the firm. I might also have been the only partner in Toronto that Robert was prepared to listen to. From early December I had been engaged in local discussion with Sonia Yung, George K, and Adam Kardash, the Toronto members of the Executive Committee. I had also maintained a regular dialogue with Marcel and with Peter Gall. After the three key departures in Montreal, I began discussions with Danny Kaufer, Eric Maldoff, and Neil Wiener about the impact this was having and the mood in Montreal and elsewhere throughout the firm.

Between December 15 and Christmas Day consensus quickly built that drastic measures had to be taken; while no one knew what those measures needed to be, I was charged with figuring it out. Even my detractors agreed that my skill set was uniquely tailored to leading us out of the quagmire. The only remaining unresolved issue was how I would be working with Kip. He might view my reinsertion into leadership as a further erosion of his authority, but despite how much Kip had been battered over the past three months, the future of the firm now hung in the balance. We had to find a way to put egos aside and work together.

I no longer had any interest in day-to-day management, and after much soul-searching and discussion, Kip and I concluded that my job would be to steer the firm through the crisis while Kip handled the everyday issues as the local managing partner. I would take on the role of Toronto chair for the year. The position would be unofficial, so I would have no seat or vote in the Executive Committee, but I would be invited to the meetings. Over the holidays I had ongoing discussions with all the members of the Executive Committee, who approved the ad hoc nature of the relationship.

In hindsight, was there any real hope for the firm at this point? Had we lost too many partners? Was the firm economically unviable? Was Robert correct in this analysis? A rational and objective advisor might have tried to convince me that an attempt to save the business was a waste of time. It did not matter, because I refused to believe it. I knew there had to be a way out when at least 165 partners and close to 1,000 people across the country and in Paris were counting on us to make this work. One thing I knew for certain was that I needed some expert professional help to find the right solutions.

I had convinced myself that my efforts could get the firm on track again, but looking back now, this was a long shot. There was also that little voice in my head telling me that if the ship went down, I needed to be at the helm until the very end. I had helped build it and if it failed, I had a moral duty to be front and centre, taking responsibility for how we dealt with that failure.

JANUARY 2014

I returned to work on January 2 with a ceremonial title and no constituted authority. In theory I was no more than an advisor to the Executive Committee. Regardless of title, within a couple of days everyone learned that I was running the firm once again. At about this time, Robert Bonhomme circulated his memo to the Executive Committee explaining why he was recommending that the firm dissolve. Most of them had either heard about it or read earlier drafts at some point in late December. Having taken that stand, he no longer had any moral authority, in any practical sense, to be leading the firm. He was done.

I called Danielle Chagnon, our COO, in Montreal to advise her that from this point forward I was running the firm and she was answerable only to me. She was both surprised and relieved. Had we not worked so closely for so many years, she might have thought to get confirmation from another source. She immediately provided me with all the current financial information and, within a week, the first set of unofficial statistics for 2013, cash flow projections for the next six months, and a status report on every aspect of the business and each of the offices. I may have been out of touch but all my instincts were working just fine. I had spoken personally with every member of the Executive Committee over the past two weeks, and they and our administrative staff were mobilized to take action; they were simply waiting for instructions. I had the full support of the Executive Committee to take whatever steps were necessary. No one yet knew what action to take, but I felt confident that within a week I would have a plan to save the organization we had built together.

While there was no time for doubt if the firm was to pull out of the death spiral, I knew, particularly in light of the most recent announced departures, there was a possibility that Robert was correct: we had no hope; we should throw in the towel, capitulate to our fate, and man the lifeboats. But too many jobs were at stake—not just the lawyers' but also those of the many loyal support staff who had given an important part, if not all, of their adult lives to us. I could not live with the idea of slinking away, tails between our legs, abandoning our support staff and their families to their own fates. As long as I could establish a battle plan, we would take on the enemy from within and fight to our last breath.

The rumours of imminent demise were unquenchable, so the first order of business was morale in Toronto. It could not have sunk any lower, and I felt we owed it to our staff to communicate with them. Kip called an impromptu staff meeting. After he reintroduced me as the new chair of the Toronto office, I stood up on my one good leg and took stock of the earnest faces around the room. I had made it my mission in the past to know most of them personally; I was on a first-name basis with at least two-thirds of the staff. I was not the faceless former leader returning to fill the room with trite statements. I knew them and they knew me; we were family and this was a family meeting to confront a family problem.

My goal was to raise the staff's morale and let them know I had returned with what my sensei would call a fighting spirit. I would work tirelessly to help get us back on our feet. I needed the support of the lawyers and told the staff I also needed their support. There would be, from this point forward, no more negatives, no more slandering of the firm's good name. We would hold our heads high, restore our reputation, and move forward together. There was to be no more talk about who was wrong or who was to blame; we would only talk about proposed solutions. I let them know that the month of December had been the strongest of the year, the billings were extraordinary, and the cash flow for the next quarter was projected to be strong. All of this was true. There was no cash crisis. They needed to hear this because this was their greatest concern, and my sole purpose was to restore their confidence in the firm. I then uttered the words that would come back to haunt us all in subsequent media coverage six weeks later: "It's time for Heenan Blaikie to once again kick ass."

I wanted all of them to leave with the same fighting spirit I felt and the same commitment I had to this endeavour. It was a theme that would reverberate in every city and in every meeting from this point forward. We needed to get our mojo back, from the receptionist through all support levels, students, associates, and lawyers. We needed to restore pride at every level of the firm. We had been the street's whipping boy for eight months, and the beating our reputation was taking had to end. The tone had to come from the top. Was I ready to kick ass? You bet, and everyone had to feel it. The old HB was back, ready to assert itself.

Next I sat down with a handful of our future leaders in Toronto, all of them mid-level and senior associates from across all the practice groups. They were savvy, but they were frightened. There could be no bull for this group, just straight facts, because the information flow to them for many months had been limited and incomplete. I had no sense of whether any of them felt any remaining loyalty to the organization given the stress we caused in their lives. My goal was to keep them in the tent and return to our roots, which meant all lawyers played a role in building the future.

I explained that we were experiencing an unprecedented difficult period, as were many other firms. The face of the profession was changing rapidly, client needs were changing, and we needed to adapt to survive. Adaptation had always been the secret of our success as an organization, and it was time for them to help us re-establish that goal. Solutions could not be legislated downward, they had to come from below. No one at the senior level understood the power of new technology, but these younger lawyers did. I wanted this group to lead the revolution in developing new processes for responding to clients. More important, I wanted them to feel a fresh energy, a revitalization, to which they would be contributing.

I could see a new spark in their eyes; I had captured their imagination. They too wanted to kick ass and once again be proud of the organization they had chosen. We needed to regain our position as thought leaders in the profession, and what better group to help achieve this than the associates, who were at the forefront of the changes in this age of technology? I could sense a new dynamism building in the group, and I knew that word of this meeting would circulate quickly. The coming year was not going to be a repeat of 2013. The HB they had joined was now reaching out to them once more to participate in an industry renaissance; I had struck a chord.

Perhaps I was living in a fantasy world, but I was going to draw every last remaining member of the firm into that world with me. I was a born dreamer and if I could get sufficient buy-in to this new vision of the firm, then all I needed was a little time and a little luck. A few new major files were looming on the horizon. If we could land them for our commercial and securities groups, the year would be off to an incredible start. In terms of building morale, no amount of adept management can replace a few huge commercial transactions or a major litigation brief.

I spent the weekend preparing for week two of 2014, which would be make or break for the entire organization. With the financial information in hand, I now had enough background to formulate a survival plan for the year. I would need to develop, elaborate, and sell it in under two weeks.

I faced an important dilemma. While I had decided to throw every ounce of energy into an attempt to save the business, I also had to face the possibility that factors outside my control would increase the rate of the tailspin and it might be too late. There was no telling who might announce they were leaving next. I was aware that at least two international firms might be interested in a presence in Toronto. DLA Piper had been in touch with Kevin and Sonia in the fall, and Ahab was aware that Dentons were very interested in speaking to us. A number of us met with both firms. DLA made it clear they were not interested in further discussion unless our firm had resolved to dissolve. Similarly we emphasized to Dentons' leadership that none of us were interested in departing from Heenan Blaikie unless the firm no longer existed. All further discussions were put on hold while we set our minds to save the enterprise. We did not keep these meetings a secret, and I am certain that some partners in Montreal may have drawn the wrong inferences about our intentions. Rumours were circulating that Toronto was planning to break away.

I committed all further efforts to the rescue. The plan was simple. We had a stark overhead problem. I had asked Danielle to take an inventory of our space usage across the country. Given the number of departures over the previous eighteen months, we had a surplus of two floors in the Toronto office. Each floor represented a $2-million annual cost to us. This meant $4 million of overhead cost before we sent the first client bill for the year. The situation was not much different in Montreal. The surplus cost there represented another $3 million annually. In other words, we were now saddled with $7 million of completely unproductive and unnecessary overhead. I was apparently the only person in the past nine months to have taken a look at these numbers, the result of the calamity we had brought upon ourselves. Management had been in such a rush to thin out the ranks that no one had seen or even considered the value in speaking with our two major landlords about the implications. Even the most basic strategic plan would have factored in the space implications of the path down which we had hurled ourselves.

As a first step, I needed a restructuring expert. While the partnership was fully exposed to the debts incurred, there were various limitations on the personal liabilities of our partners. Most landlords do not ask professional services partners to sign personally for the partnership's lease obligations. The leases are contracted with corporations, which have limited liability. This is a customary practice, in which the landlords accept the risk of the failure of the professional services firm. Partners are responsible only for their share of the lease-hold improvements to the premises financed by the landlords. This limitation of responsibility on our leases lessened the fear of many partners that by walking away from Heenan Blaikie they would be ruined financially. This was one more reason that we hoped our landlords would be co-operative. They had much at stake if we failed, so a bailout might be the best solution for all.

We would have to co-opt the landlords as partners with us in saving the firm; this would involve renegotiating our two key leases, a delicate process for which an independent and respected third party had to be retained to act as our liaison. We needed the expert to go through our books, analyze our situation, and speak to our landlords. We desperately needed to save as much of that $7 million as possible, at least for the next two to three years.

The second part of the plan required us to speak to our bankers. The amount that the partnership had borrowed was not significant, so the banks were not exposed. However, most partners had borrowed to make their capital contributions to the firm. If the firm failed, each partner was personally liable to repay his or her loan. Despite the rumours in the marketplace and the publication by the press of the most recent departures, no one in management had attended to our key banking relationships. Our line of credit was at a manageable level, and the three-month cash flows were healthy thanks to a very strong fourth-quarter billing, which was quite remarkable given the number of departures. Based on the rumours, however, our bankers must have been worrying. They needed to hear the story told from our perspective, because there was no telling what favours we were going to require over the coming twelve months.

Third, we had to deal with compensation after the previous year's debacle. The entire process had to be rethought, but we did not have eight weeks to spend on an internal review since every last minute had to be devoted to dealing with existing and prospective clients. I came up with a formula to deal with compensation that was simple, blunt, and aligned with the original values of the firm. I just needed to sell the details.

Fourth, we would be putting a six-month freeze on distributions to any partner who had departed, following which we would review our capacity to return to them the capital they had invested in the firm. Philosophically, no departed partners during this period of crisis could be put in a better position than the partners who had chosen to stay and commit themselves to pulling us out of this hole. The incumbents would not be financing the departed.

Finally, and most crucial, we needed a commitment from all the remaining partners that they would stay. I was asking for twelve months. After having lived through and managed crises in the past, I had learned the most important survival lesson: today's misery would become a distant memory in as little as six months; in twelve months we would all be pointed forward and planning on future success, a little older and a little wiser. The pain of the moment would pass, but first we had to put the chain of departures behind us. We all needed to know we could count on one another.

The meeting of the Executive Committee on January 14 to review the plan was a struggle. Robert's memo had effectively disqualified him from taking part in any discussion that involved rescuing rather than terminating the firm. The memo sat festering like two-day-old roadkill in the centre of the highway, blocking his way back to us. He placed his bet on our demise, and we all understood that the firm could no longer be run by a man advocating its dissolution.

I was worried that the firm could not survive if Robert decided to leave. His departure would have an impact on Danny Kaufer, another key leader who could not separate his practice from Robert's. On top of that there was a group of younger partners and associates who formed a considerable business unit in our Montreal labour group and who owed their livelihoods to work that Robert and Danny were generating.

I also wondered how Robert could stay at the firm after advocating for its dissolution as a logical necessity—yet I intuited that privately his heart wanted Heenan Blaikie to survive. Robert, like me, had spent his entire adult life in the firm. Regardless of what his head was telling him, there was a pride of ownership that we all shared, and that I was certain would keep him from making any rash decision to leave. That didn't mean that the rational side of his brain wasn't making contingency arrangements. I was hoping that if we could put together a plan to at least stall the decision of all remaining partners to leave, he might support it. The question I couldn't answer was whether, assuming he was planning to resign his position of leadership, his ego would allow him to stay. If I could get him to declare that he would stay and support the cause, others in Montreal would see that as a major vote of confidence.

If Robert was all about a cerebral approach and a need to be right, I was all about heart and emotion and ideals. It was no longer about what made logical sense; it was about preserving a legacy we had worked tirelessly to create, keeping jobs for hundreds of staff across the country, and standing by our obligations to our suppliers, clients, and business partners. There had to be something more noble here than dollars and cents. If the leadership stood behind the plan, we had a chance.

I had discussed strategy on an ongoing basis with David Steinberg. Sitting in my office I had my right leg propped on a chair, chilling my knee under an ice pack to reduce the post-operative swelling, while we talked.

"Where does Bonhomme stand in all this after writing that fucking memo?" David asked. He was never short on expletives, particularly when upset.

"I wish I knew. I have no idea if he's shopping for new office space for his group," I said.

David paused for a brief moment before responding.

"That wouldn't be surprising," he said. "Where does that leave the others?"

"You mean the other members of the Executive Committee?"

He nodded.

"Let's start with Wiener," I continued. "Neil's been with the firm for thirty-three years—like me, his entire career as a lawyer. He can't begin to fathom life without Heenan Blaikie. He's hard-headed, loyal, and principled. He'll never give up. He might present a dry exterior, but he's Heenan Blaikie to the core and he can't understand how we reached the current fork in the road."

"What about Marcel?"

"Aubut has been associated only with success throughout his illustrious career and couldn't bear the thought of a business failure. Sonia Yung and Adam Kardash are worn out but loyal."

"No kidding," David interjected. "Adam's grown up in the firm since the Toronto office started. I don't care how senior he is, to me he's still one of the kids. I know he's being aggressively pursued by a number of major firms."

I cut in. "A part of Heenan Blaikie is his creation, and his identity and ours have become intertwined in the same way that I'm inextricably linked to the firm."

"I've been speaking with Sonia. Regardless of how she's feeling about some of your decisions, she knows you gave her and Kevin complete autonomy to build the securities group in their image. Though the two of them have incredible offers to leave, they're loyal. Same goes for George K. Always solid and dependable." David paused for a second. "Now Peter Gall ... I don't get that guy. Where does he stand?"

"David, Peter lives and breathes for the firm. He may have some ideas that are on the outward edge of the envelope, but he's been really upset with Robert. He's with us."

"What's all this talk about him wanting to leave with the Vancouver litigators to set up a boutique? Can we trust them?"

"Unlike a lot of other partners, I feel I can trust Peter to the ends of the earth. He has his odd moments, I realize, and the last year with Robert has been very tough on him. So while he's been talking about leaving, I don't believe for a moment he will—as long as management that he trusts is in place."

I removed the ice pack. Unlike the rest of me, my knee was numb. "He's sending John Legge to represent him at the next meeting," I went on. "Now John's a realist. He understands that Robert and all the partners who left have glossed over all the shit involved in a dissolution of the firm because they're hoping to avoid the problem. John's represented other firms going through dissolution. Between possible lawsuits from major creditors, landlords, employees, and inevitable litigation between partners, we would be looking at an ugly mess that could last for years. It's almost certain every partner would lose all their capital investment in the firm ... maybe more."

David stood up and looked out my window at Lake Ontario, which was beginning to freeze over in the January cold snap. "Who else is left?" he asked.

"The tragedy is that four other members of the committee have jumped ship already: Jim Pasieka, Marie-Josée Hogue, Manon Thivierge, and Tim Lawson."

"Fuck, this is some serious shit, man. Can we save this thing?"

"With a little luck and a complete commitment from all the remaining leaders, we have a chance. I'm not ready to give up."

David gave a small smile. "That's the spirit. Where does Kaufer stand in all this?"

"Danny is the great enigma. He's been with the firm since its fourth year of existence. No one can appreciate the pain of departure more than Danny. I'm not sure if you know this, but way back he left for a couple of years—and then returned to the fold."

"He's a huge rainmaker. We can't afford to lose him. He's your old pal. Is he staying?"

I considered this. "Danny can be childish and bombastic as well as brilliant," I said, "but he ought to be an absolute supporter of the plan to move forward. However, he's closely tied to Robert, and I wonder if Robert is making plans to leave. Where would those plans leave Danny and the half-dozen lawyers who service the work they bring in?"

"I guess all will be revealed shortly."

My flight was leaving shortly for Montreal. I got out of my chair and limped to the door. I was ready to give up the cane I'd been using to help me walk. It made me look frail, and this was no time for any sign of weakness.

— • —

Robert was surprised when he was asked not to attend the meeting of the Executive Committee on the fourteenth. He was planning to resign on the seventeenth, but after seeing his memo, the Committee immediately replaced him with Robert Dupont. We spent the first hour going around the table criticizing the survival plan in order to improve it.

John Legge noted, "If the remaining partners were to walk away from the firm, it would not only be a catastrophe, it would impose an emotional and economic hardship on all parties regardless of whether they remained or left. I can see the litigants lined up at the doorstep in proportions we can't yet imagine. We have to support any plan that will keep us running."

The moment of truth arrived. I asked all the partners to confirm that they would stick it out together for one more year. I saw it as a form of loyalty oath. The tone starts at the top, and the oath had to be supported unanimously by the committee. Danny waffled. He wasn't refusing but he also wasn't committing. The rest of us closed in on Danny, pushing him for a resolution. Danny's internal emotions were tearing him up. He knew Robert's views, he didn't want to let go of the firm, and he could not bring himself to align himself one way or the other. This was a devastating blow. He knew he couldn't continue to sit on the committee, and he volunteered to resign. He simply did not want the responsibility of making the decision for others. Danny had cracked and there was no putting Humpty back together again.

Although the Executive Committee voted to approve the plan, Danny's angst left the taste of defeat in my mouth. But there was no time to think about failure. The meeting drove home to me the business imperative. We had no backup plan. Our lease guarantees were interlinked, and our bank lines covered the entire firm, so if the plan failed to carry completely in any location, that would be sufficient to defeat the whole scheme. As few as five dissenting partners could mean failure.

The next step was to sit down with the restructuring expert to determine whether a lease renegotiation with our landlords was even feasible. Kip had interviewed a couple of candidates and we agreed on Bill Aziz, who had a great reputation in the Toronto market. His assessment was that our landlords, faced with a choice of watching the firm dissolve or allowing the firm to survive and pay rent on 60 percent of our space, would likely opt for the latter. Of course there was no way to predict the outcome. If we could turn the corner, it was likely that at some point in the future we would begin to grow once more and take back all or part of the space. For the moment, though, this was all simply dreaming in technicolour. We still needed to explain the situation to our partners and get their buy-in.

We met on two successive nights, first with the partners in Toronto and the western partners attending by phone, and the following night with the partners in Quebec. Because of my knee I couldn't yet travel, so I attended the second meeting by phone. Legge made the trip in person. We outlined the prognosis and the path to survival. If they agreed to hang in for twelve months, I would work tirelessly until we were back on our feet. I could not do it alone. We would need to completely commit to one another, then put our heads down and drive forward for a year, drive until we emerged from this tunnel. It was Tuesday night in Toronto. Partners had to declare by Friday.

Given the recent defections, I was concerned about the Montreal partners. We were pleased to discover they were willing to seriously consider staying together. They had reacted to the recent departures with an intense anger that had bonded the group. They believed the decision to leave was selfish, and more than ever they wanted to make a statement. But they also insisted on a greater transparency moving forward and a greater say in the business decisions of the firm. A core group of young partners, represented by Joel Cabelli, Alex Buswell, and a few others, said they were prepared to step up and take responsibility. The Montreal approach, which had been paternalistic under Roy's leadership and Marcel's dominant influence, was going to have to change dramatically. This was the moment when the younger generation would once again make the firm its own. In many respects I could not have asked for a better result. The younger partners wanted to engage in holding the firm together.

At each of the meetings the partners asked the obvious question. How were Bill Aziz and I certain that the landlords would negotiate with us? Naturally I couldn't be certain; instead I put myself in the landlords' shoes and I couldn't imagine it was in their interest to take back all of our space if we failed. The complexity was in getting them to recognize the gravity of the situation. They needed to understand immediately that we weren't bluffing. I felt that with Bill's assistance, I could convince them that their self-interest was better served under a new arrangement that gave the firm the manoeuvring room it needed to carry on.

Bill explained to the partners that no change comes without a price, so while we might manage to persuade the landlords to take back the surplus space, that bargain might be tied to increased personal commitment from the partners. As matters stood, all of our leases were contracted by our management corporation and the individual partners were not liable for the monthly rent obligations. The partners were personally liable for the leasehold improvements, but that liability was quite limited on an individual partner basis. The question was, what additional guaranty would the landlords seek from the remaining partners in order to take back two floors? Only hard bargaining would tell the tale.

Thursday was another day of preparation at Heenan Blaikie. I had to assume that by Friday everyone was going to be committing now that they had all the information. The response from Montreal seemed to be positive, although the young partners had formed a collective and were insisting on increased power in the next version of Heenan Blaikie as a condition of their support.

I had remained in contact with Paul Wilson, who by now had impressed the remaining members of our Executive Committee and key partners in all of our cities. I had called before the partners meetings took place to let him know that he would likely be our next CEO—"provided the firm still exists in a month," I added. Paul chuckled. I was pleased to discover that neither of us had lost our sense of humour through all this. I could foresee that if we survived the immediate critical situation, I would remain in my chair role, playing the CEO function until he had enough time to adjust to the new surroundings, at which point I would hand the reins over to him while I slowly slid back into the role of business development for the firm. That was the plan, and Paul understood this would be a great challenge for him—if our partners could just hold it together.

— • —

On Friday morning, as the deadline was approaching, I had a surprise visit from Brian Burkett and Doug Gilbert. Though neither had any formal title, they were, and had always been, the leaders of the Toronto labour group. They had been shaken a year earlier when Henry Dinsdale and Jeff Goodman left. Over the course of the year other partners had left for various reasons. The greatest blow to the group had been Tim Lawson's announcement in early December 2013 that he too was leaving. Tim had been my personal choice to run the firm one day, and the loss of such a talent was devastating to the group. The load of the practice was now to be shared by five very capable partners, including Brian and Doug. John Craig was the golden boy; he managed the Telus account and was completely loyal. Greg McGinnis had been the managing partner of a labour boutique before joining us a few years earlier, and Sonia Regenbogen was a homegrown talent who was maturing into a very solid partner.

For years I had wondered why Brian and Doug had not left. They did not like the direction of the firm under my leadership, believed Roy had stayed well past his best-before date, and thought Marcel Aubut had been secretly running the firm for years. They hated everything that Jacques Bouchard represented and thought Paris was a huge mistake. Going back to the days of Jean Potvin, they always seemed to find something to criticize. Yet there they were, sadly sitting in front of me, as we possibly faced the bitter end. Ironically, while almost every partner of value was being actively solicited by other firms, Brian, Doug, and I had no intention of ever leaving. Even though our twenty-two-year ride together had been filled with tension, adversity, and anger as well as success, the factors that should have driven us apart years earlier were now the bonds holding us together. Like an old married couple who harangue one another for years yet stay together long after any rational person would have opted for divorce, we continued to be constants in each other's lives.

They hadn't come to fight or complain. They came to tell me that within the week Sonia and Greg would announce that they too were leaving for a labour boutique. They were bewildered. Half of their department had left over the past twelve months. Who would be next? It would not be either of them. We joked about how, over all these years, the idea of picking up and starting over somewhere else had never appealed to them. Their practice consisted of some of the largest national enterprises in Canada, which had been growing with them for over twenty years. Their immediate problem was the attrition they might experience without a senior team behind them to handle the files.

As Brian, Doug, and I sat there talking, I experienced a kind of revelation: our fates were inextricably linked. Despite the fact that for years they felt I did not respect the value of the labour practice; despite their fear that my dream to build us into a commercial-based firm could not co-exist with a vibrant labour practice; despite my perpetual fear that they had one foot out the door; despite my assumption that they would never support any plan that had my backing, if only because it was my plan: none of that mattered. We had been together for the key years of our professional careers, the period when we made our marks and established our reputations. Despite our bickering we had built a brand we could all be proud of. At that moment, when I had to determine whom I could count on in this time of quiet desperation, it dawned on me: the three of us could count on one another. We would continue successfully or we would go down with the ship—together.

I thought for a moment. Robert could not be counted on and Danny refused to be counted on. Ironically, though Robert had resigned as managing partner, he had not yet announced he was leaving, suggesting to me that he might not yet have made up his mind whether to leave the firm. Rumours were rampant about their plans. I was certain Adam Kardash was being pressured to leave for an offer of great financial security. I could not get a read on his level of commitment. Now, with Greg and Sonia, we were losing two more from our labour practice. The firm's survival plan could not work with this level of attrition.

I was beaten and I knew it. "Brian, Doug," I said, "go save your-selves. Leave now before your team and practice desert you." I was two and a half weeks into my return. I hadn't slept much and I had been going 24/7 since New Year's Day. My face was gaunt and I had not put back on the fifteen pounds I could ill afford to lose after my knee replacement. In short, I looked like hell. I had not yet had a first encounter with either landlord. While a core group of partners had assured their commitment, there were still too many undecided partners out there.

I no longer saw any way to save us: it was time to pull the life-support plug. The patient had been mortally wounded and had to be allowed to die, as swiftly as possible. I finally realized I had been living in what some might describe as 'distorted reality,' and I had managed to drag everyone along with me. The distortion had allowed me to convince myself and a growing number of partners that everything could work out, that HB could live to fight another day, that we all had invested too much to walk away. Brian and Doug had yanked back the curtain and reminded me there was no wizard operating the controls. "Perhaps if we had started this process in July ..." I mused aloud. But hindsight was useless now. I called my main advisors in Toronto, and then I called Marcel.

I felt remarkably calm as I began to explain my conclusion to others. It was a decision not everyone was prepared to accept. Allen Garson's first reaction was "Who gave you the right to make the decision?" Neil Wiener refused to accept it at all. They were both right. I had no authority to decide. I had no authority at all. Only the partners on recommendation of the Executive Committee had the power to dissolve the firm. Having completed the calculus, my brain had jumped ahead. I was finally in agreement with Robert.

Perhaps if we had started the fight earlier and rebuilt the hope, if we had managed to stave off the key December defections that cost us millions of dollars in lost future business and some of the stars of the firm ... perhaps then we would have had a shot. Without the commitments in place I had lost hope.

After I'd spoken to Marcel, we immediately convened an Executive Committee conference call. I laid out my reasons for believing it was too late to save the firm. Except for Neil Wiener, who would never, ever surrender, no one disagreed with my analysis. We now had to face what this meant. The decision to liquidate the firm was not one the Executive Committee could make. Only the remaining partners could make that decision, and our major creditors would want advance notice of any decision of this nature, particularly if we had to rely on their goodwill to allow an orderly wind-down. I suggested immediate discussions with our bankers and landlords. We had a partner retreat scheduled for the end of January, but it no longer made sense to spend money for no purpose. The partners, however, had to vote on the dissolution. After much debate we decided to invite all the partners to meet one last time for a half-day at the Queen Elizabeth Hotel in Montreal. We would conduct the remaining business of the firm, and then sometime after the meeting, vote on the termination of the partnership.

— • —

The final partners meeting, on the second-last weekend in January, was surreal. I arrived a day in advance to caucus with Marcel and John Legge, who would act as head of the transition team. Since we were not yet in dissolution, we needed a group to sort through the hundreds of issues that would take us from a vibrant operating business to a shell for processing claims, by and against the firm. The partners from Paris had flown in, stunned that the unthinkable had happened with them as bystanders. I began a process with Jean-François to untangle our two firms and divide up the liabilities so they could continue to practise law in Paris. It took us the better part of two days to hammer out an agreement. Ironically, when all the dust had finally settled, the Paris office continued under the name Heenan, the only remnant of the law-firm brand.

Partners flew in from all over the country for Saturday afternoon. The last time we had met was twelve months earlier to welcome the new management team and send Roy and me off with tributes. We sat passively through the business of the meeting, which was moderated by the transition committee. A formal vote would take place in the following week. Bill Aziz, our restructuring expert, addressed us on what we could expect, both before and after a formal dissolution process began. He would continue to assist us with our bankers and landlords.

The first hour was spent dispensing information, making sure partners understood the agenda for the following month. Then question period began. One by one, individual partners rose and stepped up to the microphone; rather than asking questions, each took the opportunity to express their gratitude for the years we'd spent together and for the experiences we'd shared. The speakers reflected a growing sentiment in the room that the enterprise we'd been involved with went far beyond work relationships. In English and in French they were slowly tapping into a well of emotion lying beneath the anger and frustration that had dominated their lives for the past nine months. They were recalling once more the nature of the glue that had held us together for all these years, the pride of achievement that had so quickly slipped away.

For one afternoon we managed to put all our differences aside; we refrained from trying to allocate blame for all that had happened. Our frame of mind had returned to that of the previous January when Roy and I were ushered out, when we celebrated the glory of what we had built, and recognized our collective achievements; when we ushered in a new era of Kip and Robert, wherever that was going to transport us; when it was unimaginable that in as little as twelve months the achievements of forty years would be washed away. That day we finally had a growing appreciation for what we had built together and were now about to abandon to the wolves.

Just as we look back nostalgically on our days of youthful exuberance, which can only be appreciated through the perceptive lens of hindsight, we now began to understand how magical the past had been. We had built an organization that was deliberately different and special and beyond anyone's imagination to envision. The funeral had begun and there were few dry eyes in the house during the eulogies, which were glorious and unexpected. Before the mourning process could begin, we reflected one last time on the blessing that Heenan Blaikie had been in our lives. No one touched on the many years of economic success. Instead it was all about relationships; from Sherbrooke to Vancouver, partners lauded one another for having enriched their lives. In the true spirit of Roy Heenan, Peter Blaikie, and Donald Johnston, partners focused on the friendships, the legacy of achievement, and the pride of being associated with an organization whose standard spoke of legal excellence and where respect for staff came above any elitism so common at other firms. I was never so proud to be associated with the firm as I was listening to the partners that day.

By 5 p.m. we were emotionally drained and quietly filed out of the meeting room. We said our last goodbyes knowing that for many of us it would probably be our final encounter with one another. Over the following months we would have to tear down the entire structure, all of us heading off in separate directions, but at this particular moment all that was left was the bittersweetness of the departure.

— • —

Monday morning I awoke with the dread one feels knowing that an unenviable task awaits. While Kip was responsible for winding down the Toronto operation, our first task together was to address the staff.

Neither of us was looking forward to admitting failure to our employees. It was less than a month since we'd ended our last meeting with them on a positive and aggressive note. Today the room was subdued; most remained in quiet shock, trying to absorb the news that a month hence we would close the doors for good. During the interim we would assist in job placement and try to ensure that departing lawyers made every effort to bring their assistants with them wherever they might land. Some staff, including my own loyal assistant, Mary Da Silva, would take the opportunity to retire. Others were openly angry, feeling they had been led on or lied to over the course of the previous month. A few publicly complained about this later.

The roller-coaster ride of emotions that our staff had endured while we fought to survive was regrettable, even though the entire process lasted only four weeks. I knew walking into the room that this would be a most difficult meeting to handle, not because I expected hostility, but because this group had relied on us for years for their livelihoods. Their families had counted on us for support, and I felt personally responsible for the negative effect on all these lives. We had been forthright for the past month, and we knew there would be risks, but none of that really mattered when confronting failure of such epic proportion. We answered questions for half an hour and then the meeting ended.

The group slowly filed out of the room. A number of staff stayed behind to thank me. They reminded me that this had been the best work experience of their professional lives. The emulsion of pride and embarrassment I felt was slowly choking me. I was not prepared to accept any gratitude. Perhaps some day in the future I could rationalize my emotions, but at that point, I could only accept that we were turning their lives upside down. The same was true of the associates whom we met with later that day.

— • —

The following two weeks were a blur. The group that had met at my house at the end of June would be put to the ultimate test. Would loyalty and our pledge to remain together as a unit withstand the pressure of the collapse taking place all around us? At this moment of enormous stress, would we pull together one last time in partnership or fragment? The group was raw, sleep deprived, and on edge. A few began to show signs of post-traumatic stress, which manifested itself as an inability to make decisions of any nature, a refusal to accept what was happening, and for some a kind of paralysis that prevented them from mobilizing their energies in any particular direction. A few were demonstrating classic symptoms of nervous depression.

I was charged with handling the high-level process of winding down Heenan Blaikie. I had to find time to meet with bankers, landlords, and Bill Aziz, our restructuring expert. I also had to manage our communications strategy with the media outside Quebec. We were rapidly becoming the main item in the news cycle, and I was the poster boy for the firm's responsiveness. Once the announcement of our resolution to dissolve was made public, I allowed a single interview, by Jeff Gray of *The Globe and Mail*. We had developed a solid working relationship over the years, and I felt he could come to the story without a preconceived notion as to how to write it. I turned down all other television, radio, and media requests. This was not about me. Jeff had many questions, but to my mind at the time the issue was no longer about who was to blame or how it happened. This was a tragedy of epic proportion for our staff, the people who counted on us for so many years. The social experiment I had begun in 1989, which centred on the value of a contented and valued workforce in building the backbone of an organization, was coming to an end. Now it was time to recognize that they were the real victims of this collapse. We had to do whatever was necessary to ease their pain and assist those we could to reintegrate. The partners and senior lawyers would eventually get over this and rebuild.

The following morning I showed Sharon *The Globe and Mail*, which had been delivered, as usual, to our front door. The Heenan Blaikie collapse was the main story and there was my name, above the fold on page one. I was relieved that the article captured the message I wanted to convey. A number of months later I had lunch with Phyllis Yaffe, the chair of Cineplex. We had been colleagues together on the Lions Gate board of directors and our history went back to her days building the broadcast division of Alliance Communications, at first for Robert Lantos and subsequently for Michael MacMillan. She reminded me that throughout her experience with the firm and right to the end, the one adjective that described the firm was "class." The coverage in the *Globe* was no exception.

— • —

We still had to organize the process of orderly wind-down and do our best to help staff find jobs. I sat down with Kip, who remained the loyal soldier right to the end. He was, as always, decent, engaged, and ready to run the course all the way to the finish line. There was a plethora of local issues to work out and Kip handled them all with class.

Most noble on our administrative team were André Bacchus, our head of associates, and Darci Taylor, our Toronto HR director. André could have left at any time in the final three months, but he had recruited every student and junior lawyer in the firm. He was also responsible for an incoming crew of students (among them the son of the managing partner of Torys), who were supposed to arrive in the spring but no longer had a place to work. They all needed to be placed elsewhere, along with our articling students who were midway through their clerkship. André refused to leave until every last one of them had been placed elsewhere. Most of Bay Street's legal community played a noble role in our final moments. The managing partners (with a couple of notable exceptions) stepped up to absorb our students, regardless of need. Each one felt their responsibility to the profession calling them to take action. They all went to bed at night praying to their personal gods, giving thanks they were not in my position. This was the same prayer I had said each January for allowing Heenan Blaikie to continue for one more year under my leadership.

Just days away from the final vote on our official dissolution, none of us in the firm were in a stable, unemotional state of mind, yet we all needed to make alternative working-life arrangements. Most of the partners had engaged headhunters to assist them. Ironically, that thought never occurred to me. All that mattered was landing as many as possible of the group who had pledged to remain together in a new home, where we might be able to carry on the legacy. My role was to lead. A large contingent of our commercial group had been courted by a number of firms and decided the best fit would be at Dentons in Toronto. Exhausted and emotionally battered, I poured my remaining energy into doing due diligence on our prospective firm, which we completed within a very short timeframe. We moved together, making good on the mutual promises we had made in my dining room the previous July.

I look back on those final moments and recognize that I could have been making decisions based exclusively on self-interest and self-preservation. I could have simply resigned myself to the fact that my twenty-five years of labour to create the special essence of Heenan Blaikie was about to abruptly slip away into memories. Instead I was driven relentlessly to retain the essence of the firm and embed it else-where. David Steinberg shared my vision; he too had not rested for a month while his special leadership qualities emerged. There would be no rest, no reflection on my own emotions, no giving in, until that task was completed.

On a Saturday morning in early February 2014 I had completed my due diligence of Dentons on behalf of our remaining group of about thirty-five lawyers. My final leadership task was accomplished: landing a group of lawyers whom I deeply cared about together in one spot. Dentons' offices were located in the TD Centre, where our original Toronto experiment had begun. My professional career had come full circle. As I was walking through the building lobby I ran into Mary Anne Bueschkens, one of my former partners, who was heading in for her interview with the prospective firm. She represented the best of what we had developed over the years; she had joined us as a young lawyer and was now serving as special advisor to the chair of the board of one of our significant clients. I wished her good luck as she got into the elevator. As the doors closed behind her, I turned away, took a few steps, and then I cried.

epilogue

THE **POST-MORTEM**

I reflect on the stunning demise of Heenan Blaikie, more than two years after the doors closed behind us, at a point when the intense scrutiny of the media has long since died away. I have accepted that I suffered a serious loss, akin to a death in the immediate family. I have passed through the stages of dealing with death, from mourning, to anger, and finally to acceptance. Many of these pages were written as I was passing through these stages and they mirror my emotional catharsis. While I've been able to outline what happened, I needed both time and perspective to explain *why* it happened and whether it could happen elsewhere. Heenan Blaikie is not the first Canadian firm to fail. In the United States, law-firm failure is far more prevalent. Usually economics are the root cause. Professional firms overspend, live beyond their means, or pay fortunes to buy laterals who do not perform at a level that justifies the major compensation guarantees they have been promised. While lower profitability is often a critical common factor in these failures, I believe something far more basic led to the death of our firm.

When things got rough in 2013, we abandoned our principles. The first quarter was dominated by a compensation process that left many partners feeling harshly treated and unloved. It shook the faith of many partners. Economic times had suddenly hardened and the leadership broke down, leaving the firm without direction. Robert Bonhomme thought the solution was to balkanize our offices. We were not managing the departures of people who should be leaving, and we were not communicating with other partners who began considering whether to leave because they felt undervalued. Most important, for a firm that prided itself on creating a warm environment where it was fun and exciting to come to work in the morning, a gloom had set in. The Heenan Tax was no longer an anecdote. It was a noose. We were adrift without any guiding light. People lost faith and began to leave. No one wanted to be the last out the door and there was no longer any central attraction pulling everyone inward.

Regardless of how the management is judged, a number of key partners deserted the marriage. They picked up and left. Like the deserting spouse in the marriage, their self-interest superseded their commitment to the rest of us who stayed behind. Was it greed or fear that motivated them? In my mind that really makes no difference. They left and didn't cast a backward glance, hoping that the rest of us would continue to carry the flag, save the firm, and preserve their precious capital. Some might have rationalized that risk, concluding that the decision to go to a more secure environment with better economics would eventually recompense for any capital loss. As onlookers might have put it in a post-mortem, "The run on the bank was on."

— • —

Did it really happen as quickly as appearances suggested to outsiders? In my view the cracks in the foundation began to show not long after we opened the Paris office in 2011. We endured a rogue partner, concerns over our practice activities around the world, and a flawed process to replace the leaders, which led to greater tensions between Montreal and Toronto. Add to that a chairman who stayed in his official position for too long and a Compensation Committee process that upset partners, all capped by terrible economic conditions just as management had changed. And, as the final straw, a leadership deadlocked over what to do about the growing crisis.

Still, there had been many potential turning points along the way, opportunities to recover. Robert did conceive a plan to cut back expenses, reduce staffing, and eliminate less productive lawyers in an attempt to save the firm. Regardless of whether it was a plan I would have devised, it was a call to action. However, communication and execution of that plan was lacking. Had the execution been accompanied by clear communication to the partners, Robert might have achieved the necessary buy-in to the idea. A first step would have been to ask the Executive Committee to support a detailed plan of the managing partners to carry out a firm-wide downsizing. As a second step, the plan needed to consider how we should deal with our landlords and bankers, and how to communicate with clients, suppliers, and staff. Finally, the leadership needed to meet with groups of partners and departments to explain the rationale, have them accept it, and set a timeline to execute.

Had this all been accomplished and executed crisply over ninety days it might have worked, and we could have avoided the protracted departure of partners that began as a trickle and never lost momentum, the drag downward in morale, and the loss of faith in the future of the organization. All of these factors fuelled what became, over the course of the year, an unstoppable death spiral that led to the firm's demise.

Some partners of the firm might argue that I am not shouldering enough of the responsibility for our demise—that over the previous couple of years we built too quickly, taking on too many laterals who upset the firm's chemistry; that the Toronto-office move to the Bay Adelaide Centre sent a message that the firm was committing to become the 'eighth sister' without the commercial bench strength to meet that objective; that once we had over two hundred lawyers in Toronto, the family feeling was lost; that the differences in culture between Montreal and Toronto were growing and creating problems that were not being properly addressed; that the Executive Committee led by Guy Tremblay, Roy Heenan, and me was so enamoured with the foreign markets that we lost focus on the domestic practice, which was sagging; that the premiums generated by our film-finance practice and later by our mediation practice were no more than a veneer covering weaknesses in the firm that we were ignoring. Ultimately, they would say we had built a house of cards that was just waiting for the winds of change to cause it to collapse.

I would answer that no firm is without its challenges, and managing change is part of overcoming difficult periods. Guy and I had handled the ongoing transition of our firm successfully for many years. We experimented and enjoyed periods of great success with no shortage of problems to deal with. We reached the point, however, like the prime minister who has stayed in power over eight years, where the electorate was tired and wanted change. Prime ministers Harper, Chrétien, and Trudeau all endured harsh departures from office. Why should we be any different? Simply put, our partners had enough of Guy, Roy, Marcel Aubut, and me, and it coloured their perceptions. The ongoing challenges were taking all the fun out of the day-to-day practice of law. In my final year with Robert, the two of us and our Executive Committee were sidetracked by the Bouchard crisis and the controversy over the way it was managed. The time would have been better spent focusing on a new agenda for the future. In my final year as managing partner, we were too distracted to consider where the firm should head under new leadership.

It had gotten so bad that even when we could all see the risk of collapse without effective leadership, my colleagues still did not want me involved until the eleventh hour, when it was too late. The question remains: if I had been sitting in the managing-partner chair in 2013, would all this have happened? I remain convinced, and always will, that we would have sailed the ship through the storm. In the process many partners may have stopped liking me, but they would still be at Heenan Blaikie while complaining about me.

— • —

In the end, is it worthwhile trying to pinpoint the finger of blame? In the preceding chapters I have laid out the evidence, or at least my perspectives on the evidence, that led to the collapse. I leave it to you, the reader, to make your own assessment. My own biases may be obvious.

Any assessment after the fact leaves open the inevitable armchair quarterbacking. Had times been different, might Robert and Kip Daechsel have succeeded together? Had they taken over a year or two earlier or later, without the pressure of a terrible first trimester, would they have had the luxury of time to learn how to work as a team? I recognize that they are both outstanding lawyers, and in different times might have made excellent law-firm leaders. Neither was afforded the benefit that Guy and I enjoyed in coming into the job: some time without crisis to assess and adjust to the new position and grow our political capital. Our replacements were thrown into the perfect storm and asked to navigate the ship with little experience. They both believed they were doing their best, Robert as an experienced employment lawyer and Kip as an experienced mediator. The fit was wrong for the times, and maybe completely wrong altogether. Maybe the whole notion of two leaders working together was lightning in a bottle that we had captured for fifteen years, but that inevitably had to escape and burn us all.

It was inexcusable that neither Kip nor Robert, nor the Executive Committee, nor Guy and I insisted that the newly appointed managing partners get some form of leadership training. For that we all share a portion of the blame. (Although Guy and I were given no such training, the firm was considerably smaller when he and I were learning from the school of hard knocks.) We lawyers measure acceptable behaviour by the standard of "the reasonable man," or the *"bon père de famille"* in Quebec. Any reasonable leadership should have insisted that an employment lawyer and a commercial lawyer get some leadership training when taking on a job for which they had no experience.

— • —

In the end, this is a story that culminates in a failure of leadership. In its final nine months the leadership stopped leading. Robert became disliked in Toronto and Kip was perceived as not being decisive. The Executive Committee stopped strategizing and tried to manage, and the partners stood on the sidelines and watched helplessly rather than engage in the good fight. They needed a rallying cry and there was none to be heard until it was too late.

Would the firm have survived if someone had taken the reins and led with purpose? I will always believe so. The tide could still have been turned in October 2013. By the end of December it had subsumed us. Ultimately, there is no replacement for strong leadership.

The lesson for others is simple: as soon as we forgot who we were and what we were about, we failed. Our organization made a promise to the people who joined over the years. They bought into a vision of an organization that appealed to them. They were builders; they wanted to have fun; money was not a dominant factor. When they believed that the direction was lacking, which eroded their understanding of what was being built, and that the fun was gone, they were no longer prepared to accept earning less money. As we moved away from those principles that guided us for forty years, we lost our way and then lost ourselves.

— • —

Heenan Blaikie lawyers and staff have sailed off in new directions. Each of the partners had to adjust their lifestyles to repay their capital loans, though the banks have allowed for repayment over an extended period of years. I joined Dentons, as counsel, along with a considerable core of our commercial and tax group who sat around my dining room table in July 2013. At the end of May 2016, I left the firm to begin a full-time writing career. Most of the creditor claims have now been settled and, unsurprisingly, the partners stand to lose all their capital in the firm. As concerned as we were about the collapse disrupting careers, virtually everyone has found a landing spot and gone on with their professional lives. Many of them still get together from time to time and already reminisce that Heenan Blaikie was their Camelot. They now appreciate that what we offered as a work-life experience was entirely different than what they are now experiencing elsewhere. I continue to consider the words of my mentor, Danny Levinson. We lost touch for many years after he left the firm, but after seeing the deluge of press in February 2014, he sent me an e-mail in which he wrote:

> For almost 30 years since I first left the firm, I have continued at every opportunity (some rather awkward, given where I then found myself) to extol the ever-so-rare virtues of the firm. I have never, before or since, experienced a place to work that could come close to rivalling the unique culture and blend of values that made the firm such a wonderful place to work and enjoy the company of the special individuals who were my colleagues. I thought HB was the exemplar of how a law firm should be and took a great deal of personal satisfaction from its success and in holding it up as an example of how a place where people counted more than anything else could thrive. Sure, the firm always knew it had to make money to keep the doors open, but the mission was to have fun, working with colleagues whose company we enjoyed to help clients solve their problems. The money was just a nice by-product of doing that. I know you always felt the same way, with the firm's DNA coursing through your veins when you founded the Toronto office.
>
> Sad and tragic as the firm's demise is, I have no doubt that the genetic material that was at its core will survive through those who will carry it with them elsewhere. That DNA will be

the legacy of those, like you, who worked so hard to preserve and
protect it over the years.

— ● —

Only time and experience will determine what the DNA of Heenan Blaikie will become when embedded in other firms. These are stories yet to be lived and written. If any of our lawyers and staff learned the lessons that were passed along from Roy Heenan, Peter Blaikie, and Donald Johnston, through Jean Potvin and down through Guy Tremblay and me, then in some small measure I have succeeded. In the same way that long after death our progeny carry on our legacy in ways we could never have anticipated, I can only hope that I have touched enough lives that will, in turn, touch others in the same way. If that is the case, then the legacy of Heenan Blaikie continues.

ACKNOWLEDGMENTS

Telling a story that spans forty years requires assistance in minimizing factual errors. While I acknowledge the assistance of a number of people below, any errors as to time and date of events I describe are entirely my own.

First, I would like to thank my friend, former partner, and mentor Daniel J. Levinson for helping me get the facts straight on the earliest days of the firm. More important, Danny performed the painstaking role of reading each of the quarter-million words of the original story and assisting me with the first edit of the manuscript. He also continued to ask the hard questions, pushing me to try to understand why the story unfolded as it did. He was relentless in hounding me to look into myself and into the heart of the organization to satisfy a reader's curiosity as to how this all could have happened.

My further thanks:

To my colleague Guy Tremblay, who participated so willingly in all our success and whose memory for detail and precise dates has been invaluable in recreating many scenes. To my good friend Jeff

Rayman, who contributed many helpful comments along the way. To Robert Cooper, the Los Angeles film producer, who helped point me in the right direction in terms of dramatic effect in the text when I sent him a raw first draft of the opening chapters of the story; and especially for confirming that the story itself had some merit in its telling. To Grant Roebuck, for the single valuable insight that led to the deletion of many salacious film-industry stories. (Who knows? They might appear in fiction someday.) To my daughter Meredith, who contributed valuable insight about the opening of the book. To my publisher Barlow Books and, in particular, to Sarah Scott for making some invaluable suggestions to improve the manuscript.

To my agent, Michael Levine, who needs no introduction to anyone in Canada. He reinforced the notion early on that I might actually have some talent outside the legal arena and encouraged me to discard two-thirds of the original prose in favour of a story readers might enjoy. To Marie-Lynn Hammond, my story editor, whose comments were invaluable in shaping the narrative. To my friend Shelley Theriault, whose encouragement and support nurtured my fragile artist's ego.

Finally, to the numerous partners, associates, staff, and students, including alma mater of Heenan Blaikie, and in particular to my invaluable assistants, Jocelyne Tousignant and Mary Da Silva, who were all instrumental in my success and whose contributions to the richness of the firm will always be treasured.

INDEX

Note: NB = Norman Bacal; HB = Heenan Blaikie;
italicized page numbers indicate photos or illustrations